Martine,

With love,

Dad

Xmas 2005
Ottawa

Rollercoaster

Rollercoaster

My Hectic
Years as
Jean
Chrétien's
Diplomatic
Advisor
1994–1998

JAMES BARTLEMAN

[A DOUGLAS GIBSON BOOK]

M&S

Library and Archives Canada Cataloguing in Publication

Bartleman, James, 1939–
    Rollercoaster : my hectic years as Jean Chrétien's diplomatic advisor, 1994-1998 / James Bartleman.

"A Douglas Gibson book".
ISBN 0-7710-1094-X

    1. Bartleman, James, 1939-. 2. Diplomatic etiquette--Canada.
3. Chrétien, Jean, 1934- – Travel.   4. Canada – Foreign relations – 1945-.
5. Ambassadors – Canada – Biography.   I. Title.

FC636.B37A3 2005   971.064'092   C2004-906518-1

We acknowledge the financial support of the Government of Canada through the Book Publishing Industry Development Program and that of the Government of Ontario through the Ontario Media Development Corporation's Ontario Book Initiative. We further acknowledge the support of the Canada Council for the Arts and the Ontario Arts Council for our publishing program.

Typeset in Bembo by M&S, Toronto
Printed and bound in Canada

A Douglas Gibson Book

This book is printed on acid-free paper that is
100% ancient-forest friendly (40% post-consumer recycled).

McClelland & Stewart Ltd.
The Canadian Publishers
481 University Avenue
Toronto, Ontario
M5G 2E9
www.mcclelland.com

1 2 3 4 5   09 08 07 06 05

For Marie-Jeanne, Alain, Laurent,
Anne-Pascale, Stella, and our beloved Pipen.

Contents

PART FIVE: SUMMITRY AND THE
ANTI-GLOBALIZATION MOVEMENT

Foreword

"Has this been done before?" That was Jean Chrétien's reaction when I approached him with a suggestion that I write a personal memoir of the time I spent as his diplomatic advisor. I told him that in other countries, in particular the United States and France, former politicians and diplomats wrote timely accounts of the events they had witnessed in their careers. In Canada, former foreign minister Lloyd Axworthy, and former trade minister Pat Carney had published memoirs shortly after they left office. Former fisheries minister Brian Tobin had put out a book that described his role in the fish war. By contrast, former Canadian diplomats rarely wrote memoirs, and those that did often waited twenty or thirty years before putting pen to paper, by which time they were obliged to consult dusty files to jog their memories.

I went on to say that I thought that it was high time that this tradition ended. We needed to demystify the operations of government and learn lessons from our foreign-policy successes and failures. We should not keep hidden the fascinating personalities, the clash of state-to-state interests, the drama and the intrigue, that one encounters in foreign-service life. Diplomatic history should be frankly told to make it alive and relevant, perhaps even exciting, to the public and students alike. Certainly there would be costs to greater openness. But as long as national security was not compromised, former diplomats with something to say should be encouraged not to take their insights to the grave.

Mr. Chrétien then gave me his blessing, authorizing me to consult his files and asking only that I not involve him in the process. I have respected his wishes, thank him for his indulgence, and hope that he does not live to regret his decision. I found that the events described in this book were so fresh in my memory that I had little need of documentation, other than a copy of his international agenda and of the notes that I made to remind myself of salient developments in the years after I left the Privy Council Office. I leave it to future researchers, who will have the benefit of the passage of time, to put the prime minister's foreign-policy record into historical context.

Prologue

The rollercoaster I had climbed aboard in early 1994 was a perpetual motion machine, and I loved it.

The jet jockey, more used to handling fighter aircraft than transporting his prime minister to international meetings, banked the Canadian Forces Challenger sharply first one way and then the other to line it up with the runway before coming in for a hard, gut-jarring landing at New York's La Guardia airport. It was October 24, 1995, and I was accompanying Jean Chrétien to New York as his diplomatic advisor for the fiftieth anniversary celebrations of the founding of the United Nations. Like it or not, we were on a rollercoaster in more ways than one.

It was the weekend before the referendum in Quebec and the prime minister was deeply worried. Lucien Bouchard, leader of the Bloc Québécois – a Lazarus resurrected after being written off for dead, literally, a year before and a messianic, telegenic firebrand speaker from the North – had captured the imagination of the Quebec public since he emerged as leader of the "yes" side a scant two weeks earlier. The polls indicated that he just might succeed in destroying Canada. The strategy of the "no" forces was to have the prime minister maintain a low profile, given the modest popularity scores he had registered in polling in Quebec. Although no one had confided in me, I assumed that the communications specialists thought that it would be better for the prime minister to be seen playing a statesman's role outside

Canada rather than campaigning on the ground in Quebec. If this were the case, they could not have been more wrong.

At the airport, Canada's ambassador to the United Nations, Robert Fowler, was waiting to escort us to the luxurious Pierre Hotel in midtown Manhattan, but we were in no mood to enjoy the surroundings. In his briefing, the ambassador reminded us that the United Nations was in a state of financial crisis. The Americans were refusing to pay their dues, and few of the 185 member states were meeting their obligations on time. Meanwhile, the end of the Cold War had led to an explosion of ethnic conflict in Africa and Europe. There had been genocide in Rwanda and state collapse in Zaire, Liberia, Somalia, and Angola. The wars in Bosnia and Croatia were coming to an end, but the United Nations' involvement over the years in these countries, both wrenched by violence out of the former Yugoslavia, was judged a failure. None of this was news either to the prime minister or myself. Managing Canada's involvement in these and other crises, with their constant ups and downs, had been part of the prime minister's daily fare since the general elections that had brought him to power in November 1993.

The ambassador claimed that these catastrophes were not the fault of the United Nations as an institution; rather they were the result of pusillanimous governments' unwillingness to provide the organization with the means to carry out its mandate of "saving generations from the scourge of war" as spelled out in the charter adopted by its founders in 1945.[1] The prime minister's presence in New York, he said, was an important vote of confidence in the United Nations by one of its strongest traditional supporters.

But vote of confidence or not, the next two days passed in a blur. We were all preoccupied with Quebec. My mind was only half on my work as I accompanied the prime minister on his calls. I heard but did not grasp the significance of the words of Israeli prime minister Yitzhak Rabin as he told us that peace with the Palestinians was within reach. The ruler of Kuwait, dressed from head to foot in white ceremonial desert robes, smiled enigmatically and promised to direct several major defence contracts to Canada as a sign of appreciation for our help in the 1991 Gulf War – and later reneged on his pledge. The prime minister of Norway shed crocodile tears as he bemoaned his fate in having to govern the coddled and demanding population of one of the richest countries in the world.

We left early for Ottawa as the prime minister was determined to throw all his energies into the battle for Canada at the eleventh hour. I stayed out of his way, making the final arrangements for an extensive foreign tour to start shortly after the referendum – and planned months before, when the experts were confident that winning the vote would be a piece of cake. Laurent, my son attending Queen's University, represented the Bartleman family in joining a tidal wave of Ontarians who went to a giant rally in Montreal to wave Canadian flags and appeal to Quebeckers to vote "no." Then on Monday, October 30, I sat in my Ottawa office, my team around me, watching the results come in. We had quietly prepared a contingency plan to cope with the international fallout should the separatists come out ahead. The nation then went through trauma as the referendum in Quebec was won by a whisker. Afterwards, I gratefully sent my plan to file.

The ride continued. At the end of that week, on Saturday, November 4, I telephoned the prime minister's residence at 24 Sussex Drive and insisted that the household staff rouse Canada's leader from the sleep of the exhausted to speak to me. Prime Minister Rabin, I told a thoroughly shocked Jean Chrétien, had just been assassinated. We would have to move our scheduled departure on his foreign tour forward by two days to fly to Jerusalem for the funeral. Less than twenty-four hours later, the prime minister boarded his aircraft in Ottawa, ashen-faced, to tell me that an intruder, armed with a knife, had broken into his residence in the early hours that same morning to confront his wife at the door to their bedroom. She slammed the door in his face and the police, taking their time, eventually came to their rescue. The prime minister was shaken to the core. The near death of his nation had been followed by the assassination of a respected leader whom he had just met, and then by a close call in his own house. The shocks were arriving like successive hammer blows.

Twenty-four hours later, the prime minister was pushing his way through a chaotic crowd of world leaders and their body-guards, jostling for position in the heat of the Middle Eastern sun around the grave of Israel's deceased prime minister on Jerusalem's Mount Herzl. With no time to rest, he boarded his aircraft to fly to his next international commitment – the Commonwealth summit in New Zealand. The flight eastwards across the Indian Ocean was interminable, broken only by stop-overs for fuel in the Maldives and for a brief rest at Perth, Australia. At the summit itself, allied with Nelson Mandela, he engaged in a desperate and ultimately futile and soul-destroying effort to persuade the corrupt Nigerian government to spare the life of human rights and environmental activist Ken Saro-Wiwa. Thumbing their nose at the international community, the Nigerians hanged him just as Prime Minister Chrétien was meeting with Mr. Saro-Wiwa's son. With barely a pause for grief it was then back to Australia for an official visit, this time to the capital, Canberra, before making the long flight to Osaka, Japan, for an Asia-Pacific Economic Co-operation summit.

And the world moved on – such is the nature of time and history. Staring out the window of the aircraft at the Southern Hemisphere's night sky on the long flight home with my trav-elling companions asleep, I realized that what was important to us when we started this trip – the referendum and the assassina-tion of Rabin – had already started to fade from the conscious-ness of the international community. I came to the conclusion that the breakup of Canada would matter deeply only to the United States and to France: the former because we were their largest trading partner; the latter because of the international political consequences of a unilingual French state in North America. Others would doubtless be sorry, but not viscerally. Their concern would be for the precedent separation would present for other multi-ethnic countries in a decade that had already witnessed the collapse of Yugoslavia and the Soviet Union. Our national unity problems were ours, and we would have to solve them for ourselves.

Like the Hydra in Greek mythology, which sprouted new heads when one was cut off, new challenges appeared as soon as old ones were dealt with. Within a week of our return to Canada, we were off to Benin in West Africa for a Francophonie summit where a showdown was in store between the prime minister and French president Jacques Chirac, who had not been as neutral during the Quebec referendum campaign as federalist Canadians would have wanted. Three weeks later, we departed with more than six hundred people on a historic Team Canada trade mission to Asia.

The rollercoaster I had climbed aboard in early 1994 was a perpetual motion machine, and I loved it.

PART ONE

INTRODUCTION TO THE BIG LEAGUES

I

A Shaky Start

*And one could not, in any case, even think of turning down a
request to serve Canada's prime minister.*

The Prime Minister's Nephew

"Allô Jim? How are you doing? C'est Raymond." He didn't have
to tell me who was on the line to my office at Canada's delegation to NATO where I was Canada's ambassador. It was late
November 1993 and I knew from the hoarse, friendly voice with
its distinctive accent that it was Raymond Chrétien, Canadian
ambassador to Belgium and nephew of Canada's newly elected
prime minister. We were old friends, having joined Foreign
Affairs together twenty-eight years before. I had always liked him,
appreciating his lack of phoney sophistication and his common
touch. We both enjoyed the chance to gossip whenever we could.
Despite never having served together, we had worked closely on
a number of difficult topics over the years – cleaning up a major
scam in an African post where staff members were discovered
changing dollars on the black market, and on another occasion
providing consular and humanitarian assistance to distressed
Canadians in record time following an earthquake that had
flattened parts of Mexico City.

His career path had been meteoric: Canada's ambassador to
Zaire at the age of thirty-six, ambassador to Mexico just in time
to press for the creation of NAFTA, and associate undersecretary
with the rank of deputy minister in Foreign Affairs. His uncle,

Jean Chrétien, may have been a high-profile member of successive Canadian governments when the Liberals were in power but
Raymond had earned his rapid promotion on his own through
intelligence and hard work. In fact it was Conservative prime
minister Brian Mulroney who named him ambassador to
Mexico and who brought him home to his last high-profile job
in Foreign Affairs. In recent years, however, Raymond's career
had suffered, but not through any fault of his own. He had been
forced out of Ottawa as a sacrificial lamb when his superiors
refused to accept their responsibilities in a controversial visa case
involving a prominent Iraqi named al-Mashat seeking refugee
status in Canada.[2]

Diplomatic Advisor to the Prime Minister

When he phoned me Raymond had just returned from Ottawa
where he had attended the swearing-in of the new government
as a personal guest of the prime minister. I assumed that he
wanted to share his impressions on who was who in the new
Ottawa power structure, and got ready to listen politely but
without enthusiasm. Like the majority of Canadian public servants, while not apolitical, I was not a member of a political party
and kept my political sympathies to myself. I had followed the
1993 election campaign in Canada with as much interest as any
other Canadian voter but assumed that its outcome would not
affect my future any more than the half a dozen or more elections that had taken place since I joined the foreign service.
Raymond, however, had big news. Canada's new prime minister
had told him that his exile in Brussels was to end; he was being
posted as ambassador to Washington. And, he added: "Prime
Minister Chrétien wants you, Jim, to be his diplomatic advisor."

Raymond reminded me that every world leader had such a
person, called either diplomatic or foreign-policy advisor, to
counsel him or her on foreign-policy matters. In the United States
the incumbent was the Head of the National Security Council

located in the White House. Elsewhere, foreign-service officers were borrowed from foreign ministries, designated diplomatic advisors, and assigned to work directly for their heads of state or government in their private offices. In Canada, the position had been held in recent years by ace officers from Foreign Affairs who had not yet served as ambassadors but who were marked for rapid promotion. For the past quarter century, these officers had been assigned to the government department responsible for serving the prime minister known as the Privy Council Office (PCO) and had been designated assistant secretaries to the Cabinet for foreign and defence affairs. They reported to the prime minister through the clerk of the PCO (who was also the secretary to the cabinet). Now, in a break with tradition, the new prime minister wanted to follow the approach of the other leaders. Someone who had already made it into the ambassadorial ranks, he said, should be named his advisor and report directly to him without going through the traditional bureaucratic hoops. The chosen one should also be located in the Prime Minister's Office (PMO), alongside his small team of political advisors, but would remain a non-political public servant. The fact that I was an aboriginal Canadian anglophone who spoke French was a plus, since he wished to add to his anglophone, francophone, Jewish, Croatian, Chinese, and Sikh rainbow coalition of staffers.

After swearing me to secrecy, Raymond rang off to tell another of his friends the good news. After all, what good were secrets if you could not share them?

I was dumbfounded. As a half-breed kid with an aboriginal mother and white father growing up in the 1940s in the small village of Port Carling in the heart of Ontario's cottage country, I never dreamed that I would be able to graduate from high school, let alone attend university. The first Port Carling home of the six-member Bartleman family was a tent near the village dump. Our second, occupied in the winter months, was a summer cottage so cold that when the fire in our old kitchen stove died out in the night, frost would form on the beds and snow would drift in through the cracks in the walls. Our third was a shack with one room on the ground floor and two bedrooms upstairs that my mother paid for over a number of years with family allowance cheques.[3] We turned the old building into a comfortable home and emerged from poverty when my mother got work cleaning cottages for wealthy tourists, supplementing my father's modest wages as a casual labourer.

The turning point in my life came when a generous American millionaire summoned me from my wood-cutting duties on his summer estate to join him on the porch of his summer home. He offered to provide funding to allow me to finish high school and attend university. I seized the chance, graduating in Honours history at the University of Western Ontario in 1963 and departed to spend a year as a backpacker in Europe. My interest in foreign adventure and foreign policy aroused, I wrote the exams in 1965 to join the Department of External Affairs (renamed Foreign Affairs in later years and described as such in this book), and to my surprise, was accepted as a foreign-service officer in 1966.

Now I was being given another break. And one could not, in any case, even think of turning down a request to serve Canada's prime minister. I called my wife, Marie-Jeanne, right away letting slip that I was not being recruited on the basis of any "star" qualities; it was my experience that the prime minister wanted. After a good laugh, we quickly agreed that if it was experience that was wanted, then I had plenty of it. My first posting had been to Bogotá, Colombia, where I learned Spanish, was exposed to the workings of a small embassy, and started a lifelong passion for Latin American affairs along with an abhorrence for the enormous disparities that existed between the mass of the people and the privileged upper classes in so many Third World countries. My next job was at headquarters where I was desk officer for international terrorism in October 1970 when violent separatists of the Front de Libération du Québec kidnapped a British diplomat and killed a Quebec cabinet minister before the crisis ended. I discovered in the process how easy it was for a government to deprive its citizens of their civil liberties in the face of an exaggerated threat.

Then occurred the posting that in later years I would regard as the highlight of my career. After only six years in the service, I was unexpectedly offered the chance to head my own small diplomatic mission to Bangladesh as acting High Commissioner or acting ambassador. There, at the age of thirty-two, I was exposed to human suffering on a scale I would never again encounter and, more importantly, given the chance to do something about it by working with outstanding Canadian aid officers as they funnelled massive help to desperate people. My next posting was to the Canadian delegation to NATO in Brussels as a first secretary where I became intimately exposed to the insanity of the Cold War and met and married my wife, Marie-Jeanne Rosillon. Prime Minister Pierre Trudeau was in office when I was sent to Cuba as ambassador in 1981. My wife and I admired the social and economic reforms of Castro's government but loathed the totalitarian excesses of his regime. In 1985, under Prime Minister Brian Mulroney, the government sent us to Israel where my wife and I made many friends but where we were both sickened by the senseless mayhem wreaked by Palestinians on Israelis and by Israelis on Palestinians. The posting to NATO, this time as ambassador, my most senior job to date in the public service, then followed in 1990. I learned a lot in Brussels, representing Canada as NATO reshaped its strategic doctrines to reflect the end of the Cold War, lent its support to the coalition of countries led by the United States fighting Saddam Hussein in the first Gulf War, and was sucked into the growing crisis in the Balkans. The prime minister would get the experienced ambassador he sought as an advisor, but I would also come with the intellectual and emotional baggage of almost thirty years in Canada's foreign service.

The new minister of Foreign Affairs, André Ouellet, in Brussels for a meeting of NATO foreign ministers in the first week of

December, provided more information on my new job over dinner. He started by recalling the central role Ivan Head, a former foreign-service officer and law professor, had played for Pierre Trudeau as his diplomatic advisor. Recruited in 1968, Ivan remained with the prime minister for a decade as trusted confidant and independent source of foreign-policy advice. Prime Minister Chrétien, the minister said, wanted me to perform the same role for him. I had met Ivan in 1973 when I was acting High Commissioner to Bangladesh and he visited Dhaka as a special emissary of the prime minister to discuss preparations for the Commonwealth summit being held in Ottawa that same year. We had remained in touch over the years and I had great respect for his personal and professional qualities.

The Foreign Affairs personnel division then sent me a terse message saying that my current Brussels posting was being cut short and instructing me to report for duty at the beginning of January, a mere three weeks later in Ottawa. Canada's rotational employees were often moved from continent to continent at short notice and were expected to comply without arguing when ordered to another assignment. Yet, having often been shifted from job to job in the past whatever the consequences for my family, I was reluctant to comply this time. I replied that with three children in school who would not be free to come to Canada until the end of June, I would report for work in March, thereby cutting the time of separation in half.

A furious deputy minister was immediately on the telephone, shouting into the receiver: "You have been given a job to do and you will do it! You will report to duty in Ottawa at the beginning of January" and on and on. I said nothing and did nothing. When the prime minister came to Brussels to attend a NATO summit in early January, I raised the matter with him. He said that family considerations came first. A March arrival would suit him just fine.

Ottawa 1994

Arriving in Ottawa on a snowy Thursday in late March, I moved directly into a house Marie-Jeanne and I had bought on a rush trip to the capital for that purpose some weeks before. I spent Friday consulting new colleagues and receiving briefings from Jim Judd, the incumbent assistant secretary who had served as diplomatic advisor to prime ministers Brian Mulroney and Kim Campbell. Professionally, I was in uncharted waters. Raymond Chrétien and Foreign Minister Ouellet had told me that I was being recruited to join the PMO as a public servant, but I was reluctant to follow this route. I would, I realized, become politically branded as a partisan Liberal even if everyone concerned tried to preserve my political virginity, and I would have no staff to carry out my duties other than a secretary and an officer or two. I decided to try to continue the practice that had developed in the years since the departure of Ivan Head and combine the roles of diplomatic advisor with that of assistant secretary to the Cabinet, a clearly non-political role that came with an excellent interdepartmental team of staff officers.

Jim was able to brief me on the bureaucratic role of the assistant secretary to the Cabinet in serving the prime minister: to regulate the flow of information on defence and foreign affairs matters; to prepare briefing notes with policy recommendations with the help of the departments of National Defence, Foreign Affairs, and the Canadian International Development Agency (CIDA); to chair interdepartmental task forces managing crises abroad; and to coordinate the preparation of memorandums to Cabinet. He could not, however, describe how the prime minister wanted the more personal and central role of diplomatic advisor to be carried out since the PMO had kept him at arm's length pending my arrival.

Two of the most powerful individuals in Ottawa, after making clear that they had no hand in my appointment, provided mutually exclusive advice. The clerk of the PCO (who was also head of the public service), Glen Shortliffe, explained the ambiguous intricacies of my new job. I would be expected, he said, to deal directly with the prime minister whenever I had *oral* advice to offer; *written* advice I would have to submit to him for vetting and approval. He added that there was no job description for the position of diplomatic advisor. I had traditions to uphold, however, and should model my role on that of my public service predecessors,[4] who had never forgotten that they were first and foremost members of the public service and bound by its traditional hierarchical structure. Jean Pelletier, Chief of Staff to the prime minister and head of the PMO, said that Jean Chrétien would raise no objections should I opt to remain a public servant and be part of the PCO. Should I do so, I should also consider myself to belong to the PMO family. I had to remember, however, that I was no longer working directly for the public service but was reporting directly to the prime minister. In providing advice, it would of course be helpful to indicate what the prevailing views were in Defence and Foreign Affairs on any particular issue. This should not, however, compromise my principal role – that of an independent player in decision-making, offering personal views at all times on foreign policy and international crisis management situations.[5]

My new job thus entailed being a public servant who was supposed to respect the existing bureaucratic structures and at the same time an independent advisor to the prime minister prepared to act autonomously. I opted to join the PCO and square this circle from within the bureaucracy. Optimistically, and naively, I thought that I might just manage to obtain the advantages of both worlds without the disadvantages. Needless to say, I would find myself in hot water constantly from my PCO superiors, especially from Jocelyne Bourgon who replaced Glen Shortliffe in April 1994, over the entire length of my assignment. The fact that I had spent my entire career in the foreign service, was considerably older than most other assistant secretaries, was impatient with the lengthy bureaucratic processes and endless meetings that slowed decision-making and had, I must confess, a stubborn streak beneath my mild demeanour, made it even more difficult for me to fit in.

As I was having these consultations on the Friday, a team of PCO technicians arrived at our house to install secure communications links and extra telephone lines. At the end of the day, Jim handed me his cellular telephone and pager and told me that I was now the link between the prime minister and the outside world. I would henceforth be required to remain in contact with Foreign Affairs, Defence, my colleagues in the PCO, and the PCO Intelligence Secretariat. I would have the responsibility for briefing the prime minister at any time of the night or day on developments that needed to be brought to his attention. Should any foreign leader seek to speak to the prime minister, I would be alerted by the PMO's switchboard, open twenty-four hours daily, to take appropriate action.

I handed the telephone back; I was not ready. The prime minister's work and personal schedules were still a mystery to me. On Monday morning, Jim offered me the telephone again, saying that the two of us could not be in charge. I accepted it, and climbed on the rollercoaster.

A Steep Learning Curve

I suppose I should have done something sensible – something along the lines of what presumably is spelled out in the generic best-selling books featuring smiling millionaires on their covers outlining "Ten Tips on Best Management Practices," and available at every airport bookstore for travelling businesspeople. If I had bought and read one of these books, I would have gone to see the prime minister on the Monday morning right after Jim Judd handed me the cellphone. I would have engaged him in a discussion on what he wanted to accomplish in the foreign and defence fields during his term as prime minister. And I would have sought his guidance on how he wanted me to do my new job.

But I did not – and that was my first mistake. The truth was, I had never had any interest in management matters and would have gone to sleep as soon as I opened one of the airport tomes. Moreover, as I told myself, there was no time. The prime minister was leaving that very day for an official visit to Mexico, his third official trip abroad since becoming head of government (the others were to the APEC summit in Seattle in November 1993 and to the NATO summit in Brussels in January 1994). It was all I could do to make it to the airport before his plane left. Not having been involved in the planning, I knew less about the program and objectives than the other members of the delegation. There would be ample opportunity, I assumed, to learn the ropes. I told myself that with my experience, I would fit in naturally, be able to make a contribution, and learn about my new responsibilities from participating in an official visit during my first week on the job. That was my second mistake.

Killing the Presidential Candidate

I was surprised that so many people could fit into the small aircraft parked at the Esso terminal at Ottawa International airport. Chief of Staff Jean Pelletier, Director of Communications Peter Donolo, Director of Operations Jean Carle, Chief Political Advisor Eddie Goldenberg, Executive Assistant Michael MacAdoo, and Official Photographer Jean-Marc Carisse followed an RCMP bodyguard and the Chrétiens into the small Challenger jet. It was, I thought, like one of those old movies showing how many university freshmen could fit into a Volkswagen Beetle. I am not certain, but I think a bodyguard was left behind on the snow-covered tarmac in the scramble to find room for Canada's new Ivan Head.

The trip was endless. The Challenger droned on hour after hour until at last it landed at Dallas airport for refuelling. Everyone deplaned to catch a breath of Texas spring air and then we squeezed back on for the final leg to Mexico City. The atmosphere on board was chummy – for everyone, that is, except me. Prime Minister and Mrs. Chrétien smiled at me benignly, but the others did not. They were all strong-willed, highly talented personalities who formed the heart of the political team that had led the prime minister to victory the preceding fall. In their world, everyone had to earn respect, and I had not yet paid my dues. They eyed me with curiosity. In my imagination through their body language they seemed to be saying: "So this is the great foreign-policy guru selected by Raymond Chrétien to ensure that Canada's leadership in foreign policy would be outstanding throughout the mandate. If he's so good, however, why is he not producing witty aphorisms encapsulating great thoughts, like Henry Kissinger when he was advisor to Richard Nixon or Ivan Head when sitting behind Pierre Trudeau? Why, in fact, has he not said a word throughout the entire journey?" He must be, they seemed to be thinking, either deep and silent, comatose, or plain scared.

Arriving at Mexico City airport, a staff officer was waiting to hustle Jean Pelletier and me to a waiting passenger van. I would be paired off with the Chief of Staff as a travelling companion over the next four years for no discernable reason, it seemed, other than the fact that we both had white hair. Then with much shouting and waving of flashlights, the motorcade, escorted by elite motorcycle outriders, hurtled like a primeval beast toward the centre of the city. Sirens wailed into the polluted night air, vehicles on the highway were pushed to one side, and orders barked into a microphone by an operations officer in a police car poured forth from the radio sets installed in each vehicle. As we approached our destination, a gigantic luxury hotel, his disembodied voice provided a countdown to arrival worthy of a space shuttle launch. "Three minutes out! Two minutes out! One minute out!" The tension and excitement in his voice reached a fever pitch.

"Thirty seconds out! Twenty seconds out! Ten seconds out!" We roared, tires screaming, into the entranceway.

Waiting officials jerked the car doors open. The official photographer sprinted forward as if his life depended on it – to catch a shot of the prime minister shaking hands with the hotel manager. Staff officers yelled for everyone to hurry. All and sundry stumbled forward, encumbered with briefcases filled with secret documents and overcoats that would be of no use until we returned to the winter blasts of Canada. There was then a scramble to share the elevator with the prime minister. The fortunate few rode up, basking in reflected glory alongside Canada's bemused prime minister and his wife, who simply wanted to go to bed. The rest of us waited anxiously for another elevator, certain that momentous decisions were being made by those who had managed to accompany the prime minister to his suite and worried that we were not there to provide our indispensable advice!

At last we arrived at the delegation office, our operations centre for the duration of the visit. There had, in fact, been no particular need to rush from the airport. But rushing was apparently how the programs of world leaders were organized and I had better get used to it! Besides, now that everyone's adrenalin was pumping, the official visit could really begin. My new colleagues, familiar with the routine, picked up thick files and immediately started to work on the hot domestic issues that followed them around the globe. There were no files marked for my attention. Eventually, Peter Donolo announced to no one in particular that it was time to meet the press. He headed out the door, accompanied by Canada's ambassador, David Winfield. Peter did not invite me. I followed along and watched as the ambassador briefed the press on Canada's relations with Mexico and Peter fielded questions on Canadian domestic issues. Returning to the office, Peter wordlessly handed me copies of the speeches the prime minister was scheduled to give the next day. Then he disappeared.

Attending the briefing session for the prime minister the next morning, I sought to outline the day's program but no one, including the prime minister, seemed particularly interested in what I had to say. Eventually, the ambassador produced a small card, obviously prepared for his personal use, on which he had scribbled a number of points and from which he gave the prime minister an overview of Canada-Mexico relations. The director of operations reviewed protocol questions and Peter Donolo discussed media-related issues. As the meeting broke up, the prime minister, perhaps sensing that he needed better preparation, grabbed the card that the ambassador had used and stuffed it into his pocket.

The schedule for the first day would set the pattern for most future official visits abroad: laying of a wreath at the tomb of the unknown soldier, inspection of a guard of honour, official talks with the head of government, luncheon with a major speech before a large business audience, meeting with the local mayor, visit to a local Canadian business venture, attendance at a cultural event featuring Canadian artists, meeting with the employees and families of the Canadian embassy, question and answer session with the press by the prime minister, and state dinner. I came with a bulging, heavily annotated briefing book in accordance with the practice of generations of foreign-service officers who had prepared ministers and prime ministers for diplomatic negotiations. The prime minister politely ignored the book. Instead, prior to each event, he pulled out the ambassador's by now tattered card to remind himself of the issues to be addressed, and relied on his memory of the morning's disjointed discussion to carry him through his official talks. I likewise was given little opportunity to prepare him to meet the media; instead, the other officers jumped in, talking at the same time and competing, it seemed, to provide the best analyses of the day's highlights.

The major event that evening was a state banquet offered by President Carlos Salinas de Gortari at Los Pinos, his magnificent residence, in the presence of his cabinet ministers, key members of Congress, big businessmen and businesswomen, university rectors, newspaper magnates, and senior members of the Mexican public service. The Canadian delegation departed on schedule from the hotel to attend the dinner. In accordance with local protocol practice, the Chrétiens were to follow later in a different motorcade, meet privately with the president, and then join the assembled guests for cocktails prior to leading the way into the banquet hall. As we disembarked from our vehicles, it was obvious that something was wrong. The Mexican protocol officers were nervous and the Mexican notables waiting in the large ballroom were talking to each other in excited and hushed tones. We soon learned that Luis Donaldo Colosio Murrieta, the candidate for president selected by the ruling Institutional Revolutionary Party, had just been assassinated. The Mexican public was as yet unaware of the news. The elites assembled in the room were deeply worried that the killing, one of the most dramatic to occur in Mexico in the past half century, taking place in the middle of the election campaign, could destabilize Mexico politically and economically.

After a prolonged wait and much milling around, the president and his wife appeared, accompanied by the prime minister and Mrs. Chrétien, to announce that the dinner was cancelled. Returning to the hotel, my colleagues went to work drafting a press release for the approval of the prime minister expressing condolences to the family of the assassinated leader and confidence in the ability of Mexico to weather the crisis. They did not seek to involve me and I, as the new boy, hesitated to intervene.

The next day, most official functions were cancelled. With time on his hands, the prime minister asked his team whether it would be appropriate for him to pay his respects to the remains of Colosio, moved overnight from Tijuana, where he had been killed, to the headquarters of the ruling party. No one demurred, although someone should have. Departing in our motorcade for the headquarters of the Institutional Revolutionary Party, I was placed once again with Jean Pelletier in the minivan behind the prime minister's car. As we approached the headquarters, the drivers forced their way, sirens wailing, through crowds of weeping mourners, until we could go no further. At this point the prime minister opened his car door and plunged into the crowd, accompanied only by his RCMP bodyguard.

I hesitated. Was it the job of the diplomatic advisor to risk his life to accompany the Canadian head of government into a sea of grief-stricken Mexican followers of an assassinated leader? I decided that it was not. I stayed put and watched the prime minister disappear. About thirty minutes later, he re-emerged, fighting his way through the mob, followed by his RCMP bodyguard who, as always, let the prime minister open the way.

That evening, we gathered at the residence of the ambassador for an excellent meal and a review of the disrupted visit. The depth of passion in the streets and the concern of the Mexican establishment puzzled us. Were we simply witnessing Latin emotions run wild, or had something more profound that would affect the future of Mexico happened? No one knew. It was only later, reflecting on the events of those dramatic days, that I came to the conclusion that it was the latter – an outpouring of hysteria and public revulsion against criminal overlords united in an unholy alliance with dishonest politicians who were confident enough to kill a presidential candidate in front of the television cameras. The fact that the candidate was himself selected in an undemocratic process by party bosses seeking to perpetuate a political system rotten for seventy years merely made the establishment look ineffectual. The collapse of the peso later in the year, the growing power of the drug cartels, and the general descent of Mexico into new lows of corruption were foreshadowed by the events we had just observed.

Called on the Carpet

Before we left Mexico an unhappy Jean Pelletier gave me some less than fatherly advice. The advisor, and no one else, not even the local ambassador, was responsible for ensuring that the prime minister was properly briefed each morning during trips abroad! The advisor, and no one else, must prepare the prime minister for each of the meetings he would have in the course of an official visit, remaining close to him at all times to be of assistance during discussions! The advisor, and no one else, was to provide the substance for press releases on foreign-policy developments! The advisor, and no one else, furnished definitive government positions on foreign-policy matters to the press! The PMO, he said, was composed of a limited number of officers, each with major domestic responsibilities. Not one of them had my foreign-policy background; all had been instructed not to meddle in foreign affairs, which was my exclusive sphere of authority. No one had intervened to help me since it was up to me to take charge. Everyone on the prime minister's team, and that included Jim Bartleman, had to produce or get out!

At least I knew where I stood. There would be no breaking-in period for me. I returned to my lonely house in Ottawa, my tail between my legs, regretting that this wisdom had not been given to me at the beginning rather than at the end of the trip to Mexico – perhaps I would have stayed at home. The reality I now had to face, however, was that after only a few days on the job, I was already in trouble. The senior ranks of the bureaucracy in Foreign Affairs and the PCO, not having had a hand in my selection, were suspicious of and in some cases actually hostile to my appointment. The people in the PMO did not know me and could not be counted on for support until I had earned their confidence.

2

Setting the Agenda

The Canadian people, in their collective wisdom, have more often than not elected leaders with the foreign-policy skills that met the needs of the times.

Government Policy

Returning to my office, I gave myself two months to get a grip. My first task was to draw up a draft work schedule for the prime minister's approval. But in order to do so, I had to be clear on the foreign-policy priorities of the new government and to learn which issues Canada's leader intended to leave to his foreign minister to handle and which he would run with alone. The success or failure of the prime minister's management of foreign policy over the life of the government depended on getting a handle on these matters at the outset of his mandate. I looked first for a clear statement of government policy and was disappointed. In the election campaign of 1993, the Liberal Party published a Red Book detailing the new foreign and defence directions it intended the country to follow should it win, but it was not specific enough for my purposes. Think-tanks, in particular the Canada 21 Council and the National Forum on Canada's International Relations, were feverishly pouring out studies and recommendations for the Foreign Affairs, Defence, and parliamentary policy wonks. Their conclusions were too vague, however, to be of immediate practical use. Foreign Affairs was labouring away on a policy review but it would not be finished until almost a year later (when it would

be issued as the Government Statement on Foreign Policy entitled *Canada in the World*). The Defence review would not come
out until December 1994, as a White Paper on Defence. The
Special Joint Committee of the House of Commons and Senate
on Canada's foreign policy were holding public consultations, but
their reports would not be ready before the end of 1994.

I could not, however, wait for months or even years for a
policy consensus to emerge, and I had neither the temperament
nor the time to commission major studies. A number of items
were already inscribed in pencil on the prime minister's schedule,
and decisions had to be taken on which ones to confirm. Likewise
messages were pouring in from foreign leaders, inviting the prime
minister to their countries, or angling for invitations to come to
Canada. I decided to sound out as many informed people as possible and to consult the prime minister on his priorities before
drawing up an agenda.

The Mood in Canada's Capital

The morale of the public service was terrible in the spring of
1994, and had been so for years. The personnel in Foreign Affairs,
Defence, and CIDA were even more despondent than their con-
freres elsewhere. For the past decade, successive governments had
piled additional burdens on them while freezing their salaries,
cutting their numbers and not replacing staff who were resign-
ing in droves. The previous government had also named two
ardent Quebec nationalists, Marcel Masse and Monique Vézina,
as minister of defence and minister of state for External Affairs
and Development respectively. Their nominations were part of
the *beau risque* strategy that sought to co-opt members of the
nationalist camp in Quebec to the federal cause by offering them
high-profile jobs in the government (the strategy also involved
making Lucien Bouchard the senior minister from Quebec). The
well-meaning approach had been a failure. Marcel Masse I knew
well from my days as ambassador to NATO when he attended the

semi–annual meetings of NATO defence ministers. While he was personally charming, I had to grit my teeth whenever he told me that the days of Canada, as it existed, were numbered. His support and that of Monique Vézina for an independent Quebec, no matter how carefully they camouflaged their views in public when they ostensibly represented a united country, can only have damaged Canada internationally, and was certainly demoralizing for the public servants who worked for them.

All three organizations faced crises of purpose. In Foreign Affairs, staff laboured in a world in which Canada's relative global position had been falling for a generation. The profession of foreign–service officer had also lost its lustre, made worse by a few individuals being caught submitting exaggerated expense claims and by management tolerating cost overruns in the construction of embassies abroad that became widely publicized. The perception had taken root in the greater public and in the public service that Foreign Affairs personnel had become pampered fat cats who enjoyed a lifestyle abroad that other Canadians could only dream about. The reality that the majority of staff worked most of their careers in unhealthy, difficult, and often dangerous environments was overlooked in the rush to condemn the handful who abused the system.

The Defence department faced much bigger problems. While the end of the Cold War had drastically reduced the risk of cataclysmic war in Europe, the world had become a more dangerous place for Canada's men and women in the military. Small hot wars, often ethnically based, were proliferating not just in the Balkans, but in Africa and Asia. Canada had rushed to collect its peace dividend by slashing its already small defence budget and reducing the size of its minuscule armed forces. The professionals knew, however, that they would soon be called upon to provide even larger numbers of men and women to help bring peace to more regions in conflict than in the past, but in circumstances where risks to their lives would be much greater than during the Cold War. Canada, they well knew, needed multi-purpose, well-equipped armed forces with the capability to deploy heavily armed peacekeeping units into areas of conflict and maintain them in the field. A strong lobby led by members of the academic community and other non-governmental organizations, however, had the government's ear and argued that there was no longer a requirement for Canada to maintain such a capability. Some even claimed that all Canada needed was a militia that could be used for civil defence at home, fighting forest fires and combating flooding, while taking on light peacekeeping duties abroad. There was little public pressure to have Defence re-equip the army with better armoured personnel carriers and the navy with modern submarines. And no one, other than a few retired military officers and a handful of academic commentators, protested the decision of the incoming government to cancel an order placed by the outgoing government for state-of-the-art EH-101 Cormorant helicopters to replace its ancient Sea King fleet.

Then there was the Somalia controversy. The Canadian Airborne Regiment, reinforced by an armoured squadron from the Royal Canadian Dragoons, had deployed into Somalia in late 1993 and early 1994 as part of an American-led and U.N.-authorized military operation to help aid agencies assist starving people in conditions of endemic clan warfare. Rotten apples within the ranks were caught torturing and killing prisoners. There was a cover-up and a subsequent Commission of Inquiry. The defence minister dismantled the Airborne, scattering its parachute companies to other combat formations,[6] amidst a scandal that thoroughly demoralized the Canadian Forces. The baby, however, was thrown out with the bath water. Canada had only ten combat battalions to start with, and the scrapping of the Airborne reduced the army's front-line capability by 10 per cent just as demands for Canada to participate in tough peacekeeping operations were growing.

CIDA, already reeling from drastic cuts to its budget, was in the midst of a mid-life crisis. Like most development agencies worldwide, it was trying to come to terms with the reality that aid programs in many countries, since their inception in the period of decolonization in the 1950s and 1960s, had been costly failures,[7] in the words of scathing assessments from the World Bank itself. Corruption, poor governance, and other factors still being evaluated had wasted billions of taxpayers' dollars. For example, Canada provided large sums of money to Zaire over the years, indirectly allowing President Mobutu Sese Seko to keep his cronies supplied with new luxury cars. When I was ambassador in Israel in the late 1980s, my newly appointed Zairean colleague called on me to say that he had served for over ten years as head of the president's bodyguards in Kinshasa. Those had been good years, he said. Each year, as Christmas presents, President Mobutu gave each of the members of his inner circle a new Mercedes. The cost to the Zairean treasury was some $20 million annually, a sum equal to that allocated each year in development assistance by Canada. From his eager smile, he obviously thought I would share his gratitude in having benefited from the rotten system. And in another notorious case, at least a billion dollars was spent in Tanzania for roads and Canadian-style wheat farms, all of which fell to pieces when the Canadian experts departed.

A new wave of gurus in the development field were espousing "tough love" doctrines, saying that private investment flows rather than traditional aid programs were the way of the future, but their theories were unproven. New strategies were required to help marginalized countries develop better systems of governance and better capacities to absorb aid. Until this was done, it was unlikely that the prime minister, who was personally supportive of a strong Canadian aid program, would champion CIDA's cause within Cabinet.[8]

The Prime Minister

In these circumstances, how suited was the new prime minister to tackle these and the other foreign-policy challenges facing Canada in the 1990s? The Canadian people, in their collective wisdom, have more often than not elected leaders with the foreign-policy skills that met the needs of the times. At the height of the Cold War and during the era of decolonization in the 1960s, Lester Pearson, a great internationalist, made Canada proud in the councils of the world. In a more nationalist period, Pierre Trudeau followed brilliant, elitist, somewhat anti-American, and often iconoclastic policies. Brian Mulroney led the fight against apartheid in the Commonwealth and took the tough decisions to pursue Free Trade and NAFTA agreements with the United States in the late 1980s and early 1990s, a time when Canada needed to protect its privileged access to the world's largest market. In Jean Chrétien, Canada was getting someone who understood economics, was comfortable with the business community, and had the personality that made it easy to forge close personal ties with the world leaders whose countries counted the most to Canada. His background as minister in numerous portfolios – including stints in the departments of Industry, Trade and Commerce, National Revenue, Finance, Natural Resources, Indian and Northern Affairs, Justice, Foreign Affairs, and Treasury Board – as well as his private-sector experience when out of office, prepared him well for such a role. With his high personal ratings in the polls, he had the credibility with the public to persuade them to embrace rather than to seek to hide from the economic currents of the mid-1990s. With the Cold War over, he would be able to focus on preparing the country for a profound transformation to a knowledge-based economy built on global competition, flexible labour markets, innovation, information technology, a growing service sector, and for a world in which the United States had become the sole superpower.

By the end of May, I was familiar with the views of the major players around town, had met many times with the prime minister, knew where he stood on the big issues, and had a better feel for how I could be of help to him. He had thought long and hard about Canada's position in the world, had specific objectives he intended to pursue and ideas on how to achieve them. The greatest and most immediate threats facing Canada as the millennium came to a close, he said, were economic and psychological. The country was mired in the deepest recession it had faced in decades, unemployment was at record levels, and economic growth was not producing new jobs. The public had lost faith in politicians, in the public service, and in itself. There was a perception that Canada was at the mercy of the impersonal forces of globalization and risked losing its place as one of the most prosperous countries in the world.

The state of the economy, the prime minister believed, was the most pressing problem. There was fear that the Free Trade Agreement, signed by Prime Minister Brian Mulroney and President Ronald Reagan in 1988, and the NAFTA agreement negotiated with Presidents Bill Clinton and Carlos Salinas de Gortari, had tied Canada to an American economy in terminal decline, and to a Mexican one with uncompetitively low wage rates. The public was convinced that Canadian factories would relocate to Mexico and to the United States and that jobs would be lost in Canada. The prime minister was also worried at the size of the debt and deficit. "Young men in red suspenders," he repeated to me constantly, might exploit these weak economic indicators and manipulate the currency markets in New York, London, and Tokyo and force a collapse of the Canadian dollar. It was a serious threat. The *Wall Street Journal* even ran a story at this time about Canada becoming an honorary member of the Third World.

Ironically, the state of Canadian national unity was one bright spot in this world of gloom. Or at least that was the conventional wisdom, shared by the prime minister, in the spring of 1994. The people of Quebec, by a sixty to forty margin had voted against sovereignty in a referendum on May 20, 1980, and the issue had languished on the backburner of Quebec politics for years. Everyone recognized, however, that sooner or later the people of Quebec would grow tired of the incumbent provincial-federalist Liberal government and vote it out of office. The incoming administration would be led by the Parti Québécois, and it had promised to hold another referendum. The prime minister, however, was not unduly worried at this prospect since opinion surveys in these early days indicated that Quebeckers would massively reject sovereignty when they went to the polls. Just to be on the safe side, however, he intended to spend time and effort lobbying foreign leaders to reject overtures from a future Quebec government to support a sovereign Quebec.

Strategic Objectives

The prime minister's strategic objectives, as I understood them, were to make Canadians proud of their country and a model for other nations to look up to. He would stimulate export-led growth, reverse the decline in our international position, and establish better balanced ties with the United States. Under his leadership, Canada would take full advantage of our membership in the Group of Seven major industrialized democracies (G7) to influence global macroeconomic policies to Canada's benefit, to consolidate bilateral ties of privilege with the big countries, to work hard to have Canada emerge as the leader of the so-called middle powers that were barking at our heels, and to embrace rather than shy away from globalization.

In so doing, Canada would have a more influential economic and political voice on the world stage, obtain the reforms in the multilateral system that were crucial to our economic well-being, and more subtly, create a network of linkages to help balance Canada's increasing economic and political dependency on the United States. Canadians were, he admitted, concerned that NAFTA could lead to a greater dominance of Canada's markets by the United States. His answer to this legitimate fear was to expand NAFTA to include all the countries of the Americas in a giant Free Trade Association. This would be a win–win situation; trade and prosperity would grow throughout the hemisphere and Canada would not be left alone in the company of Mexico to confront the giant United States in its trade disputes. Perhaps most important of all, he would give Canadians a common international goal that everyone could work together to achieve in a decade of growing uncertainty and great global change.

The G7

An immediate challenge, he said, was to consolidate Canada's position in the G7 and to use our membership to defend aggressively our global economic position. The exclusive club of the world's major industrialized democracies had been founded in 1975 by the United States, France, the United Kingdom, Germany, and Japan to discuss world economic matters, but the agenda had grown over the years to include political issues and Italy and Canada had joined one year later. The prime minister was aware that Canada had gained admittance the following year, largely at the insistence of the Americans who wanted to add another North American voice to an organization dominated in numbers by the Europeans. No one had yet challenged Canada's membership. But the Netherlands had let it be known that its external trade figures came close to matching those of Canada. Spain and major industrializing countries such as India, China, Mexico, Brazil were not shy in complaining that their economies had caught up and in some cases exceeded that of Canada in the years since 1976. Academics had mused that the time had come for the entity either to become larger to take in these new economic powers or to become a smaller grouping restricted to the United States, the European Union, and Japan.

Prime Minister Chrétien took these possibilities seriously. The Europeans were making enormous strides in these years in their drive for greater economic and political unity, and a decision, however far in the future, to let the country holding the presidency of their union represent and speak for them in the G7 could not be excluded. The approach that he announced to Foreign Affairs Undersecretary Gordon Smith and me, and which he pursued assiduously in the coming years, was to push his colleagues to admit Russia and turn the G7 into a G8.[9] (Russia already attended the second day of the summits as a member of the Political Eight or P-8 when world political matters were discussed.) In so doing, he would, he reckoned, achieve two goals: integrate an old enemy state into a powerful mainstream multilateral structure, and eliminate the possibility that the big European states, the Americans, and the Japanese might opt to convert the G7 to a G3 that shut out Canada.

Losing its place as a member of the G7, the prime minister well knew, would be a calamitous setback for Canada's image internationally and would confirm the predictions of the *Wall Street Journal* about the decline of the nation. For the G7 was one of the two most powerful multilateral structures on the world scene in the 1990s. The United Nations Security Council, paramount in dealing with world peace and security, was the other one. The New York–based body, however, had no role to play in world economic affairs – the new centre of gravity in the post–Cold War world. That was the domain of the G7. Moreover, the Security Council, the prime minister was well aware, was dominated by a caucus of permanent members – the five big power victors of the Second World War: the United States, Russia, China, Britain, and France. Canada could hope to be elected to it once every decade, if lucky, and our influence in the United Nations as a whole, while considerable, was not based on belonging to any inner group. Our membership in the G7, therefore, was our trump card for international influence. In addition to prestige, it gave us a means, not available to other middle powers, to influence global economic policies to our advantage.

And the advantage the prime minister sought was to use the G7 to reform the Bretton Woods institutions – the International Monetary Fund (IMF) and the World Bank – set up in July 1944 to regulate the post-war financial system. The two institutions had evolved over the years, the first as the guardian of international financial order and the second as a key source of development capital for the Third World. Should currency speculators take a run at the Canadian dollar, it would be the IMF that would be charged with restoring order. Its record in recent years had not been stellar, however, and everyone admitted that it and its sister institution badly needed reform. It was essential therefore that Canada use its membership in the G7 to strengthen these institutions.

Embracing Globalization

The prime minister told me that he would take full advantage of Canada's geographic location, with its Pacific and Atlantic coasts and its border with the United States, its multicultural, well-educated, and disciplined population at home to attract foreign investment and find new markets for our exporters. He would also lead Team Canada trade missions, rallying Canadians from the worlds of business, academia, and provincial, federal, and municipal governments in a common cause to make Canada better known internationally and to draw the attention of ordinary citizens to the markets which were becoming more accessible as a result of globalization. The prime minister knew that the challenge was great, but it was not in his nature to shy away from a fight. Supported in his plans by Mrs. Chrétien, who provided unofficial and unsung counsel on many of these issues, he had enormous and passionate faith that Canadians would rise to the challenges he was setting for them.

The Agenda

In late May, I called on Jean Pelletier armed with my recommendations on strategic priorities and international obligations the prime minister should adopt not just for the coming months but for the years to come. He provided helpful suggestions and incorporated my programming proposals into a draft master long-term schedule. We then trekked up Parliament Hill to discuss my findings with Canada's leader. I told him that Foreign Affairs, Defence, and Parliament would eventually submit to him the results of their reviews. Having talked to staff officers who were working on the Foreign Affairs review that was expected to set the tone for the others, I told him that they would say that governments had three core foreign-policy responsibilities: to ensure the security of the state, to provide for the economic well-being of their citizens, and to project internationally the values of the nation. The first two constituted irreducible vital national interests that all governments, regardless of their political colouring, were bound by their compact with the electorate to promote and defend; and the third was desirable if the resources were available but not essential like the first two. The big challenge facing the drafters, I told him, was to translate these general goals into specific policy initiatives, and that would take time.

But, I suggested, that delay should not prove to be much of a problem. The prime minister already knew what he wanted to accomplish and I was feeding his perspectives, especially his views on Canada's role as a middle power, into the Foreign Affairs policy review process.

I started my advice with a general caution. As an old foreign-service hand, I said that good judgement and common sense were more useful than theoretical models in handling the overwhelming majority of foreign-policy problems that governments had to deal with. Good judgement, I recalled, and not a conceptual framework had been the key to allowing him to deal with pressures from the Americans to launch a NATO bombing campaign in Bosnia that would have imperilled Canadian peacekeepers blocked in Srebrenica during his first NATO summit in Brussels just four months earlier.[10] Beautifully formulated lists of areas of geographic and substantive priorities, short-, medium-, and long-term goals or visions of Canada's place in the world would be of little use if not accompanied by common sense.

I then provided my thinking on a conceptual framework. Canada's foreign horizons, I told the prime minister, had traditionally been limited to the United States, Europe, and Japan in that order of importance. In my proposed ranking, the United States would remain at the top, followed by the Asia–Pacific region, Europe, Latin America, and Russia. Canada's relations with the United States outweighed by far the importance of our ties with any other country, or for that matter, any group of countries, in economic, security, and cultural terms. However, the time had come to accord greater attention to the newly emerging countries of the Asia–Pacific region, Russia, and Latin America. The Asia–Pacific region followed the United States because it was the zone of greatest global economic growth and hence the one with the greatest potential for expanding Canadian trade. It was also the most important source of new immigrants and of fee-paying overseas students.

Although I had dropped Europe into third place behind the Asia–Pacific region, the old continent remained important because it was an area of instability, and large numbers of Canadian troops were committed to peacekeeping operations in the Balkans. It also remained an important source of foreign direct investment and had shared values which needed cultivating. We also needed to be in a position to pre-empt any effort by France to influence our national unity debate. Latin America followed Europe and merited cultivation because all of its governments, with the exception of Cuba, were democratic for the first time in history, providing us with a unique opportunity to establish close political links and to strengthen our trade and investment ties with their fast-growing economies in the process. And Russia, while undergoing a difficult transition from half a century of communist rule to democracy and a market economy, was still the world's largest country, with enormous potential for growth. The Middle East and Africa, I said, should be left to his ministers to deal with for the time being. He would have more than enough on his plate in tackling his initial priorities.

The draft work schedule I proposed reflected this geographic ordering of priorities and was built around the summit meetings he would be obliged to attend each year. Canada, I said, probably belonged to more international clubs than any other country of its size. And the number was growing, making it necessary for Canada's leader to attend far more international meetings than his predecessors. There were the annual summits of the G7 and of the eighteen-member Asia-Pacific Economic Co-operation forum (APEC). Every other year, there were meetings of the fifty-three-member Commonwealth, the fifty-member Francophonie, and the fifty-five-member Organization for Security and Co-operation in Europe (OSCE). The United States had just proposed convening a summit of all the democratic countries of the Americas for later in the year to discuss establishing a Free Trade Area in the Americas (FTAA) and follow-up meetings could be expected. The United Nations could be counted on to convene a summit at least once every two years and NATO about once every three years. APEC, the OSCE, and the Summit of the Americas meetings were obligations that previous Canadian leaders had not had to assume. Canada was also a member of the Organization of American States (OAS), which it had joined in 1990, but no meetings at the level of head of state or government were planned for the foreseeable future.

I told him that I had reviewed the agendas of his predecessors and built in extra time to take care of the growing demands the management of foreign affairs would take. My rough estimate was that he would need to be on the road between six and eight weeks each year. That should allow him to attend obligatory summits and fit in six or seven official or unofficial visits to individual countries. There would also be major calls on his time at home. The leading events looming on the horizon were the obligations to host the G7 summit of 1995 and the APEC and Francophonie summits in 1997 and 1999 respectively. He should also plan to receive six or seven heads of state or government each year on official or state visits. Finally, he would want to see a certain number of distinguished visitors such as foreign ministers, heads of international organizations, and senior members of sister parliaments for thirty-minute courtesy calls in his House of Commons office; these could be limited to three per week. At least 20 per cent of his time, I hesitantly noted, would have to be devoted to international relations – a figure that would have seemed amazingly high to Lester Pearson, the prime minister when I joined Foreign Affairs three decades earlier. (And my forecasts would prove to be conservative.)

The prime minister gave his approval to the proposed long-term work schedule. We could fine-tune his agenda, he said, as time went on. He then instructed me to begin preparations immediately for the first Team Canada mission to go to China later in 1994. He also expressed strong interest in becoming personally involved in deepening links with Latin America, which he knew well from his days as minister of Trade and Commerce. He was a strong believer in personal diplomacy and intended to make the establishment of ties with leaders of our partners in the G7 and in major developing economies an early priority.

Sharing Responsibilities

The prime minister discouraged the notion that there could be any division of labour between himself and his ministers on Trade, Foreign Affairs, and Defence matters. He would decide on a case-by-case basis which matters he would handle and which he would leave to others. A head of government could not in good conscience simply delegate issues in these sensitive fields to others; the public expected their prime minister to be in charge and to be seen to be in charge.

The ministers who served him in these years respected these rules while focusing on areas of their specific interests, carving out space and reputations for themselves in the process. Roy MacLaren, a former trade commissioner and successful business-man, followed by Art Eggleton, previously the mayor of Toronto, were the trade ministers; they would find a kindred spirit in Jean Chrétien, arguably the most activist promoter of Canadian trade and investment among Canada's prime ministers since Confed-eration. André Ouellet and Lloyd Axworthy were the foreign ministers. Ouellet and the prime minister had been close friends and political allies for decades prior to the 1984 leadership contest to replace Pierre Trudeau as head of the Liberal Party. After promising to support Chrétien, Ouellet changed his mind and backed John Turner for the job, which angered Chrétien. In time, their relations improved but the highly efficient Ouellet never seemed entirely comfortable in dealing directly with Chrétien in the years I saw them in action. Ouellet (who went on to be a controversial head of Canada Post) was particularly close to the business community, and he used all the tools at his disposition, including the Industrial Co-operation Program of CIDA, to promote Canadian exports. He was also an early supporter of banning anti-personnel mines.

Lloyd Axworthy, who succeeded him, was from the left wing of the Liberal Party and was much more comfortable in dealing with Jean Chrétien. He championed the doctrines of soft power and human security, an approach highly popular among Canadians, with their sense that the conduct of foreign affairs should have a strong moral basis. In Axworthy's view, many people misunderstand the concept and think that adherence to soft power obviates the need to spend money on Canada's armed forces to obtain hard power and state security.[11] Perhaps Canada's most imaginative foreign minister since his hero Lester Pearson in the 1950s, he would at times overshadow the prime minister with his imaginative initiatives, helping to create an International

Criminal Court, stemming the trade in small arms, and fighting the use of child soldiers. His decision to carry on the work on anti-personnel mines, working closely with the prime minister to ensure its success, was the highlight of his term in office. In general, the prime minister had the confidence to give his ministers wide latitude to pursue their business and human-security initiatives that appealed to powerful domestic constituencies and served the national interest.

Crisis Management

Finally, the prime minister was mindful of the need to ensure that international crises affecting Canada were properly managed. He appreciated that the head of government was ultimately responsible for national security and must be directly involved in the management of international emergencies affecting the safety of the state and its citizens. The consequence was that when a crisis occurred, he made room to deal with it whether by day or night to the exclusion of whatever else was on his agenda. It was my job to provide him all the assistance I could. I chaired inter-departmental working groups, arranged for the convening of ad hoc meetings of Cabinet, and activated back-channel contacts with my opposite numbers at the White House in Washington, 10 Downing Street in London, the Elysée in Paris, and the Office of the Chancellor in Bonn. This network provided the latest information on breaking developments to which foreign ministries were often not privy. This was critical for crisis management purposes when decisions often have to be made with incomplete data, and facilitated direct communications between the heads of government themselves. The wars in the Balkans were a constant concern in 1994 and 1995. The fish dispute with Spain also dominated 1995, Canada's involvement in Eastern Zaire was the single greatest problem in 1996, and the effort to bring about democratic change in Cuba was a priority from 1996 to 1998.

3

The Grip Is Got

Early June found me somewhere over the Atlantic accompanying the prime minister as he travelled to Europe to participate in the fiftieth anniversary of the Normandy landings and to see the troops in Bosnia.

The Horsemen of the Apocalypse

By June, the initial planning process was over. The world had not, however, stood still while I worked on the prime minister's policy agenda and work schedule. In April, two events occurred that were to have far-reaching consequences for international relations and for Canadian foreign policy. First, the presidents of Burundi and Rwanda were killed when their aircraft was shot down at Kigali airport. The situation in Burundi remained calm but in Rwanda, a death-squad militia, called the Interhamwe, drawn from the majority Hutu population, began killing members of the Tutsi minority. It was soon evident that what was going on was not random killing. Rivers filled with bloated corpses soon became our evening television fare as the killing went on and on. Insulated from the sound, sight, and smell of death by the cold medium of television, none of us could grasp the horror, befitting Joseph Conrad's *Heart of Darkness* or Francis Ford Coppola's *Apocalypse Now*. Incomprehension marked the faces of everyone I spoke to that week in April, including those of my colleagues on the senior management committee of the PCO. They looked at me blankly when I briefed them, clearly not even certain where Rwanda was on the map. I asked myself, not for the first time in a career where I had been exposed to human indifference and mayhem, what made people do evil things? With the Nazis, it was a mix of perversion in the direction of modern society, the industrial means of extermination, and anti-Semitism that led to Dachau. In Africa, these factors were not in play. How was it possible for tens of thousands of ordinary people to hack to death hundreds of thousands of other ordinary people – often neighbours – taking lunch breaks among the dead and dying before starting again? And day after day, and week after week!

And no one, especially world leaders, wanted to do anything. We were living in the post–Cold War era where economic benefit, rather than East-West security and ideological competition, was the ruling standard for international behaviour. Rwanda was poor, overpopulated, and had no natural resources worth exploiting. There was even reluctance to call the butchery "genocide" since that might make governments feel obliged to do something to stop it. And Rwanda was not Iraq. Why risk the lives of young Europeans and North Americans to save the lives of civilians in a land that did not even have oil or gas reserves? The failure of the international community to act would turn out to be a crime against humanity as grievous, in its own way, as the behaviour of the Hutu executioners. The prime minister would not forget. When the world appeared to be faced with a similar disaster in Eastern Zaire in November 1996, he was more than willing to have Canada do its share to head off another catastrophe.

Second, the situation in Bosnia flared up. In early April, the Bosnian Serbs took hostage sixty-five United Nations Protection Force (UNPROFOR) officers, including sixteen Canadians, in retaliation for the bombing by NATO aircraft of Serb army positions. Canada's foreign and defence ministers contacted their opposite numbers but the prime minister took the lead, working the telephones, consulting his French, British, and American colleagues as well as the United Nations Secretary-General. They had little to suggest other than a pious hope that the stalled peace process might bring results. But the Serbs held all the cards. Canada had to accept that our forces did not have the authority or equipment to fight; there was nothing that we or our allies could do other than to cave in to the Serb demands. The United Nations, with as much dignity as possible in the circumstances, which was not much, quietly gave the word to NATO to stop the bombing for the time being and the hostages were released. It was now evident that the United Nations peacekeeping forces on the ground, including the Canadian battalions in Croatia and Bosnia, had become virtual military and political prisoners. The prime minister intended to visit Bosnia as soon as possible to see conditions on the ground for himself.

May brought a visit that would have a lasting effect on Canadian foreign policy. The president of the International Committee of the Red Cross (ICRC), Cornelio Sommaruga, the bespectacled, heavily built former foreign minister of Switzerland, called on the prime minister in his Centre Block office, raised the issue of anti-personnel mines, and said something had to be done to ban their use. Having worked with the ICRC in Bangladesh, where it ran refugee camps housing millions, and in Israel, where it monitored the treatment of Palestinian prisoners, I knew the organization and a number of its senior officers. One of its top officials, Frédéric Maurice, with whom I had developed particularly close ties, had just been killed by Serb artillery fire as he led a convoy of trucks laden with humanitarian aid into Sarajevo. When I expressed my heartfelt condolences, Sommaruga's eyes filled with tears.

Sommaruga told the prime minister that his organization's mandate included reunifying families divided by war and bringing help to prisoners of war. It was also, he said, to press governments to eliminate weapons of war that cause indiscriminate or unnecessary suffering. Thousands of people were being killed and maimed each year and huge areas of fertile farming land rendered useless for cultivation by one particular blind instrument:

mines scattered by rampaging armies during the proliferating conflicts of the Third World. Civil society in the form of more than a thousand non-governmental organizations from countries around the world and loosely grouped under a steering committee of the International Campaign to Ban Mines, headed by an American, Jody Williams, was mobilizing international public opinion. Governments were starting to move; growing numbers were banning the export of any type of mine. Toothless provisions governing their use were already on the books – in the form of the 1980 Convention on Certain Conventional Weapons. An international treaty banning their use, however, was needed. Thus introduced to the issue, the prime minister made the crusade against anti-personnel mines a national and personal policy priority, becoming one of the first heads of government to adopt the cause.

Organizing the Prime Minister

Early June found me somewhere over the Atlantic accompanying the prime minister as he travelled to Europe to participate in the fiftieth anniversary of the Normandy landings and to see the troops in Bosnia. The amateurish administrative arrangements that had caused grief on earlier trips were now a thing of the past. A Canadian Forces Airbus with ample space for PMO staff, technicians, RCMP bodyguards, and press was the means of transportation, rather than a small Challenger jet. There were three sections: a forward one for the prime minister, his wife, and senior advisors; a central one for communications people plus technicians and bodyguards; and a large third one for media. Seats in the first two sections had been configured for work, which was what most of us did throughout the journey. I sat in the forward section across an aisle from the chief of staff to be able to discuss foreign-policy issues with the prime minister. The atmosphere on board, set by the prime minister, was businesslike and friendly, as it would be on all future flights.

My relations with the team in the PMO had changed dramatically and rapidly for the better after I followed Jean Pelletier's advice, taking charge of the foreign and defence files and then guarding them like a hungry dog his bone. Peter Donolo and Eddie Goldenberg I now counted as friends. I had established good ties as well with the other members of the PMO who had missed the trip to Mexico: Director of Policy Planning Chaviva Hosek and Press Secretary Patrick Parisot. I had also solidified links with my team in the Foreign and Defence Policy Secretariat. Just as important, I had discovered allies among the army of Foreign Affairs and Defence colleagues at the so-called working level – junior, middle-ranking, and senior officers – whom I had come to know during almost three decades in a dozen postings around the globe. They were Canada's real experts on the policy issues, they knew and trusted me, and would work their hearts out whenever I sought their help.

Shortly after takeoff, Peter Donolo came to me with the latest drafts of the speeches the prime minister would deliver in the course of the coming visit. We went over the text, line by line, and he accepted the changes I suggested with good grace. They were then retyped and handed to the prime minister for his comments; by the time we landed, there would be a consensus on the messages. I then reread the briefing books that I had forwarded to the prime minister some days earlier, and delved more deeply into the substance by reading files on specific issues that my team had prepared for background. My object was to be as well informed as the local head of post on problems that could come up, since I would have the job of dealing with them should they intrude into the program.

When we arrived in London, a staff officer mounted the stairs to escort the Chrétiens to a waiting British minister who provided the official welcome and accompanied them past the obligatory guard of honour on the requisite red carpet to their car. I now knew the drill. I joined the others in ignoring the assembled

protocol officers and staff from the High Commission and proceeded directly to my place in the motorcade; if I dawdled, I
would be left behind. Motorcycle police cleared the way through
the evening traffic to the Inn on the Park hotel where we would
stay during this, and all subsequent visits to London. At the delegation office in the hotel, there was a bulging file of messages for
me that I set aside to read later. Peter Donolo, High Commissioner
Fred Eaton, and I then briefed the press; happily, I knew many of
them from my days at NATO and they were friendly. I returned to
the office to deal with my pile of messages, to call my deputy in
Ottawa to seek his advice on a difficult matter and to eat a room-
service meal. Before retiring, I prepared notes to brief the prime
minister the next morning, and handwritten cue cards with key
points for each meeting he would have in the course of the day.

The next morning, I checked overnight developments in the
office and made for the intimate room used to brief the prime
minister. Accompanied by his executive assistant, the prime minister entered exactly on time and sat down without saying a word;
he was always punctual, and his staff followed his example. He had
read his briefing book, but like a senior lawyer preparing a case
he wanted to review the details beforehand. This time, after giving
the head of post an opportunity to say a few words of welcome,
I took the lead. The approach adopted at this meeting would set
the pattern for all future briefing sessions. Having seen in Mexico
City that the prime minister had an uncanny memory, was
intensely focused, and used cue cards well, I shot insights, facts,
figures, and biographical information at him as if I were manning
a machine gun and he was the target. I knew that he would
remember every detail. The cue cards provided only the names of
the people he would meet and a list of topics to be raised.

In twenty minutes, the briefing was over and the prime minister left to join his motorcade at the main entrance, the rest of
us hurrying along behind. I slipped him his first card as we arrived
for his first appointment at 10 Downing Street with Prime

Minister John Major. It was then up the stairs past a portrait of a former occupant, Winston Churchill, whose funeral I attended in 1964 when I happened to be living in London as a penniless adventurer.[12] A smiling official ushered us into a small conference room where a butler in formal attire promptly served tea. The two leaders, meeting officially for the first time, sized each other up and liked what they saw. Both were self-made men from humble backgrounds: Jean Chrétien, son of a mill worker from Shawinigan, was meeting John Major, son of a circus performer.

The prime minister pulled the cue card, written in my scrawling handwriting, out of his pocket and was ready for business. His British host opened a voluminous briefing book, searched for the right chapter, and began the discussion. They brought each other up to date on their respective domestic, political, and economic situations. John Major wanted to know how the battle for national unity was going; Jean Chrétien was interested in the growing strength of regionalism in Europe. Major lobbied for a British company seeking a government contract in Canada and Chrétien did the same for a Canadian firm seeking entry to the United Kingdom market. They then discussed the situation in Bosnia, criticizing the Americans who offered free advice and use of their air force to bomb the Serbs from twenty thousand feet but refused to deploy their ground troops into harm's way. Both said that they would like to pull out their forces, but believed that they would be abandoning innocent civilians if they did. Chrétien told Major that he wanted leaders at the Naples G7 summit to discuss the impact speculators were having on otherwise sound national currencies. Major had no objection, all too aware that the British pound had been forced to its knees in 1992 by the money-market manipulations of George Soros, the famous Hungarian-born American financier, but he doubted that the problem could be fixed. Chrétien said that the time had come for Russia to be admitted to the club as a full member, turning the G7 into the G8. John Major demurred – "not yet."

D-Day Commemorations and the Royals

An hour later, at our next event at Green Park to mark the inauguration of a memorial to Canadian war dead, I watched from my place two rows back as a happy Princess Diana, separated but not yet divorced from Prince Charles, took her seat beside Prince Andrew. They had been friends since childhood when she lived with her parents on the royal estate at Sandringham and their spectacular marital problems had been splashed across the newspapers for years. But if there was any pain, it was not evident on this sunny, cool day in London as we waited for the arrival of Her Majesty and Prince Philip to start the official ceremonies. They launched into a playful conversation with much joking and laughing but I tried not to listen – it was their business. What a contrast to the cold, almost sullen Princess Diana whom Marie-Jeanne and I had met some years earlier at a diplomatic reception in Brussels. I did not blame her at the time; the event was just another dull gathering to promote British exports which, to tell the truth, we attended only to meet the famous spouse of Prince Charles. I was to think of this day in London when I heard the news reports of her death on Labour Day weekend in 1997. And again in May 2003 when as Lieutenant-Governor of Ontario, I hosted Prince Andrew at an official luncheon at Queen's Park in Toronto.

We spent the weekend at Gosport on the south coast of England, attending ceremonies to mark the embarkation of the more than fifteen thousand Canadian troops that stormed ashore at Juno Beach on June 6, 1944. The chill pouring rain did not bother our British hosts in the slightest. Desperately cold and damp, Eddie Goldenberg and I sought shelter under the platform holding the official party, but were soaked anyway from water dripping through the cracks. Prime Minister Chrétien was allowed to take one bodyguard and one flunky on the ceremonial crossing of the Channel the next day on the Royal Yacht HMS *Britannia*. I was the flunky. We went on board in good class-conscious British style. Flunkies and bodyguards negotiated the service gangway, leading into a lower deck close to the kitchen, to be greeted by cheerful ordinary seamen. The leaders and their spouses strolled aboard on a magnificent walkway to the upper deck, to be met with formal whistles and salutes by the captain and his officers in full-braid uniform. After I had been confined to a cabin with an RCMP officer long enough to make sure that I knew my station in life, an equerry of the Queen came to get me, saying that Her Majesty had decided to allow diplomatic advisors to mix with the others. I abandoned my new-found RCMP friend to her lonely existence in the cabin and headed for the action. In the main stateroom, Her Majesty was issuing last-minute instructions to the serving staff on how to receive her distinguished guests. Her conscientious attention to detail and concern for the well-being of her invitees aroused my admiration, a feeling reinforced when Marie-Jeanne and I called on her in Buckingham Palace shortly after I had assumed my duties as her representative in Ontario in 2002.

The guests were fifty-two in number and included assorted kings, queens, presidents, prime ministers, and foreign ministers who represented the coalition that defeated Germany in the Second World War. The Germans and Austrians had pointedly not been invited. Soon a gaggle of the great of the world congregated for morning tea. The British Royal family was out in force and threw themselves energetically into playing the role of good hosts. I drank my tea with the other advisors, all of us casting furtive glances in the direction of our particular leaders in case he or she had need of our wisdom.

The guests then moved outside to watch as HMS *Britannia* took the salute from one of the greatest arrays of warships assembled for review in British waters since the war – fifty-five destroyers, frigates, aircraft carriers, and landing craft plus ten merchant ships. Finally, modern fast military jets from eighteen nations, followed by thirteen different types of World War II aircraft, including Swordfish, Lancasters, Hurricanes, and Spitfires, flew by in a show of air power and nostalgia. In mid-Channel, President Clinton departed to board the American aircraft carrier *George Washington* – it would not do, it seemed, for the president of the United States to arrive in France to commemorate D-Day on a British ship, when it was the Americans and not the British who sustained the greatest losses exactly fifty years earlier coming ashore on the beaches.

The host at my table for lunch was Princess Margaret, Countess of Snowdon, the Queen's sister, who showed no sign of the illness that would end her life a few years later. Lech Walesa, president of Poland, and Douglas Hurd, British foreign secretary, both of whom I had met at NATO when I was ambassador there, were among the eight lucky guests at my table who feasted on what my souvenir menu tells me was *Couronne de Tomates à l'homard, Suprême de Volaille Edouard VII*, and *Framboises St. Georges* washed down by Gewürztraminer Grand Cru Altenberg 1989 and Pauillac Château Latour 1990. The Duke of Edinburgh presided over a dinner of similar quality later that evening when our table for eight included Prime Minister Paul Keating of Australia and President Václav Havel of the Czech Republic. In all of this I should not have been surprised when I discovered that royals enjoy talking about everyday matters just like the rest of us, but of course I was. And just when I was beginning to believe that it was my natural lot in life to consort with the great and famous, the Queen's equerry came to remind me and the other diplomatic advisors that we should not forget to use the servant gangway when exiting the ship.

Normandy, June 1994

In Normandy, I took my place in the crowd at Omaha Beach to watch the victors of the Second World War, led by presidents Mitterrand and Clinton, solemnly commemorate the landings which spelled the beginning of the end for Hitler in 1944. It was raining and cold but the assembled veterans, now old men, did not mind; they knew that this would be the last pilgrimage to France for most of them. Charles Lynch, a Southam news columnist and a former war correspondent whose work I had admired for years, ignored the weather in his medal-bedecked blazer, and stood laughing with another old veteran, Michel Gauvin, winner of the DSO and a retired Canadian ambassador. Both would pass away shortly afterwards.

Our group headed for Courseulles-sur-Mer where the Canadians came ashore, making greater gains than either the Americans or the British before being bogged down in the fighting further inland. I thought of my mother's cousin from the Mujikaning First Nation, wounded as he parachuted in the dark behind enemy lines fifty years before with his mates. I thought of a boyhood friend of my mother, Sanford Stinson also from Mujikaning, who had been killed in the fighting at Caen several weeks after D-Day. His son, a long-time and progressive chief of his First Nation, had never seen his father's grave, and had asked me to take a picture of it for him. I arrived early at the Commonwealth War Cemetery where commemorative ceremonies led by the prime minister of Canada and the president of France would be held later in the morning. Sanford Stinson's tombstone, I saw, was adorned with flowers among the freshly cut grass and chairs set up for the Canadian war veterans coming later to honour their fallen comrades. The son, I noted, was now twice the age his father had been when he had died. The father, I also thought, would have been proud to have known that his son had grown up to be a leader of his people.

When he arrived I called the prime minister aside to speak to him about the sacrifice native soldiers had made for their country in the wars of the twentieth century. My own Indian great-grandfather had been wounded in the First World War and returned to die on the reserve, his lungs ravaged by mustard gas. I told him that native soldiers were wounded or died for a Canada which, in those days, treated them as second-class citizens and did not accord them the same benefits as white veterans when they returned from overseas. The prime minister was pleased to include a reference to Sanford Stinson in the speech he delivered in a broadcast direct to Canada from Juno Beach early in the afternoon.

Bosnia, June 1994

Rounding out this European tour with the prime minister, I accompanied him to Bosnia. We were the only ones in the forward compartment of the Airbus leaving Paris at four in the morning for Split on the Croatian coast. He was not in the best of moods and waved me away when I tried to impart some of my knowledge on what he would encounter on arrival. Perhaps I should not have woken him up. The sole occupant in the middle compartment was Peter Donolo. In the rear were a handful of disgruntled reporters. They were mad because we had informed them of the Bosnia portion of the tour at the last minute and rejected our explanation that we could not tell them earlier for security reasons. They were also grouchy because there was not enough room on the helicopters we would use to get from Split to Visoko, the Canadian base near Sarajevo, for all of the large media contingent that was participating in the prime minister's spring tour of Europe.

Major-General John Arch MacInnis, the most senior Canadian officer in the theatre, and Sam Hanson, chargé d'affaires at the Canadian embassy in Zagreb, were on the tarmac to greet us. Both were old friends: Sam, from when we served together at NATO in the 1970s; and John Arch, from my stint as High Commissioner accredited to Cyprus from Israel in the late 1980s when he was deputy force commander at U.N. headquarters in Nicosia. They rapidly brought the prime minister up to date on the latest developments. It was, they said, a depressing time. UNPROFOR had been unable to halt the conflict, and had no coherent strategy. The Muslims and Croats had just stopped fighting each other and were united in a common alliance under a new political entity called the Federation, to fight the Serbs. Their war goals included maintaining the territorial integrity of Bosnia and obtaining 58 per cent of the land for their peoples. The Serbs wanted separation from the newly independent state and union with their fellow Serbs in Croatia and Serbia in a "Greater Serbia." They also wanted as much as they could keep of the 72 per cent of the country they controlled and had ethnically cleansed. Having just humiliated UNPROFOR forces and prevailed to date in the fighting with the Croats and Muslims, they had the wind in their sails.

John Arch then led us into the terminal where we changed quickly into military uniform. I was quite proud of myself, wearing a uniform for the first time, until I glanced in the mirror to see only a white-haired public servant impersonating a soldier. We then boarded two British Sea King helicopters – the press in one, and the rest of us in the other, sitting on our bulletproof vests to protect ourselves from possible hostile fire from below, which made us feel even more vulnerable. Heavily armed members of Canada's Joint Task Force Two, an elite military formation trained for hostage rescue and commando-type operations, modelled on the British Special Air Service Regiment, were our bodyguards. The countryside was deceptively peaceful as we flew low over village after village of gutted and deserted houses. The helicopter with the press scooted ahead to land before us and to take photos for the morning papers in Canada. Arriving at our destination, we scrambled out in fine military style, but the prime minister's helmet was on backwards. The media were now happy; they had a story and revenge in the first minute of the visit. I simply did not care about this so-called media flop. I was more interested in seeing how our troops were coping.

The setting was familiar to me, having served twice at NATO headquarters and lived in war zones as a diplomat. This time, however, the soldiers were Canadian and I felt vicarious pride for their accomplishments in difficult conditions. There were more than two thousand Canadian military personnel on two ships offshore, on the NATO airbase in Ancona, Italy, and in battalions in Croatia and Bosnia. The soldiers we met were responsible for providing security for humanitarian relief convoys in central Bosnia, when the Serbs allowed, and for monitoring the regularly broken ceasefire agreements in the region. They were unwilling and helpless witnesses to the most abhorrent human rights abuses and all too aware of the hopeless nature of UNPROFOR's overextended missions; now they stood silently as the prime minister announced that Cabinet had decided to renew their mandate for another six months. In June 1994, the still prevailing philosophy among senior military and civilian officers at headquarters was that real men did not suffer from combat stress. Soldiers were encouraged to keep their feelings to themselves. Many of these soldiers would suffer from post-traumatic stress syndrome on return to Canada.

We moved on to Sarajevo, a much more dangerous place. Our bodyguards met us in armoured personnel carriers on the airport tarmac, an area exposed to sniper fire and mortar shelling from both Serbs and Muslims, and whisked us to the terminal building, where we exchanged our uniforms for our civilian clothes. Two armoured cars, their back doors open and their motors running, waited for us when we re-emerged. Lieutenant General Sir Michael Rose, UNPROFOR commander, joined the prime minister in one. The rest of us piled into the other. It was then a "hell-bent for leather" ride into town to avoid sniper fire, the two vehicles roaring abreast at top speed down the road, the drivers blowing their horns to force oncoming traffic out of the way. We rolled past burnt-out buildings, walls pockmarked by machine-gun fire, and twisted wrecks of trolley-cars and vehicles till we reached the shell-marked presidency building.

President Alija Izetbegovic, wearing a heavy overcoat, unsmiling and impassive, greeted us at the entrance of his dreary unheated office, its shattered windows covered with metal plates for protection against Serb shrapnel. A Muslim intellectual, he had been jailed by Tito for defending the people of his faith and seemed inured to suffering. An aide entered to offer us Turkish coffee and water. Bosnia, the president said, was a multicultural and multiracial nation despite the fighting among its Serbian, Croatian, and Muslim peoples, and his government would never accept partition. Almost as an afterthought, and after being reminded by the prime minister that he had just visited young Canadians in Visoko who were putting their lives at risk every day for the cause of peace in his country, he expressed thanks for Canada's peacekeeping contribution.

On the return flight to Paris, Peter Donolo told us that the helmet incident, rather than the substance of the visit to Bosnia, dominated the news coverage that day in Canada. The prime minister laughed.

PART TWO

CANADA AND
THE OLD WORLD

4

The Europeans

Who wanted to do business anyway with the Europeans, who seemed determined to steal our fish, ban our furs, restrict the import of our lumber, and refuse to drink our wine?

On the Nature of Leadership

Before I joined Foreign Affairs in Ottawa as a junior foreign-service officer in 1966, I had met no world leaders. My view of them was formed from my university studies in history, from my travels as a backpacker in Europe in the early 1960s, and from the media. What, I wondered, set them apart from ordinary mortals? My education started when a senior parliamentary delegation from a friendly nation came on an official visit to the nation's capital shortly after I reported for work. I was appointed liaison officer. One leader asked me to join him for morning prayers; another sought my help in finding a prostitute. Leaders, I discovered, could be saints or sinners, or more often, a combination of both, just like the rest of us.

They could also be skilful backroom operators like Pierre Trudeau, whom I witnessed lobbying his colleagues to obtain changes in Canada's position on the recognition of the People's Republic of China at the General Assembly of the United Nations in the fall of 1966. They could be humane and witty diplomats, as I found watching Lester Pearson in action from my lowly position as junior protocol officer during Canada's centennial year. They could be engaging demagogues like Sheik Mujibur Rahman of Bangladesh or Fidel Castro of Cuba to whose countries I was posted in the 1970s and 1980s. They could be powerful powdered leaders with brilliant insights into the workings of the international order but with enormous moral blind spots like Richard Nixon, who visited NATO when I was at Canada's delegation in 1974. They could be intellectuals like Václav Havel, workers like Lech Walesa, or soldiers like Yitzhak Rabin, all of whom I had encountered professionally at one time or other in my career. None of them was poured from the same mould. All were, however, historic figures, for better or worse, in the lives of their nations, and uniformly interesting to an amateur student of history and professional diplomat such as myself.[13] And the first ones I would see in action in my role as the prime minister's silent notetaker would be the Europeans.

Monory, Chirac, Balladur, and Mitterrand

After attending the fiftieth anniversary commemorations of D–Day, the prime minister set out to get to know the Europeans. His first call was on his old friend, French senator René Monory, in the beautiful region of the Loire, southwest of Paris. Monory, whom he had come to know many years before when both were ministers of finance, was now president of the French senate and a good and influential contact in his own right. At Monory's hometown, Loudun, we were treated to French hospitality at its rural best. The dinner was held at the *mairie* or town hall where we dined with the local supporters of the senator, a fascinating cross-section of notables including the village doctor, the notary, and the veterinarian. The wines were superb and the food, local specialties, was succulent. Our hosts told us that they had a reputation to uphold. The most famous son of Loudun, they claimed, was actually not the president of the French senate: it was Rabelais, author of *Gargantua*, the most famous epicurean in French history. Afterwards, the prime minister and Mrs. Chrétien retired to spend the night as guests at the country house of the senator. Eddie Goldenberg and I went back to the home of Monory's daughter and son-in-law to admire their exotic carp collection and to talk until the early hours of the morning in the soft French night air over coffee and cognac. We then joined the others in the local one-star hotel for a short night's sleep before departing for Paris on a state-of-the-art high-speed train to call on Jacques Chirac, the mayor.

I was the only anglophone in the party when the prime minister paid his courtesy call at the ornate *mairie*. A conservative populist, founder of the Rally of the Republic Movement, inheritor of the mantle of Charles de Gaulle, former prime minister, and strong contender for the post of president in the forthcoming elections, Chirac was no run-of-the-mill municipal politician. Jean Pelletier was one of his intimate friends from the days when the prime minister's chief of staff was mayor of Quebec City. In private discussions going back more than fourteen years, Pelletier had persuaded Chirac to drop the traditional Gaullist support for Quebec separation and now was anxious to introduce his old friend to Canada's new prime minister.

The two leaders shook hands at the entrance and sized each other up. They were both more alike than they would probably have cared to admit: political beings of the same generation; tall, strongly built physiques; direct and frank styles of expression; earthy senses of humour; and dominant, highly competitive personalities. It was not for nothing that Chirac was known as *le bull-dozer* and Chrétien as *le bagarreur*. Chirac led the prime minister into a reception room, invited him to take a seat, and welcomed him officially to Paris. The discussion got off to a good start, with Chirac declaring that *le fait français dans le monde* would be better supported by a bilingual united Canada that vigorously defended French culture and language around the globe than by a unilingual English-speaking Canada and an independent Quebec. The jousting then started. The mayor proudly described his frequent travels to Canada, betraying a woeful ignorance about the situation of the French language outside of Quebec and other pertinent facts relating to the French reality of Canada. The prime minister set him straight. The mayor, used to being right, and surrounded by a bevy of aides who hesitated to correct him, grimaced. It would not be easy, I decided, for these two to establish good relations but if they did, their friendship would be firm.

After the June 1994 trip, we returned to France many times in the coming years, since the Chrétiens knew and liked Paris. Our two countries continued to endure an intense love-hate relationship. On both sides of the Atlantic, leaders spoke of our important economic ties. In fact, cultural and political relations trumped everything else. Canada's exports to South Korea, for example, were greater than those to France. Canada was, however, home to the *Québécois*, the cousins of the French and part of the family. The downside was that Canada was also homeland of *les canadiens anglais*, seen as too close for comfort in its foreign policies to the distrusted Americans. The unease was shared by many Canadians: France was the motherland of Canada's francophone population, which was good, but also the potential source of support for separatism in Quebec, which was not. For both countries, it was a relationship that was often in crisis.

In December, we were back in Paris. The Airbus pulled up to the VIP terminal at Charles de Gaulle airport, a guard of honour lined up for inspection, and we were off to the Hotel Intercontinental through the evening traffic with motorcycle escorts, their sirens wailing, rushing to get us to our destination at top speed to meet no particular deadline. A smiling Canadian ambassador, Benoît Bouchard, greeted me as an old friend when I walked into the delegation office. Mistaking the signal, I used the familiar *tu* rather than the more formal *vous* when responding, since we had met several times before and had even shared a meal. The ambassador winced, making clear that we were neither friends nor social equals. I had blundered across a linguistic red line.

I didn't waste time brooding on my faux pas, for we had business to attend to. The prime minister was scheduled to attend an

HIV/AIDS summit and René Monory had invited him to address the French senate. After a war of words between the PMO and the embassy in Paris over the contents of the speech, the prime minister decided to speak on the need for a NAFTA-Europe Free Trade Agreement.[14] He recognized that France, with its desire to protect its agricultural sector and its fear of American competition, would be the least likely of all European countries to agree to our proposal. With trade with Europe stagnating, however, he wanted a frontal attack on the citadel of resistance. The response he received was polite interest but nothing more. The French and their fellow Europeans had other priorities.

The French leadership, however, was willing to meet our prime minister even though his visit was an unofficial one. The first call was on Prime Minister Edouard Balladur at the Matignon, and was a failure. Even to his friends, France's prime minister, a conservative cohabiting politically with a socialist president, was an insufferable snob. He seemed to relish the opportunity to talk down to Canada's leader, pretending that he could not understand what Chrétien was saying and rushing through the agenda. He had not read his briefing book, opened it at the wrong place, and began complaining about a problem that had already been resolved. Canada's prime minister shrugged off Balladur's nastiness with a smile, showing everyone who was the real gentleman. Balladur was odds-on favourite to win the presidential elections at the time of the prime minister's visit but would lose in May 1995 to Jacques Chirac and fade into political obscurity.

The next call was on President François Mitterrand at the Elysée. The prime minister had met him during his initial trip to France in January en route to Brussels to attend a NATO summit. At that time, he achieved a diplomatic coup of sorts by persuading the president to accompany him to see *Starmania*, a rock opera authored by Quebecker Luc Plamondon. He met him again at the June D-Day ceremonies in Normandy. Mitterrand was a friend of Canada. After he came to power in 1981, he put an end

to the campaigns of previous French governments to rally international support for Quebec independence. He treated the prime
minister with genuine affection, making a determined effort to
be a good host despite the awful state of his health. Ravaged by
prostate cancer, his condition had deteriorated markedly since I
saw him last in Normandy addressing Canadian veterans at the
Bény-sur-Mer Commonwealth war cemetery. Now his face had
the pallor of death. There were dark splotches under his washed-
out brown eyes, his lips were purple, the skin on his sallow face
hung slackly, and his neatly combed black-and-white hair was
thinner than I remembered. Obviously in pain, he shuffled his
legs and shifted his position in his chair in an attempt to be more
comfortable. He would, I was certain, have willingly traded his
elegant office with Louis XVI furniture, ancient tapestries on the
walls, giant crystal chandeliers, and gilt over everything for just a
moment's peace.

Mitterrand, one of the giants of post-war French political
life, was a man of contradictions. A one-time right-wing supporter of Vichy France in the early days of the war, he joined the
Resistance, emerging at the liberation of France as a leading
socialist. After his election as president, he moved his party to the
right economically and shed his early reliance on the Communist
party to gain a second seven-year term as president. He was a
strong supporter of Israel over the years and confidant of Israeli
leaders as different politically as Golda Meir, Menachem Begin,
Moshe Dayan, and Igal Alon, yet he quietly protected former
Vichy officials guilty of sending French Jews to death camps
during the war. René Bousquet, Maurice Papon, and Paul
Touvier, who were compressed into one character played by
Michael Caine in the movie *The Statement*, are three of the notorious anti-Semitic Vichy-era officials associated, fairly or not, with
the French president. And defying conventional morality, he
fathered a child with his mistress, at no cost to his relations with
the media or with the French public.

When I was Canada's ambassador to NATO, I had seen Mitterrand in action at summit meetings in Rome and Brussels in the early 1990s when I had the impression that his peers listened to his pronouncements with superficial respect, hiding a sense that they were in the presence of a lame duck leader who was over the hill. It was only later, when I sat in on his discussion with Canada's prime minister in Paris, and read his *Memoir in Two Voices*, written jointly with Elie Wiesel, Auschwitz survivor and Nobel Peace Prize winner, that I saw the depth of his wisdom and the warm and caring side of his nature. But by December 1994, everyone, himself included, knew he was dying. The newspapers and weekly magazines were filled with retrospective examinations of his life that were premature quasi-obituaries in another guise. Far from being offended, the president was making his own farewells on French television, seeking to justify his protection of Vichy-era war criminals, and formally presenting his illegitimate daughter to the French people. I would think of François Mitterrand when I called on Fidel Castro in 1996 and again in 1998 as a secret envoy seeking to persuade the Cuban leader to introduce democratic reforms to his country. The same medicinal odour was pervasive in his private office. And Castro, like Mitterrand, looked like a shadow of his former self at the time. Mitterrand died in January 1996, but Castro fought his way back to health.

After the December 1994 visit, Canada-France relations entered into a difficult period marked by missteps and farce. The problems started with the January 1995 visit to Paris of Quebec premier Jacques Parizeau, the hard-line separatist Parti Québécois leader who had defeated Daniel Johnson, the federalist Liberal Party leader, in the provincial elections of September 12, 1994. The new premier promptly announced that a referendum on Quebec sovereignty would be held within a year and set out to persuade the people of Quebec to vote "yes." Part of his strategy involved seeking international backing for his plan, in particular from France, *la mère patrie*. There was, however, little enthusiasm in France about getting involved in the perennial debate in Canada and Quebec on the nature of their relations. Most French leaders shared the view expressed to Prime Minister Chrétien by Jacques Chirac that their interests were well served by a united, bilingual Canada. And they certainly did not want to return to the days of de Gaulle, when France actively sought the breakup of our country.

While in Paris, the new Quebec premier lobbied hard to obtain an appointment with Chirac. The mayor of Paris, however, was disinclined to meet him, aware that Parizeau would want to drag him into the referendum campaign. Then, in an unfortunate gaffe, Canadian ambassador Benoît Bouchard put the cat among the pigeons by describing Philippe Séguin, president of the French National Assembly, and political ally of Chirac, as a "loose cannon" in what he thought was a private briefing to members of the press in Paris. With great glee, they ran to tell Séguin; mortally offended, he obtained revenge by personally intervening with Chirac to arrange a last-minute meeting for Parizeau. At the conclusion of the session, Chirac told the press that while it was not for France to intervene in Quebec's affairs, if the "yes" side won the referendum, France would want to be the first country to recognize an independent Quebec. The press accompanying Parizeau focused only on the second part of the comment, causing an uproar in Canada.[15] An irritated Canadian prime minister, at that time on the first of his major missions to Latin America, lashed back from Santiago de Chile that Chirac had no more chance of winning the French presidential elections than the Quebec separatists had of winning the referendum – a comment he certainly later regretted, being wrong on one count and almost on the other as well! And to make matters worse, just before the referendum in October, President Chirac made comments during a Larry King CNN interview that seemed to violate the long-standing French policy position of "*non-ingérence, non-indifférence*."

With rocky relations at the top, bilateral relations also entered into a difficult phase. Canada was angry because France refused to buy its asbestos and blocked the importation into Europe of genetically modified canola worth hundreds of millions of dollars annually. France was furious because Canada had opted to re-equip its armed forces with search-and-rescue helicopters from an Anglo-Italian consortium rather than from a Franco-German one, and had voted in the United Nations to condemn France for nuclear testing in the Pacific. On this last point, I went to see the prime minister at 24 Sussex Drive just before the critical United Nations vote to see whether he would be prepared to accept a compromise position of my own making that might satisfy France. I often called on him to discuss knotty foreign-policy issues, and we were used to the drill. He was, as always, friendly until I made my proposal. He then became so angry his face turned white.

"Jim, we must do what is right. Not what is expedient!"

Chirac vowed to make us pay, and was rude and insulting to the prime minister at the Francophonie summit held shortly afterwards in Cotonou, the commercial capital of Benin, in December 1995. The president arrived in the hot, humid, malarial, and mosquito-infested underarm of West Africa looking for revenge and made a speech warning darkly about a global anglophone menace that I found hard to swallow. He then ostentatiously snubbed Canada's leader in public, even engaging in a loud discussion with another president on the platform as the prime minister delivered his keynote speech.

Meeting later in the day with the prime minister, the French president was at his bullying best, complaining loud and long about Canada's vote on nuclear testing and vowing that Canada would pay a price for not selecting Franco-German helicopters. Chrétien, however, had his own bone to pick and was not shy in telling the president that he had not been sufficiently neutral in the referendum debate. How would you like it, he said, if I was to go to a region of France where there was a strong separatist movement and called for its independence? As the free and frank exchange of views continued they raised their voices in anger. But I obviously missed something – the two emerged from the raucous meeting red-faced, but with better personal relations and a heightened respect for each other.

As for me, the lone anglophone witnessing this battle in French, when he said goodbye, the president shook my hand and called me, "*cher ami*" and addressed me as "*tu*" – leaving me thoroughly confused, and wondering if I would ever grasp the nuances of my other official language.

The two leaders cemented their personal ties at a working dinner of leaders on the eve of the G7 summit hosted by President Chirac in Lyon in June 1996. Chirac then received Prime Minister Chrétien in Paris on an official visit with all the honours in January 1997, initiating a friendship that would deepen with time.[16] Most of the details of their discussions that day over lunch at the Palais de l'Elysée with only the ambassadors and diplomatic advisors present, I have long forgotten. My attention was devoted to the *Rouget farci au pistou, gigot, pâtes fraîches au parmesan, fromages, glace au lait d'amandes et citron vert*, Châteauneuf-du-Pape, Château Lynch-Bages and Champagne. What I do remember was that Chirac raised helicopters and Chrétien asbestos, but without the rancour of past exchanges. The president drank beer rather than wine and was interested in picking up some tips on the Canadian model of economic governance. Canada, by this time, had eliminated its deficit, reduced its debt, dramatically expanded exports, and added hundreds of thousands to its employment rolls. France, for its part, was saddled with growing unemployment and a stagnating economy. And the French people refused to accept any restrictions on the hard-won rights of the workers in the interest of restructuring and modernizing an economy faced with the competition of a globalized world. Every time the French government made modest proposals for change, the group affected

– whether teachers, truckers, farmers, or railway personnel – immediately took to the streets and shut down the country. Chirac's rueful conclusion at the end of the discussion was that Canada's model was not exportable to France. The French were inherently not as disciplined as Canadians.

Pope John Paul II

We flew into Rome in the scorching heat of the Italian summer in July 1994 to make official calls at the Vatican. For the Holy City of the Roman Catholic faithful is also a sovereign European state with a national territory, a superb diplomatic corps, a foreign policy, and excellent bilateral relations with Canada. And the Holy Father, in addition to being the spiritual head of the church, is also a head of state. Ambassador Leonard Legault told us that while frail, the Holy Father was maintaining a full work schedule. He was, however, tired and would depart for a summer of rest at his retreat at Castel Gandolpho following his meeting with our party.

The next day, the prime minister's team – Catholics, Protestants, and Jews – accompanied the Chrétiens to the Vatican. Everyone except for Peter Donolo, looking uncomfortable in an electric blue suit, was dressed soberly for the occasion. Members of the Papal Guard in sixteenth-century Swiss military uniform and lay members of the papal court in striped pants, white ties, and swallow-tailed jackets with elaborately decorated silver chains holding papal medals of high distinction hanging from their necks, received us with full protocol honours. They escorted us up wide marble staircases and along long gilt-painted corridors adorned with statues and Renaissance frescoes to an antechamber outside the private quarters of the pontiff. We waited while the Chrétiens were received in private audience. Time dragged on. An RCMP bodyguard stumbled against a priceless Ming vase that rocked back and forth, almost causing heart attacks among our elegantly dressed escort officers, but it did not fall over. I filled in the time admiring the rooftops of Rome and staring down on Saint Peter's Square, seeing in my mind's eye the multitudes of pilgrims that gathered there on great religious occasions to receive the blessing of the pope.

I was tremendously excited at the prospect of meeting the Holy Father, a person of deep and fervent religious faith whose spiritual strength had touched the lives of millions. And although not a Roman Catholic, I recognized the enormous role played by the Church in the lives of individuals and societies through-out the ages and in the world of the twentieth century. During my first posting as a junior foreign-service officer to Canada's embassy in Bogotá, Colombia, in the late 1960s, I had watched with admiration the rise of Liberation theology in the Latin American Catholic Church of the period. Exposed to the bru-tality of the rigid and unjust social and economic conditions imposed on the average Colombian of the period, I had hailed the emergence within the Catholic Church of theologians who took the side of the poor and agitated for social economic change. A highlight of my time was climbing to the roof of my apartment building to join a crowd of pious maids, who had emerged via the servants' stairs from the luxury apartments where they quietly toiled for starvation wages, to watch Pope Paul VI go by in an open car en route to the 1968 Latin American Conference of Bishops at the cathedral of Bogotá. They hoped that the Church would be a force for social and economic change. And Paul VI did not disappoint them, openly denouncing the lack of justice in their society.

John Paul II, for his part, was no fan of Liberation theology, perhaps judging it too heavily influenced by Marxist doctrines of the type he had fought against for many years in his native land. He was, however, a fierce defender of social, political, and eco-nomic justice in Poland, supporting materially and spiritually Father Jerzy Popieluszko and other church leaders who were resisting communism. I was sure that the 263rd Roman pontiff, born Karol Wojtyla and the first non-Italian elected pope since 1522, would go down in the history books with Ronald Reagan and Mikhail Gorbachev for helping tear down the Iron Curtain by supporting Poland's solidarity movement. And his influence extended beyond Europe. When the pope visited Cuba in January 1998, he praised the socialist ideals of the people while calling for greater religious freedom. Fidel Castro was still under the force of his personality and message when I called on him to make arrangements for Prime Minister Chrétien to visit Cuba shortly after the Sovereign Pontiff left Havana. In the course of a night-long conversation, he returned time and again to the subject of John Paul II, speaking of him with the greatest reverence. What irony, I thought, one charismatic leader devoted to a credo of dialectical materialism overwhelmed by another whose life was dedicated to the spiritual.

Then it was time for us to file in to meet John Paul II. The ladies anxiously pulled their veils into place and the men adjusted their ties. Everyone was solemn as the prime minister introduced his entourage. There were no speeches. The pope looked older than I expected, his shoulders were stooped and his hands trembled as he handed over small gifts of rosaries and medallions. Aware that we all wanted souvenir photographs, he twisted his body to be able to make direct contact with us from his one good eye, kindly taking care that the Vatican photographer captured the moment for our scrapbooks. In this, and in three subsequent brief encounters in the coming years, I found him as impressive in person as he was in reputation despite his failing health.

The audience over, the prime minister, the chief of staff, the ambassador, and I went on to call on Cardinal Angelo Sodano, secretary of state and prime minister of the Vatican in its temporal capacity. The others returned to the hotel. The cardinal, accompanied by Archbishop Jean-Louis Tauran, officially known as the Vatican secretary for relations with states but in reality the Vatican foreign minister, pressed the prime minister to have

Canada adopt a conservative position on family planning at a United Nations conference in Cairo. The discussion was animated but the tone was subdued and my mind wandered. The black cassocks, wide red sashes, purple silk trimmings, and skull caps, together with the heavy gold pectoral crosses and chains of the two clerics, I saw, matched in elegance the decor of the office with its pink marble floors, white marble tables, plush carpets, antique furniture, and paintings and tapestries on religious themes. The room was hot and airless. A faint smell of roses hung in the air although there were no flowers to be seen, leading me to imagine that a busy nun had hurriedly removed a vase filled with dead blossoms just before we arrived. I listened to the quiet ticking of a grandfather clock and examined an El Greco picture of Christ, seeing but neither feeling the passion nor understanding the genius of the Spanish artist. Except for the telephone on the table in front of the cardinal, incongruously coloured green, white, and red, the decor of the room did not seem to have changed in three hundred years.

Chancellor Kohl

That same week in July 1994, the prime minister called on Chancellor Helmut Kohl at his residence in Bonn. I was familiar with the chancellor from his reputation and from seeing him in action at NATO summit meetings. He would be remembered, I appreciated, for his role in integrating East Germany into the Federal Republic after the fall of the Berlin Wall in 1989. He had displayed leadership and steadfastness when the German people themselves had their doubts and when British prime minister Margaret Thatcher, and his ostensible friend François Mitterrand had actively opposed the historic project. From what I had seen of him, however, he was a bully. At one summit meeting, he chose to humiliate Manfred Woerner, the mild-mannered and conscientious secretary-general of NATO for no apparent reason, other than to show everyone who was boss. I disliked him instinctively and could not stand his ponderous manner of lecturing others. But my job was to ensure that the prime minister was well prepared to discuss Canadian–German relations, and to take notes while keeping my feelings to myself.

The chancellor's office was huge, airy, and filled with modern sculptures, modern art, and photographs of the mighty of the world shaking hands with him. Enormous picture windows covered one wall. A large deep-green lawn, waterlogged from the rains that soak Bonn year-round, sloped gently down to the Rhine. Kohl was a good host, showing the prime minister to a comfortable easy chair and pulling up another close to him. There were only five of us in the room – the two leaders, their two advisors, and a French-German interpreter. Kohl said he detested large meetings since they inhibited frank exchanges of views.

This time the two had little to say about Canadian–German relations. The single most important link between the two countries had disappeared with the end of the Cold War and the closure of Canada's NATO military bases at Lahr and Baden-Baden. After agreeing that trade was down and tourism was up, they moved on to the real purpose of their meeting – becoming acquainted. They hit it off. Both were veteran, plain-talking populist leaders. Kohl would eventually be Germany's longest-serving chancellor since Otto Von Bismarck and Jean Chrétien would be one of Canada's most senior parliamentarians and prime ministers. Both had been consistently underestimated over the years by their political opponents – who now littered the political wilderness.

The chancellor spoke with passion about his youth in Hitler's Germany, the suffering of the German people, the generosity of the Americans in the post-war era, and the role played by Konrad Adenauer and Charles de Gaulle in driving forward the process of European unity in the 1950s and 1960s – a mission that he and President Mitterrand had picked up again in the 1980s and were carrying forward throughout the 1990s. The discussion was animated and the two leaders were soon on a first-name basis. The chancellor was, however, used to being surrounded by yes-men. And Jean Chrétien did not play by those rules. During the discussion on the Balkans, he said that the bloodshed in the former Yugoslavia might have been avoided had Germany not been so hasty in recognizing Slovenia and Croatia as independent countries in 1991. Kohl was outraged. He was clearly not used to being contradicted even by new friends and launched into an energetic and unconvincing rebuttal. Nevertheless, the friendship he would form with Prime Minister Chrétien in July 1994 would make him a powerful friend of Canada until he was forced out of office for alleged corruption in 1998. I would sit in on similar sessions with Kohl at least half a dozen times in the coming years, even accompanying him and the prime minister on a trip to Baffin Island, which allowed me to see a different aspect of his personality.

In June 1995, he accepted an invitation from the prime minister to spend a few days following the Halifax summit in Canada's Eastern Arctic. Like many Europeans, Chancellor Kohl was fascinated by ecological tourism. He was attracted by Inuit sculpture and wanted to thank his personal staff of interpreters, diplomatic and domestic policy advisors, and secretaries for their hard work at the summit by treating them to a Canadian Arctic experience.

The two leaders, each on his own aircraft, left Halifax as soon as they could for Iqaluit, capital of the Eastern Arctic, arriving in the early hours of the morning. Given his enormous size, Kohl was transported to the hotel in an old school bus where he took up a row of seats by himself. As our little convoy of Canadians followed the Germans, I wondered what Kohl would make of the garbage-strewn streets and graffiti-covered buildings all too typical of Canadian northern communities. At the hotel, I asked myself whether the chancellor and his entourage would be satisfied with the rudimentary if functional accommodations. I was well aware from living so many years in Europe that Europeans were used to Club Med–style luxury even when visiting the wilds of the Third World. I need not have worried. Over breakfast the next day, munching on giant portions of overcooked bacon and eggs, accompanied by burnt toast and jam washed down with warm orange juice straight from a can, Kohl was ecstatic. He loved his school bus, saying that nowhere else had his hosts provided a vehicle that met his special needs so well. His accommodations were, he said, exactly what was required in a rugged northern environment. He looked forward enthusiastically to seeing the sights and meeting the local people. He made no mention of the public squalor to be seen under Iqaluit's midnight sun. Perhaps, I thought, Kohl was not so bad after all.

The prime minister was justifiably proud of Canada's Arctic, which was familiar to him from his days as minister of Indian Affairs and Northern Development. And it was with evident delight that he took the chancellor from Iqaluit on day tours to Cape Dorset, the foremost centre for soapstone carving, and to Pangnirtung, gateway to a magnificent fjord and national park. The chancellor bought dozens of carvings, sat in on performances of Inuit throat-singing and dancing, petted fierce sleigh dogs, and went hiking in a remote fjord. The highlight of his trip was meeting the local Inuit at lunches and dinners. They told him that they would gain greater control of their destiny when the new territory of Nunavut was hived off from the Northwest Territories in April 1999. They pointed out, however, that unemployment in the Arctic was prohibitively high and the Europeans were about to make the situation worse. New regulations, they said, were being put into place by the European Commission in Brussels to ban leghold trapping. This would destroy one of the few remaining means of livelihood, and they appealed to the chancellor to intervene with the bureaucrats in Brussels.

Jack Anawak, member of Parliament for the Eastern Arctic was the first to raise the matter. "And what meat do you eat for dinner in Germany, Mr. Chancellor?" he asked, politely setting his own trap.

"Why beef or pork, of course. Why do you ask?"

"Me, I eat seal. And my friends and family sell the skins of the seal, fox, wolf, and other animals to the Europeans for the fur industry."

Jack, standing beside a polar bear skin stretched out to dry, then explained to the sympathetic chancellor the harmful impact the animal welfare movement in Europe was having on the traditional ways of life of native peoples. There were, he pointed out, from forty thousand to fifty thousand native people across Canada who would be deprived of one of their few remaining livelihoods if they could no longer sell their furs. Equally important, their way of life would be crippled. I followed up by briefing the accompanying German media on the role trapping played in the life of my aboriginal grandfather and other native relatives. The money they earned from beaver and muskrat pelts had often been their only source of revenue. When I was a child, the meat from the skinned carcasses that they shared with my parents was often their only source of protein.

The prime minister, who had been lobbying his European colleagues on this issue since he assumed office, provided background information to the chancellor, who was not familiar with the subject. In 1988, he explained, pressed by the anti-fur lobby, the European parliament passed a resolution calling for action by the European Commission to ban the importation of furs obtained from leghold traps. In January 1991, the Commission decreed that furs of thirteen species of animals harvested with this type of trap would not be allowed into the European Union effective January 1, 1995. Fierce lobbying by aboriginal groups and industry representatives, backed up by pressure from Canadian ministers and the prime minister, had persuaded the Europeans to postpone implementation of their regulation. The Canadians undertook to phase out steel leghold traps in favour of more humane ones, but needed time to develop and implement new technologies.

The chancellor's visit in June 1995 thus took place as the battle raged in Europe between supporters and opponents of taking a hard line with Canada. Whether he intervened personally in the debate after his return to Germany to support Canada, I do not know. But certainly a key to eventual victory was the intervention in the battle by the aboriginal community who had many supporters in the European environmental world and even among animal rights activists. In 1997, after much acrimony, we would get our way. The Canadian and European sides would agree to the continuation of the fur trade, with Canada given two years to phase out its conventional steel-jawed traps.

Jacques Delors and the New Europe

After his private talks with Canada's prime minister, in June 1994 in his Bonn residence, Helmut Kohl led a discussion on Canada–European Union relations. Jacques Delors, president of the European Commission, who had flown in from Brussels for the occasion, joined us around the dining-room table for a working lunch. A host of officials, ambassadors, and notetakers then materialized. It was a law of nature, apparently, that whenever and wherever European Union matters were discussed, the room must immediately fill with Eurocrats.

Delors, who was just finishing his third term in office, will go down in history as one of the giants of the construction of Europe. It was he who ensured that Europe completed its goal to create one genuine single internal market and to establish a timetable for a common currency. A technocrat, he reminded me of a younger Mitchell Sharp.[17] From a modest background (his father was a bank messenger), he joined the Bank of France at the bottom and worked his way up through the ranks. A Christian Socialist supporter of Mitterrand, he was rewarded by being appointed minister of Finance in 1981 and was then nominated to be president of the Commission in Brussels in 1984. Such was his success in his Brussels post, he could have easily been the socialist candidate to replace Mitterrand in 1995, but he did not have the fire in his belly to fight for the job.

The discussion with Delors and his team of Eurocrats on Canada–European Union relations did not take long. There were only trade problems on the table and no solutions. The most prickly issue, and the one that would return to haunt us before a year was up, was fish. Canadians blamed the Europeans for ravaging East Coast stocks and Europeans denounced Canada for shutting Spain and Portugal out of their traditional fishing grounds. A Canada–European Union fisheries agreement had, however, been negotiated to deal with these problems and had been ratified by all levels in the European system. Both sides had agreed that Jean Chrétien, Jacques Delors, and Helmut Kohl should sign it during the prime minister's visit to Bonn. Our side had begged off at the last minute, saying that we were not ready. Delors sought an explanation, but the prime minister could not tell him that Fisheries Minister Brian Tobin had won an interdepartmental fight to dump the agreement just before we left for Europe. André Ouellet had argued that the agreement should be signed, since it contained a dispute settlement mechanism to resolve the growing fishing quarrels with the Europeans. Tobin, speaking as the Newfoundland political boss, said the draft agreement was unpopular in Newfoundland where the people simply did not trust the Europeans. Should the prime minister sign the deal, he said, there would be an uproar. Tobin won, but the stage was set for the defining event in Canada's relations with the new Europe of the 1990s – the fish crisis with Spain and the European Union of March and April 1995.

The Widening Atlantic
The heart of the matter was that Canada and the new Europe were not as important to each other as they were during the Cold

War. Few Canadians knew the details of Europe's latest drive for integration and enlargement, and fewer cared. When Canadians thought about Europe, it was usually in response to television coverage of instability and war in the Balkans or to complaints from Canada's farming sector that the Common Agricultural Policy was ruining export markets. There was thus something odd about this summit in Bonn and the subsequent ones between the prime minister of Canada and the leadership of the new Europe. Ironically, as the substance in the relationship declined, the two sides stepped up the frequency of their meetings at the top. Form was replacing substance as irritants increased in number and transatlantic drift accelerated.

To the prime minister, Europe in 1994 must have seemed like a set of problems to be solved rather than opportunities to be exploited. Canada–Europe trade disputes over aluminum, canola, softwood lumber, wine, and other matters lingered unresolved for years. Canada's image remained that of a supplier of raw materials even though manufactured goods had long dominated Canadian export sales. This "branding" problem made it that much harder for Canadian exporters of high technology products to penetrate the European market, and discouraged European investment in our hi-tech sector. Moreover, with the end of the Cold War and the closure of our last NATO bases in 1992, Canada was no longer needed to defend Europe against a communist menace to the east. We were providing peacekeeping forces in the Balkans, but our contribution was regarded as "nice" and "useful" but not essential. After all, Bangladesh and the Czech Republic provided almost as many soldiers as Canada. And economically, to Europe Canada was just another mid-size industrialized nation, ranking somewhere between Taiwan and Singapore as an export market.

It was thus no accident that Team Canada did not go to Europe in the 1990s. The prime minister, provincial premiers, and business community believed that the opportunities for trade and investment in the areas of Canada's economic strength (transportation, telecommunications, insurance, construction management, and energy) were greater in Asia and Latin America. Who wanted to do business anyway with the Europeans, who seemed determined to steal our fish, ban our furs, restrict the import of our lumber, and refuse to drink our wine? Besides, they seemed to have forgotten that one hundred thousand Canadian war dead were buried on their continent, and might be inclined to laugh at our gung-ho provincial enthusiasm.

Despite these problems, the fact remained that Europe was still a region of great interest to Canada. A new postmodern empire was emerging on the other side of the Atlantic that defied definition. It was pulling into its orbit the countries of Central Europe and the Mediterranean who wanted to become members, countries of the former Soviet Union who were seeking investment, former colonies who sought trade preferences and greater aid flows, and major emerging economies such as South Africa and Mexico who were hunting for better trade access. Geopolitical reality dictated that Canada could not afford to ignore Europe even if Europe could ignore Canada. Prime Minister Chrétien thus went out of his way to establish good personal ties with the leaders of Europe. They were prepared to talk endlessly about their project to build a new Europe and to listen as the prime minister provided his insights on the situation in Bosnia and other international issues. On the case for a united Canada, which the prime minister raised in virtually all meetings before and after the 1995 referendum, all, including the French (despite their nuanced approach), gave assurances that they supported the federalist position. Other Canadian priorities, including initiatives to deal with trade irritants, global free trade, and the genocide in Rwanda, were of less interest.

Canada in the American Orbit

Another geopolitical reality was that by 1994, the Europeans considered that Canada, having joined NAFTA, was firmly fixed in the gravitational pull of the United States, Europe's rival for economic supremacy in the post–Cold War world. Future developments would prove the Europeans wrong at least as far as domestic political, societal, and religious values were concerned,[18] and on some, but not all, major political-security issues. A decade later, for example, in perhaps its greatest foreign-policy disagreement with the United States since the Vietnam conflict, Canada said no when asked to participate in the war on Iraq. The Europeans were generally right, however, when it came to trade matters. In many disputes, such as genetically modified foods and beef hormones, Canada was on the same side of the barricades as the United States. The Europeans were also aware that Ottawa, despite protesting that it followed made-in-Canada trade policies, actually rode Washington's coattails whenever the Americans sought to forge closer institutional ties with the European Union. Canada may not have had much trade with Europe, but the United States did, and American businesses wanted to protect their access. Moreover, the United States, the dominant member of NATO during the Cold War, wished to safeguard its political position as Europe strengthened its mechanisms for speaking with one voice on the international scene.

Accordingly, in 1990 and again in 1995, the United States pushed to regularize and deepen high-level political contacts with the Europeans in an effort to manage trade disputes and to consult on world issues. In each case, alarmed Canadian officials and ministers intervened with the Americans and Europeans to have Canada included, fearing that Canada's interests could be affected if Canada were not a partner to the negotiations. In the face of American reluctance to involve Canada and a less than enthusiastic reception on the part of the Europeans, Canada settled for separate but similar arrangements with the Europeans. In November 1990, Prime Minister Mulroney and Italian prime minister Giulio Andreotti, representing the European Council, issued a Declaration on European Community-Canada Relations, one day before a similar statement was issued by the Italian leader and President Clinton. Then in December 1996, after the Europeans made Canada wait one year as a price for playing hardball in the fish war, Irish prime minister John Bruton, representing the European Union, and Prime Minister Chrétien signed a Political Declaration and Action Plan in Ottawa that mirrored texts issued between the Europeans and Americans in 1995.

Relations gradually improved. The personal friendships Prime Minister Chrétien established with European leaders – Helmut Kohl, Jacques Chirac, Romano Prodi, John Major, and then Tony Blair – whom he met at the G7 and at semi-annual meetings with the presidents of the European Commission and European Council, did much to improve the atmosphere. Britain, France, Germany, and Italy, we discovered, were occasionally prepared to speak up for Canada in the deliberations of the European Council and in our disputes with the Commission. The accession of Sweden, Finland, and Austria in 1995 then brought into the European Union countries that had much in common with Canada in foreign-policy outlook and domestic policy. The Political Declaration and Action Plan provided a framework for a systematic and calm discussion of economic problems, even if few of them were ever resolved. And they also prepared the ground for the evolution of a new agenda. For the European Union was becoming progressively more involved in areas of social policy. Both the European and Canadian sides were inter-ested in learning more from each other on health care, tobacco and drug abuse, and the problems of aging societies. Canada and the European Union, pushed by its new Scandinavian members, also launched a program of co-operation on Arctic social and environmental issues. Police and immigration services on both sides of the Atlantic improved their collaboration on interna-tional criminality and illegal migrant flows.

Ties were strengthened in the more traditional foreign-policy areas for which the European Union was acquiring new foreign

The week from hell on the rollercoaster, October 1995. Prime
Minister Jean Chrétien and James Bartleman (left) arrive in New York
to attend the U.N., but with the Quebec referendum on their minds.

On board the Airbus in November 1995, en route to Yitzhak Rabin's
funeral. Raymond Chan, an unknown aide, Sheila Finestone, and
James Bartleman listen in horror as the PM describes finding an armed
intruder outside his bedroom in the early hours of that morning.

When the prime minister's party travelled on the official Airbus, they socialized (above), or worked, as here where the PM and James Bartleman consult with Patrick Parisot (left), the press secretary.

A private consultation between James Bartleman and the
prime minister at the Miami summit, December 1994.

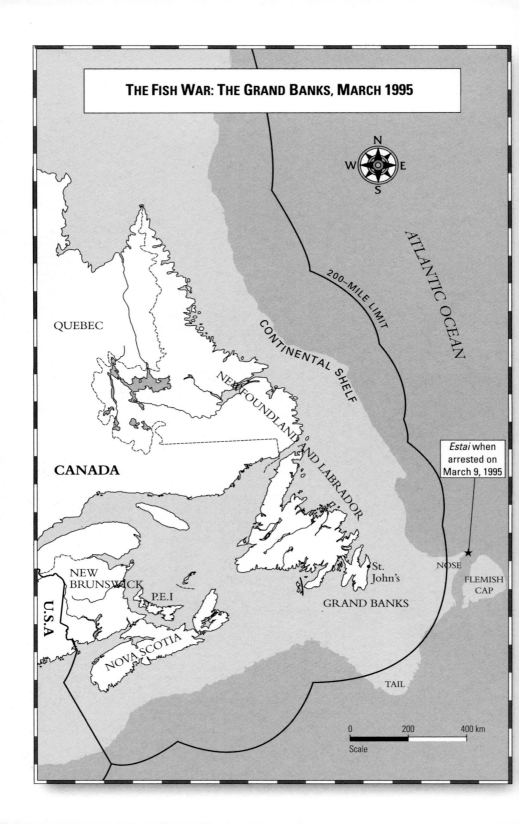

THE FISH WAR: THE GRAND BANKS, MARCH 1995

QUEBEC

CANADA

NEWFOUNDLAND AND LABRADOR

200-MILE LIMIT

CONTINENTAL SHELF

ATLANTIC OCEAN

Estai when arrested on March 9, 1995

NEW
BRUNSWICK

P.E.I

U.S.A

NOVA SCOTIA

St.
John's

GRAND BANKS

NOSE

FLEMISH
CAP

TAIL

0   200   400 km

Scale

and security responsibilities. Given the small size of our armed forces, they were unenthusiastic about collaborating with us on hard or military security issues. Our views on human security matters, such as on anti-personnel mines and the International Criminal Court, which struck a chord with the European public and civil society, became of greater interest to European foreign ministries as the decade progressed. Likewise, consultations on trade policy questions were mutually profitable – both sides holding membership in a coveted inner caucus with the United States and Japan, known as the quad, that heavily influenced the work program of the World Trade Organization.

By the time I took my leave of the prime minister in 1998, Canada and the European Union had started to tackle a number of long-standing irritants in a more positive spirit; there was even some half-hearted talk of exhuming old proposals for a free-trade deal. The reality was, however, that the Atlantic remained as wide in June 1998 as it had been in 1993 when the prime minister took office.[19] The close personal relations the prime minister had developed with the leaders of Europe had not – or at least had not yet – proven strong enough to overcome a generation of mutually exclusive continentalism. And Spanish bitterness towards Canada from the 1995 fish war still lingered.

5

Anatomy of a Fish War

The duty officer then announced that after four bursts of fifty-
millimetre machine-gun fire, the Estai *had come to a stop in the*
water. . . . The easy part was over.

An Irate Ambassador
Spanish ambassador Enrique Costa José Luis Pardos did not take
the news well. He had arrived at my Blackburn Building office
on Sparks Street on short notice on Friday, March 3, 1995, to
warn the Canadian government not to apply the provisions of the
Coastal Fisheries Protection Act to Spanish fishing boats operating beyond the two-hundred-mile limit on the continental shelf
on the Grand Banks of Newfoundland. I could not provide the
assurances he sought. In fact, I was aware that as we were meeting,
a PCO official was walking from one minister's office to another
seeking the requisite four signatures on an Order-in-Council
document to amend the Act. Before the end of the day, Spanish
(and Portuguese) fishing vessels would be barred from what until
then had been international waters off Canada's east coast. I
therefore reiterated Canada's well-known position: Spanish fishermen were destroying the last commercially available groundfish
off the Grand Banks of Newfoundland. Canada had negotiated
an international agreement to conserve the stock, which Spain
and the European Union were ignoring. We intended to arrest
offending fishing vessels if need be.

Pardos stared at me for a long, silent minute. He then carefully put down his cup of coffee, rose to his feet, hitched up his

trousers, clenched his hands into fists, and approached. Fierce and distraught, he towered over me; in my imagination, he was trying to decide whether to throttle or to smack me. I braced myself and held tightly to my coffee mug. Fortunately, he picked a non-violent but very surprising option. Dropping to one knee, he thrust out his jaw, pounded his chest with his right fist, and told me "as a Spaniard" that his country would never accept the jurisdiction of Canada on the high seas. If Canada's "gunboats" tried to arrest Spain's fishing vessels, "Canada would bear the consequences." He then rose to his feet and stalked out the door, muttering that I harboured a personal anti-Spanish bias and was doing everything possible to punish his country for innocently fishing off Canada's east coast.[20]

Thus began the endgame in Canada's dispute with the European Union, acting on behalf of Spain, over fishing rights in the Northwest Atlantic. For the first time in its peacetime history, Canada would resort to force to impose its will rather than use diplomacy to settle a dispute. Latecomers to Bismarckian tactics, we learned the dark arts quickly, and progressively raised the stakes until some of us did not know when to stop, coming within hours of conflict with Spain on the high seas after Madrid had conceded victory. Lester Pearson must have turned over in his grave.

How could relations have become so bad? How was it possible that Canada, which in the subconscious view of many of its citizens still considered itself to be a mid-Atlantic nation with special historic ties to Britain and France, could have become so estranged from the new Europe? Why did the Chrétien government depart from the prudent step-by-step, pragmatic approach that was the hallmark of Canada's management of its foreign relations since the 1930s? Why did so many Canadians, taught from their earliest years that Canada's mission in the world was to be peacekeeper and peacemaker, whip themselves into a jingoistic fever? How could Canadians reconcile our embrace of the use of force with our espousal internationally of soft power? How was it possible that large numbers of print, television, and radio journalists, so critical of gunboat initiatives when coming from the United States, would wave Canada's flag so vigorously? Why did Canada's political leadership, federally and provincially, unanimously support a hard-line approach?

There are, I think, two explanations. The first is intuitive. Based on thirty-five years experience as a Canadian diplomat observing human societies interact, I long ago came to the conclusion that whenever countries quarrel over a natural resource, whether water, wood, or fish, people temporarily lose their reason. Atavistic instincts dominate our thinking and our animal natures come to the fore. To indulge in a few stereotypes, it does not matter whether we are polite Canadians, proud Spaniards, cool Icelanders, hot-headed Latin Americans, or patriotic Americans, we somehow feel that we are engaged in a life and death, fang and claw struggle for existence. The other side is always the aggressor. At the same time, we see no contradiction between our bellicose behaviour and our image of ourselves as peace-loving, justice-seeking, family-oriented individuals. The second answer is more conventional, and is rooted in the long history of Spanish-Canadian relations in the troubled East Coast fishery – not to mention the estrangement of the new Europe from Canada in the post–Cold War era of the 1990s, which I have just described.

From Riches to Rags
Up to the 1960s, it was thought that the fish resources located on the continental shelf off Canada's east coast were inexhaustible. For hundreds of years, fishermen from Newfoundland and elsewhere, mainly from northern Spain and Portugal, had been taking large quantities of fish, mainly cod, using traditional labour-intensive technologies. In the late 1960s, Spanish fishing companies introduced huge stern trawlers up to eighty-five metres in length with a capacity to hold up to 2,500 tons of fish. Equipped with nets hundreds of metres in length, they dragged

the bottom, sweeping up all fish, large and small, from acres of seabed at a time. Fish stocks declined precipitously. Canada and other coastal states similarly affected by foreign fishing fleets then obtained recognition in the 1977 Law of the Sea Convention for jurisdiction over two hundred nautical miles extending out from their coasts as Exclusive Economic Zones. As a result, foreign fishermen were excluded from the continental shelf off Canada with the exception of small areas called the Nose, Tail, and Flemish Cap that extended beyond the two-hundred-mile limit. This did not, however, resolve the problem. Canadian fishermen, supported by heavy government subsidies, bought modern trawlers, moved into the areas vacated by the foreign fishing fleets and massively overfished the Northern cod.

The Spaniards and the Portuguese, now excluded from Canadian waters, concentrated their massive fleet just outside. They scooped up huge quantities of groundfish, especially cod, which migrated from the Canadian-controlled two-hundred-mile zone into the Nose, Tail, and Flemish Cap. No attention was paid to quotas set by the Northwest Atlantic Fisheries Organization (NAFO, the intergovernmental organization responsible for managing fish stocks outside the two-hundred-mile limit). Spanish capacity increased dramatically in the late 1980s with the arrival in the Northwest Atlantic of their ultra-modern factory trawler fleet from waters off the coast of Namibia, where they had been ravaging the hake fishery until their expulsion by the newly independent state. Overfishing by Canadian and foreign fishermen alike, combined with changes in water temperatures and a massive growth in the seal population, had ruined the fishery by 1990. In 1992, the Canadian government imposed a moratorium on fishing Northern cod.

The Crisis of 1994
In March 1994, when I reported for work in Ottawa, the public mood in Newfoundland was sour. Some thirty thousand fishermen

and fish-plant workers were unemployed. Massive government subsidies, including the 1.9-billion dollar Atlantic Groundfish Strategy, were not only a heavy burden on the federal budget in a period of recession, but were regarded as humiliating by the recipients. All the federal Progressive Conservative members of Parliament in Newfoundland had been turfed out in the 1993 elections and the population looked to the new Liberal government to solve a problem that was blamed entirely on foreign overfishing. Conditions were thus ripe for a confrontation with the Europeans. It was not long in coming. On December 20, 1993, the Canadian government extended the moratorium on the cod fishery and drastically reduced the quotas for most other groundfish.

The only commercially viable groundfish then left to catch was the Greenland halibut or turbot. In the late 1980s, the Spanish fishing fleet had located large schools of this bottom-feeder in the deeper waters of the continental shelf and took an average of 37,000 tons annually from 1991 to 1993. Canadian fishermen were not as well-equipped for fishing in such deep waters and their annual catch was only 6,400 tons. Russia, Japan, and others took another 6,000 tons. At this time, there was no limit to the total allowable catch. In early 1994, however, the NAFO Scientific Council announced that the turbot stock was being depleted by overfishing and that conservation measures were required to prevent it from going the way of the cod. In September, pressed hard by Canada, the NAFO Fisheries Commission agreed to establish a limit on the amount of turbot which could be taken in 1995 at 27,000 tons – or some 23,000 tons less than what was taken in 1993.

The Coming Storm
The stage was now set for the clash. Canada and the European Union (representing Spain and Portugal) each wanted the lion's share of the reduced catch. Fisheries Minister Brian Tobin lobbied

hard at a special NAFO meeting on February 1, 1995, on the critical issue of how the catch would be apportioned. Canada came out the winner with an allocation of 16,300 tons or 60 per cent of the total. The European Union was the loser, receiving only 3,400 tons or 13 per cent. The other members of NAFO got the rest. In a conciliatory move, Tobin sent a letter to the European Union fisheries commissioner offering to make available a substantial share of Canada's allocation to ease the transition from the large catch the European Union had made in previous years to the low share provided by NAFO for 1995.

An outraged European Union rejected the offer and vowed that it would not accept the results. It claimed that the jobs of ten thousand Spanish fish workers were at stake, as was Spanish pride. Tempers flared in Canada, where many noted loudly that thirty thousand workers were unemployed as a result of rapacious European Union fishing practices. Tobin issued an inflammatory press release on February 15 warning that Canada "would not allow the European Union to devastate turbot the way it had devastated American plaice, yellowtail flounder, witch flounder, redfish, and cod species in the 1980s." The European Union responded by formally "objecting," or declaring itself to be not formally bound by the NAFO allocation decision, as it was allowed to do under the organization's rules. At a meeting of the European Council of Ministers on March 1, it unilaterally gave itself a quota of 18,630 tons, or 69 per cent of the total.

Canada Acts
The Canadian government had been preparing for this moment since the Liberals had taken office in November 1993. In May 1994, Parliament approved Bill C-29 which amended the Coastal Fisheries Protection Act and the accompanying regulations to assert Canadian jurisdiction over the continental shelf beyond Canada's two-hundred-mile economic zone. In a key provision, fishery protection officers were authorized under section 8.1 of

the Act to use force. To prevent the European Union from chal-
lenging the validity of the new law before the International
Court of Justice, Canada entered a "reservation," unilaterally
removing the legislation from the purview of the court.

Only ships flying flags of convenience – registered in a third
country such as Belize or the Cayman Islands but owned by citizens of other countries who were seeking to take advantage of
the absence of jurisdiction on the high seas – were targeted in the
summer of 1994. Fisheries arrested one boat registered in Panama
and chased away the others. Spain and Portugal had not yet been
directly targeted, but they knew that it would only be a matter of
time before Fisheries turned its attention to them. The European
Union accordingly made strong pre-emptive diplomatic representations saying Canada's actions in asserting jurisdiction beyond
two hundred miles were illegal under international law. It made
the point, repeated many times over to Canadian ministers and
officials, that no state could legitimately submit any part of the
high seas to its sovereignty. The only exceptions permitted under
international law, they said, were to combat piracy, the slave
trade, and drug trafficking. Entering a reservation before the
International Court of Justice demonstrated to them that Canada
recognized that Bill C-29 had no basis in international law. In
the European Union's eyes, Canada's real objective was to seize
control of part of the high seas and not to conserve fish stocks as
we claimed.[21]

European Miscalculations

The European Union must have thought that its warnings to
Canada not to apply Bill C-29 to any of its member states would
be heeded. After all, the European Union was an economic
superpower with a combined population and gross domestic
product rivalling that of the United States. In any contest, the
European Union would hold the moral high ground since international law was on its side. It also had more levers of power, for

example, to apply economic sanctions on Canada, whereas there was little scope for Canada to retaliate. Canada in their eyes was, after all, only a middle power which barely qualified for G7 membership. To the Europeans, or at least to a jaded minority, our country was also the quintessential civilized, postmodern nation that seemed to believe that war had gone out of style. No one could have imagined that Canadians, of all people, would be prepared to use force against traditional friends and NATO allies in pursuit of such an old-fashioned objective – one of the principal causes of the two world wars – the control of a natural resource.

The Europeans thus probably thought that the matter would end at this point. The Spaniards would catch their 18,630 tons (plus cheat for a little more) and Canada, after making strong objections, would also take what it wanted. So what if the 27,000 total allowable catch set by NAFO was exceeded and the turbot stock was depleted? Spain, a difficult partner in the European Union on fisheries issues in general, would be satisfied. European Union member states which had large fisheries industries would also be happy, since the Spanish fishing fleet currently operating on the Grand Banks would not be forced to relocate into their waters.

But they could not have been more mistaken.

Countdown to Conflict
On March 3, Canada's ambassadors accredited to every capital of the European Union were ordered to stand by for urgent instructions from the prime minister himself. When they came in late in the day, the surprised diplomats saw that they were being instructed to deliver a veiled ultimatum in the form of personal letters to the heads of state and government of the fifteen countries of the European Union and to the president of the European Commission. Canada, the prime minister said, would not allow the turbot stock to be destroyed and he threatened unspecified measures should European fishing boats not immediately stop

fishing off Canada's northeast coast. To sweeten the pill, he proposed that all countries should accept a sixty-day moratorium on
the fishing of turbot and that negotiations begin as soon as the
Iberians complied. The concession would not have cost us anything since Canadian fishermen were not scheduled to depart for
their turbot fishing grounds until the end of April – sixty days
hence. The prime minister then followed up his letters by trying
to call key European leaders who, warned by their embassies in
Ottawa of the likely content of his message, were either unavail-
able or noncommittal. All were soon outraged or baffled. No
country, other than perhaps the U.S.S.R. in the bad old days, had
ever issued an ultimatum to Europe. And on a weekend!

Emma Bonino, the fiery commissioner for Fisheries and the
Environment, had assumed the Fisheries portion of her portfo-
lio some months previously, but had not, it seemed, mastered the
detail of her new responsibilities. She was spending a quiet
weekend in Rome and despite being briefed on the seriousness
of the situation, was not disposed to consult her colleagues on the
Commission until Monday, when she would be back in Brussels.
Jacques Santer, president of the European Commission, who
some years later would be driven from office for incompetence,
had not been well briefed, did not take our ultimatum seriously,
and wanted to enjoy his weekend.

When Canada's ambassador to the European Union, Jacques
Roy, managed to contact Commission officials over the weekend,
they told him to be realistic. They reminded him that three
different European entities, each jealous of its authority, had participated in the European decision to award itself the bulk of the
catch: the Commission with its twenty commissioners, each with
responsibilities roughly equivalent to those of a Canadian cabinet
minister; the Council of Ministers with a membership drawn
from the individual countries of Europe; and the European parliament with its hundreds of members directly elected in every
member state.

They told him that even if the European Union wanted to comply with the ultimatum, which was unlikely, the process of undoing decisions taken by these three different European jurisdictions could not be completed by March 6. First the Commission would have to meet and agree. The Council of Ministers would then have to review the decision of the Commission. However, before that could happen, the ambassadors to the Committee of Permanent Representatives (COREPER) would have to seek instructions from their capitals and prepare recommendations for their ministers. Spain and Portugal could be expected to block any move to back down in the face of the Canadian ultimatum. Finally, the European parliament would have to vote to reverse itself on an issue on which it had just pronounced.

This was all theoretical, because the European Union was not, in any case, willing to be accommodating. In a toughly worded press release issued at the end of the day on March 6, the Council of Ministers vigorously denounced Canada's actions in extending its jurisdiction onto the high seas. It also defended its position in allocating to itself a quota in excess of what NAFO had authorized and called for bilateral negotiations in Brussels to resolve the dispute. Canada rejected the European Union proposal, insisting that the Spaniards and Portuguese first withdraw their fishing vessels from the Nose, Tail, and Flemish Cap. We were, however, prepared to hold discreet "talks," but not "negotiations," over the telephone.

From Wimps to Warriors
The "talks" led nowhere and the Canadian government moved its plans to arrest a Spanish fishing vessel into high gear. Incredibly, no interdepartmentally agreed upon strategy existed to manage the crisis. Fisheries, the lead department, had done internal planning, and according to Tobin's memoirs,[22] had worked directly with naval officers to draw up rules of engagement to arrest offending fishing boats; concerns about international law

and about the impact of such action on Canada's relations with Europe were given short shrift. Clearly the government needed to have a balanced picture of the risks and advantages of the course of action it was considering. After consulting the clerk, Jocelyne Bourgon, I established a senior task force of deputy ministers from Fisheries, Foreign Affairs, Solicitor General, Transport, Defence, and Justice plus the Chief of the Defence Staff and the Commissioner of the RCMP to prepare recommendations for the government and help manage the crisis.

Unfortunately, the system broke down at the first meeting. The case for taking action was outlined by Bill Rowat, deputy minister of Fisheries. Under Canada's informal system of checks and balances, it was then up to a senior officer from Foreign Affairs to spell out the case against. In a move that he probably regretted when passions had cooled, he threw his instructions on the table, announcing that although he was supposed to counsel constraint, he personally supported a tough line.

I was as outraged as any of my public-service colleagues at the Spanish and Portuguese overfishing but I wanted the response to be properly managed. I thus spoke up to fill the policy void, saying the government deserved answers to several key questions. Had we exhausted all peaceful means of achieving our objective? Could we revive the fishing agreement containing a dispute settlement mechanism that we had negotiated with the European Union in 1992 and refused to sign in 1994? Could we wait until the United Nations "Convention on Straddling Stocks and other Highly Migratory Fish Stocks," which included mechanisms to resolve differences between nations on fishing on the high seas, entered into force? (Negotiations on the final text were in their final phase in New York and it was expected that the agreement would be opened for ratification in the coming summer.) What would happen if we arrested a European Union vessel and the European Union did not back down? Would we be prepared to accept the economic costs of the sanctions which the European

Union could impose on us? While it was true that the United States absorbed the bulk of our exports, European Union countries still bought more than 400 million dollars in seafood products and several billion in newsprint. Loss of the European Union market for these exports would hurt the East Coast economy. What would we do if Spain were to send warships to defend its fishing fleet? Were we prepared to fight? Would our position as a member of the G7 and host of the forthcoming summit in Halifax be jeopardized? Spain now matched Canada in terms of GDP; might it take our place in the G7? The foundation of Canada's foreign policy and leadership internationally was based on respect for the rule of law. How could we keep the moral high ground?

The questions fell on deaf ears. Normally pacific public servants had suddenly become warriors. With the exception of George Thompson, deputy minister of Justice, senior officials listened without hearing, the blood roaring too loudly. They agreed, however, that these questions should be dealt with in the strategy papers being prepared for the government.

Tobin sat in on a discussion I had with the prime minister. Foreign Minister Ouellet, who favoured going the extra mile to obtain a negotiated settlement, perhaps frustrated by the hard-line atmosphere that pervaded Ottawa, had by that time largely abandoned the field. What was my opinion, asked the prime minister. I reviewed the options and concluded by saying that at the end of the day, the government would have to be satisfied that the national interest would be served by using force and risking the lives of young Canadians and Spaniards. Tobin had already raked over the coals other senior public servants, notably Ambassador Roy, and Foreign Affairs Undersecretary Gordon Smith for signs of independent thinking. It was now my turn. His eyes blazing, he said nothing to me while the prime minister was present. But he telephoned me in a rage soon afterwards to administer a vicious tongue-lashing at high volume. Before I could open my mouth, he began shouting that he wanted no voices counselling restraint with the prime minister. He called me a "gutless do-nothing, know-nothing Central Canadian who never had to fish for a living and wouldn't know one end of a fish from the other even if it was laid out before your eyes." After warning me never to cross him again, he slammed the telephone down without hearing me out as I tried to tell him that Central Canadians were not so bad. Some were even fishermen, including my father and grandfather. I said nothing to the prime minister about his attempt to muzzle me, but continued to provide advice as before.[23]

In addition to working on a general strategy paper, the task force turned its attention to reviewing the operational plan drafted by Fisheries. We established subgroups, each headed by an assistant deputy minister, to monitor and provide ongoing advice to the main task force on matters ranging from legal questions to media relations. An early recommendation was that our efforts be directed at the Spanish fishing fleet since it was more guilty than the Portuguese in overfishing turbot, and we doubted our capacity to deal with two outraged governments at the same time. We also recommended that our strategic objective should be to apply force to save the last commercially viable groundfish stock within and without Canada's two-hundred-mile limit. The quota issue, we could worry about later. In this way, Canada would strike a blow for conservation and appeal over the heads of governments in Europe to their civil societies. The government endorsed these general principles and directed that a Spanish fishing boat be arrested forthwith.

The Arrest
Fisheries, wrongly as it turned out, was confident that an arrest could be made without difficulty. Forty-two Fisheries protection officers and a RCMP team were embarked on two protection patrol vessels: the *Cape Roger* and the *Leonard J. Cowley* as well as on the Coast Guard vessel *Sir Wilfred Grenville*. The *Cape Roger* was

designated lead vessel. Crew members, trained by the Canadian Forces, manned fifty-calibre machine guns on the vessels that had been on station waiting for a call to action since March 4. The personnel were highly experienced, having participated in numerous armed boardings since 1986. At that time, the government had approved the arming of patrol vessels after a humiliating incident in which Fisheries officers were held against their will on a Spanish fishing boat that fled to the Azores rather than obey orders to proceed to St. John's. A Canadian Forces frigate, the HMCS *Terra Nova*, was situated over the horizon in Canadian waters as backup.

On the morning of March 9, after one last effort to achieve a deal with the European Union through telephone talks had failed, the government gave the order to proceed with an arrest. Tobin invited Gordon Smith and me to join him and Bill Rowat in the Fisheries operations centre, a room filled with every modern gadget imaginable for managing a crisis. Lights were flashing on various consoles and television sets programmed to news channels were blaring out news on the action on the Grand Banks. Duty officers sat grimly at their places, taking down blow-by-blow descriptions of the action from the skippers on the high seas. By the time we arrived, the chase had been on for several hours. Testosterone filled the room as the skipper of the *Cape Roger* pursued his prey, the *Estai*, a sixty-five metre Spanish trawler, in fog and drizzle through what for all members of the world community save Canada were international waters on the nose of the Grand Banks. Intoxicated by the excitement and mesmerized by the glittering lights, I entered into the spirit of the pursuit. In my imagination, the skipper of the *Cape Roger* was Captain Ahab of *Moby Dick*. He had harpooned the Great White Whale and was being dragged in his longboat through the seas to his fate.

The *Estai* had already cut its warps, the cables attaching fishing gear to the trawler, dropping its net into the sea, liberating itself to flee. It had fought off one armed party trying to climb aboard from a Zodiac boat, by throwing the ladders into the water. Now it was heading eastwards through four-metre seas whipped up by winds of twenty-five kilometres an hour. The *Cape Roger* was being helped by a surveillance aircraft and from some distance away, by its sister ships. Five Spanish fishing vessels kept pace with pursued and pursuer, bringing moral support to their fellow countrymen on board the *Estai* and threatening the *Cape Roger* by crowding in close to her until they were driven off by water cannon. The one European Union inspection vessel in the area, the *Kommander Amalie*, stayed well clear of the action.

Brigadier-General George Macdonald, my deputy in the PCO, called periodically to keep me up to date on the reactions of the European Union, Spain, and the media. Strong diplomatic protests, he told me, were being registered repeatedly by Spain, each more frantic than the last, accusing the Canadian government of recklessness and piracy. The media, citing news stories originating in Brussels, gave details of the failed boarding attempt on the *Estai*. I provided progress reports to the clerk and prime minister. Tension continued to build. A duty officer anxiously told us that the skipper of the *Cape Roger* had just reported that the fog was closing in, and there was less than one hour of light left before the chase would have to be broken off.

"He wants permission to use his weapons to fire across the bow, and if that does not work, to shoot out the propellers."

The minister turned to Bill Rowat, Gordon Smith, and me, asking us to sign a written order authorizing the skipper of the *Cape Roger* to fire warning shots over the bow; if the *Estai* did not stop, he would be authorized to blow away the propellers. I worried over one detail, but thought it would be too dovish to ask aloud how the skipper could be sure that he could hit the propellers in heavy four-metre seas without sinking the ship. And even though my signature was not required to make the document legal, and I suspected that Tobin only wanted me to inscribe my name to implicate the prime minister in the decision in case matters turned out badly, I joined the others in signing. Actually, by this time, I was so absorbed in the chase that this type of consideration meant little to me. The order was issued and there was a short silence. The duty officer then announced that after four bursts of fifty-millimetre machine-gun fire, the *Estai* had come to a stop in the water. A triumphant Tobin shook hands with all of us, a huge grin on his face. The easy part was over.

Horrified Europeans

Would the seizure of the *Estai* induce the European Union and Spain to agree to our key demands? Or would it lead to the imposition of sanctions? The Spanish fishing fleet had left the area but we expected it to return, this time under the protection of a Spanish navy patrol vessel named the *Vigia* that would arrive on station on the Grand Banks in a week. We had a short window to try to resolve the crisis diplomatically before the Spanish and Canadian navies confronted each other on the high seas. In Canada, there was crowing. In Spain, there were cries for retaliation. But with the exception of Spain and Portugal, the European governments and media had other matters on their minds in March of 1995. In Bosnia, scores were dying every week. In Northern Ireland, the peace process was once again at a critical juncture. These were the crises that counted – not a Canada-Spain dust-up over turbot.

To the surprise of many in Ottawa, not one country spoke up in favour of Canada. The European governments without exception told our ambassadors that they disagreed with our flouting of international law. The United States maintained a studied silence in public, but in private told us that, if asked, they would say that the arrest of the *Estai* was illegal.

No one asked. I called my opposite numbers in London, Paris, and Bonn. All three said the same thing. "What do you crazy Canadians think you are doing? You are acting like pirates, violating international law. Don't ask us to take your side in your quarrel with Spain. European Union solidarity takes precedence. But you can count on us to help behind the scenes." And they did.

Fortunately for Canada, the European Union was incapable of proper crisis management. Decision-making was divided among the Commission, the Council, and the Parliament, and its aspirations to develop a Common Security and Defence Identity, which would have given it a capacity to handle crises, remained in the realm of dreams. NATO had handled Europe's crisis management problems for almost fifty years but the Cold War was over and the vital national interests of the West would not be affected one way or another by the outcome of Canada's quarrel with Spain. In any case, it would have been ludicrous to ask NATO to settle a dispute between two of its most democratic members.

Spain, backed by Portugal (whose fleet was quietly and illegally fishing for cod just outside the two-hundred-mile limit), was screaming for the European Union to slap heavy trade sanctions on Canada immediately. The European Commission, however, restricted its response to issuing a relatively mild press release explaining in pedantic tones the background to the confrontation from its perspective. It was once again Friday in Brussels and a weekend with family, friends, and dogs was in the offing. The matter could wait until Monday morning, but our reprieve would not last long. The European Union decision-making process could be likened to the progress of an ocean liner: slow to start and to turn, but once headed your way difficult to stop or deflect. If by Monday Canada had not done something to counter the Spanish demands for retaliation, we could be in trouble. Making matters worse, the *Estai* was scheduled to be escorted into St. John's early in the week. If the crew was not treated with respect, Spain would have more ammunition to attack us in the European Union, and relations between Canada and Spain would become even more inflamed.

Alfred Siefer-Gaillardin, France's ambassador to Canada, was the first to recognize the danger. As the local representative of the country holding the European Union presidency, he worked hard to find a way out. His personal advice was to send a negotiating team immediately to Brussels, even if uninvited, to make the Canadian case on the ground and mitigate the pressure for European Union retaliatory action on Monday morning. I called the prime minister who gave his approval as well as authority to use a government aircraft. Canada had several of its most capable public servants working on the issues. Gordon Smith's most recent diplomatic appointment abroad was as ambassador to the European Union. He still knew many of the major players and enjoyed a well-deserved reputation as a skilled negotiator. Bill Rowat had an intimate knowledge of the Canadian fishing industry and was trusted by Tobin. And Jacques Roy, prior to becoming Canada's ambassador to the European Union had managed many crises in his long career.

Gordon, Bill, and I departed late Friday afternoon on March 10 for Brussels on a Challenger aircraft with overly optimistic instructions to bring the dispute to a negotiated settlement before the Spanish fleet returned. We knew that there was little chance of success but hoped that our presence would limit the damage. As we were flying over Iceland, the captain called Gordon forward to take an urgent message from our ambassador who told Gordon that Commission officials had asked that we cancel our trip and return to Canada. We were unwelcome in Brussels. We decided to carry on anyway and use our personal contacts to try to open channels with the Europeans. The European Union, we knew, would find it hard to refuse to receive us. If the Commission persisted in its position, we would go public and tell the media that the Europeans had passed up an opportunity to meet emissaries coming to bury the hatchet.

After our arrival in Brussels, Gordon telephoned Horst Krenzler, the director general of the directorate responsible for relations with Canada. Krenzler was our key contact, assigned the task of coordinating the positions of the various European Union directorates in coping with the crisis. He reported to Sir Leon Brittan, the commissioner responsible for North America and International Trade. Sir Leon in turn worked closely with Commissioner Bonino, responsible for fisheries issues. Krenzler had been one of Gordon's closest contacts during his recent posting to Brussels as ambassador and so agreed to meet him alone for a discreet lunch. With much reluctance, Krenzler then cautiously met us on Sunday morning for informal talks. (He could have been fired for agreeing to meet with "the enemy" without the consent of the Council of Ministers.) Little was accomplished other than providing the director general with the opportunity to blow off steam.

On Monday, the Council of Ministers froze relations with Canada, suspending ongoing negotiations on science and technology, education, competition policy, customs, mutual recognition of standards, and veterinary matters and so on. We had escaped lightly: our friends on the Council had deflected calls from Spain and Portugal for the imposition of economic sanctions. The Council also authorized Krenzler to continue informal talks as long as we understood that they were not formal negotiations. Furthermore, the Council also stipulated, any conclusions we might reach could not be finalized before the *Estai* and her crew were released. Canada had insisted in the days leading up to the arrest of the *Estai* that we would hold only informal talks and not negotiations as long as the Spaniards and Portuguese were fishing on the Nose, Tail, and Flemish Cap. The Europeans were now imposing the same terms on us, but linked to the release of the *Estai*. The two sides would maintain these positions, at least publicly, to keep the pressure on the other until the crisis was eventually resolved.

At the ensuing meeting our European hosts were stiff and cold. No coffee was served. They lectured us on the piratical behaviour of our government and rebuked us for Canada's refusal to allow the International Court of Justice to adjudicate the dispute, saying "civilized states always put their disputes to the courts and obey the rule of law." The mood at these meetings degenerated further when the *Estai* was met by a large, booing and heckling crowd in St. John's. We had appealed to Ottawa to ensure that the Spanish vessel was taken to a dock well away from the public, but our advice was ignored. The Newfoundland crowd had to be appeased and the ship was tied up in front of the mob. The ambassadors of France, Germany, and Spain, who had gone to St. John's in a show of European solidarity, were jostled, and the German ambassador was hit by an egg.

We apologized for the rough treatment of the European envoys and somehow kept the talks going until Friday, March 17, when we returned to Ottawa. Our presence in Brussels had served at least one purpose. Our allies, the ambassadors of the United Kingdom, France, and Germany, were able to point out that the Canadians were in town seeking to resolve the matter peacefully and thereby to stave off repeated demands from Spain to impose economic sanctions. We also made some progress on enforcement matters. It was agreed that talks would continue in Brussels with Ambassador Roy representing Canada.

Spain Ups the Ante
Ten Spanish fishing vessels, escorted by the *Vigia*, returned to the area on March 21, precipitating the most dangerous phase of the crisis. The Spanish government informed us courteously but firmly by communication from the Spanish defence ministry that the *Vigia* had been authorized to use "deadly force" by opening fire to protect its fishing vessels operating on the high seas from further arrest. No one had foreseen this, and I sat down with the prime minister to discuss the implications. The dynamics of the confrontation would change dramatically, I told him, once the first blood was spilled. He told me that as prime minister, he had the

duty and responsibility to take the tough decisions in the national interest, even if lives were lost.

At this time, Jocelyne Bourgon, without telling me why, replaced me (as was her right) with Ian Glen, one of her deputies, as head of the task force. Ian also became her principal PCO contact on the ongoing crisis. If I had been in a normal public service job, I would have taken the hint, returned to my home department, and resumed my life as a career foreign-service officer. The inherent contradictions in my position had come home to roost; even though I had been all but fired, I could not in good conscience simply walk away. The prime minister would have to be told why I was leaving. And with nerves fraying in both the PCO and the PMO, nobody needed the added distraction of trying to find a new diplomatic advisor for him in the middle of the crisis. So I soldiered on, feeding information to Ian to pass to the clerk and continuing to work with the prime minister as before. I also had great respect for Jocelyne and knew she would not have dumped me without good reason. And she could well have been unhappy with some of my initiatives.

On the last point, for example, I thought that there were lessons Canada could learn from the November 1975 to June 1976 Britain-Iceland cod war that I had observed first-hand during a posting to NATO. In response to declining cod stocks, Iceland had declared that only Icelandic fishing boats could fish in waters up to two hundred nautical miles from its shores. In those days, the Law of the Sea Convention according such rights to coastal states had not yet come into force. Britain thus considered itself justified under international law in ignoring the Icelandic claim and sent its trawlers, protected by Royal Navy frigates, into the area. Iceland resisted by deploying its small coast guard, including ice-breaking ships. Britain was eventually forced to back down after several of its frigates were rammed and Iceland threatened to close the NATO base at Keflavik. Why not, I suggested, follow the example of Iceland and deploy an icebreaker, not to ram a

Spanish ship but to keep the pressure on the Spanish fishing fleet without raising tensions unduly with Spain. Icebreakers, after all, carried no armaments and were not warships. The prime minister liked the idea, but Jocelyne did not. In the end, the giant *Sir John Franklin* was reassigned from ice-breaking duties to become an integral part of Canada's makeshift fleet off Newfoundland.

The Media Campaign
Despite our threat to walk out of the talks in Brussels if fishing resumed, we allowed our ambassador to carry on discussions while we considered what our next steps should be. The first thing we did was to ratchet up our media campaign in Europe, bombarding newspapers, television stations, members of legislatures, and organizations such as Greenpeace with a heavy flow of information on the perilous state of the world's oceans and the depletion of fish stocks as the result of Spanish overfishing. Our messages hit a responsive chord among non-governmental organizations abroad who cared about conservation issues, and several came out in support of the arrest of the *Estai*. Canadian non-governmental organizations were already on side. The endorsements in Europe were muted since these same organizations smelled a rat. Canada, in their view, had long been an environmentally unfriendly country that permitted the slaughter of baby seals to obtain their penises for export to China as aphrodisiacs, engaged in clear-cutting of old-growth timber, exported dangerous heavy metals such as cadmium and mercury, and allowed the trapping of animals by cruel leghold traps.

With the exception of coverage in the United Kingdom (pro-Canada) and the Iberian countries (anti-Canada), media coverage in Europe was relatively balanced. We were lauded with muted praise by the environmental lobby and criticized by editorial writers for disregarding international law. Although we engaged in a lot of wishful thinking in Ottawa, there was little justification for believing that our media campaign would force governments, other than that of the United Kingdom, to support our cause. The Spanish and Portuguese press, as expected, were scorching in their criticism of Canada for trying to deny their fishermen access to fishing grounds that they had been exploiting for more than five hundred years. They were equally disgusted with their own governments for not standing up to Canada more strongly, and angry with the European Union for not penalizing Canada for violating international law. Portuguese rancour diminished considerably after we told them that Canada had no intention of targeting their ships. Our media campaign would make no headway in these countries.

Things were very different in Britain. Fishermen along England's southern coast had bitterly fought Spain's addition to the European Union in 1986, out of fear that Spanish fishing boats would obtain access to traditional British fishing grounds. They had not succeeded in blocking Spanish entry but had obtained agreement that the Spanish fleet would not fish in their waters for ten years or until 1996. It was now 1995 and Spanish competition for already scarce fish would start in less than twelve months. Canadian press releases on the nefarious activities of the Spaniards confirmed their worst suspicions. They remembered their wartime solidarity with Canada and the dastardly attempt of the Spanish Armada to invade England with a fleet of 130 ships in 1588. The fishermen loudly called on Whitehall to support Canada, making the British government's position of trying to maintain solidarity with Spain in the European Union publicly while supporting Canada behind the scenes all the more difficult.

Tobin then pulled off a publicity coup which dramatized the plight of the world's fisheries and undermined the Spanish claims that there was no basis to Canada's complaint that Spanish fishing boats were violating NAFO conservation rules. Canada's Fisheries minister took the *Estai*'s net as well as a liner with a small mesh designed to catch juvenile fish to New York and displayed it on a barge on the East River, across from the United Nations headquarters building where an international conference on straddling fish stocks was in progress. Emma Bonino had just made a passionate speech to the conference condemning Canada's behaviour on the high seas and had challenged Canada to prove its allegations on Spanish overfishing. She was made to look ridiculous as Tobin rubbed it in, holding up a baby turbot and lamenting its fate with all the bathos of an over-acting diva in a bad eighteenth-century Italian opera.

Applying Pressure

The European Union then tried to outflank us diplomatically by proposing that a special meeting of NAFO countries be held to take a fresh look at quotas. This we rejected since it was likely that European Union pressure would lead NAFO members, who had supported Canada at the February 1 meeting, to change their positions and support the European Union. We replied that we would agree to a special NAFO meeting after and not before Canada and the European Union had worked out their differences on enforcement, conservation, and quota allocations. We had no intention of easing up on the pressure before we locked in lasting reforms.

The Spanish fishing vessels, under the watchful eye of the *Vigia*, continued to fish in prohibited waters, arousing the ire of the Newfoundland public. The *Cape Roger* and her sister patrol boats went to work making harassing runs through the Spanish fleet, cutting the warps of *Pescamors Uno* and dropping its net into the sea. A confrontation with the *Vigia* ensued, with the Spanish ship interposing itself between the *Cape Roger* and the *Pescamors Uno* in a vain attempt to shield its piglet from the Canadian wolf. The *Cape Roger* made no attempt to arrest its prey and the *Vigia* did not resort to its armament. While the Spanish government and press bitterly criticized the European Union for not reacting strongly, demonstrators from Galicia, the home base of the Spanish fishing fleet, travelled to Madrid to pelt the Canadian embassy with eggs and other missiles. Worse, the Spanish government imposed visa restrictions on Canadian visitors, and Spanish companies cancelled several large business deals with their Canadian counterparts.

Elements of a Deal

Despite the fireworks elsewhere, Ambassador Roy and his team, supplemented by periodic visits by Bill Rowat and Fisheries officials from headquarters, quietly hammered out the elements of a deal in Brussels by early April. They first resolved the issues of enforcement and conservation, our key concerns. The European Union accepted our demand that observers be stationed on all fishing vessels and agreed to the establishment of a pilot project placing ground-satellite transponders on 35 per cent of the fleet, to help eliminate cheating by tracking the movements of individual ships. We also gave our word that once all the elements of an agreement were in place, the charges against the skipper of the *Estai* would be dropped and the regulations pursuant to the Coastal Fisheries Protection Act amended to remove Spain and Portugal from their purview.

The two sides also reached agreement on how much fish each would receive in a multi-year plan starting in 1996. The sticking point remained how much fish Spain would be allowed to take in 1995. There was agreement that Canada and Spain would each obtain 10,000 of the total allowable catch of 27,000 tons. But Canada said that Spain had already taken much more than it had reported to NAFO since the beginning of the fishing season in 1995 and this actual amount should form the basis for calculating the allotment given for the year. Spain defended its figures and held out for receiving a greater share than Canada, continually moving the yardsticks, agreeing with certain quota levels one day and seeking even more the next. By this time, I had opened up a secret back-channel link into the internal deliberations of the

European Union ambassadors in Brussels dealing with the fish dispute. My contact, Deep Throat, told me that the tide had turned against Spain. Canada's focus on conservation and our willingness to compromise on shares had gained it sympathizers. Spanish intransigence and complaining had done the rest.

Despite this progress, there were those on the Canadian side who were wedded to the concept of using force to bull our way through to final victory. One team of officials – Eddie Goldenberg, Gordon Smith, Ian Glen, and myself – the "peace camp," met every day in my office in the Blackburn Building. Another, the "war camp" – Tobin and Bill Rowat – met in the Fisheries head-quarters building in the Centennial Tower at 200 Sparks Street. Each side established its own direct link to the prime minister via the PMO switchboard at 24 Sussex Drive. The prime minister listened to both camps and took his own decisions. Meanwhile, the task force toiled away in some forgotten corner of the Langevin Block.

Almost everyone outside of the "peace camp" favoured taking a tough line. The use of force had put the Europeans on the defensive. Why not raise the stakes and hit the Spaniards again? There was even half-serious talk of deploying Canada's CF-18 fighter aircraft to Newfoundland, presumably to bomb the small Spanish fisheries protection ships if they dared interfere in a further arrest of a Spanish fishing boat. Fisheries, reading the jingoistic mood around town, no longer consulted the rest of us, and sent independent orders to the skippers of the makeshift civilian navy to make periodic harassing runs through the Spanish fleet. The European Union screamed bloody murder but remained at the negotiating table.

The last forty-eight hours of the crisis were the most dramatic. Ambassador Roy and his European Union counterparts reached agreement on all substantive outstanding issues at meetings on April 13 and 14. There was jubilation in Canada followed by intense disappointment and anger when Spain reneged on its word. The government then gave orders that another arrest be made on April 15, Easter Saturday.

The OK Corral

When the Canadian and Spanish armadas squared off on the Grand Banks the weather could not have been better for a fight. Winds were low, seas were moderate, and visibility was fair. In one corner was the Canadian fleet, composed of a motley collection of civilian and military ships operating under a confusing variety of legal authorities. The Fisheries patrol boats, *Cape Roger*, *Cygnus*, and *Chebucto*, were manned by personnel possessing peace-officer status and legally entitled to use force to effect arrests in accordance with Canadian law. Two Coast Guard vessels, the supply ship *J. E. Bernier* and the icebreaker *Sir John Franklin*, were in the line of battle ready to take on the might of Spain. Their personnel, who were not peace officers, probably wondered what they were doing in the middle of a possible shootout out in the Atlantic. HMCS *Gatineau*, which had replaced HMCS *Terra Nova* as military backup, was steaming towards the zone of possible action from its hull-down position within Canada's two-hundred-mile zone. A second frigate, HMCS *Nipigon*, was preparing to set sail from Halifax to join the battle. By this time, keeping up the pressure on the Spanish military, the head of Canada's navy served notice to his Spanish counterpart that he intended to deploy submarines in the contested zone. Then on Good Friday, the Chief of Defence, after obtaining Cabinet approval, issued instructions to the commanders of the frigates to use deadly force to defend any Canadian civilian vessel threatened by a Spanish warship as it sought to make an arrest.

In the other corner was "the enemy" – a Spanish armada composed of eighteen factory trawlers under orders from their owners to carry on fishing. Backing them up were two small Spanish navy patrol boats, *Vigia* and *Centinella*, whose normal role was inspecting fishing boats in Spanish coastal waters. Another small naval patrol boat, *Atalaya*, was on its way from Spain to join the fray. All three had been similarly ordered to use deadly force to protect the Spanish fishing fleet. The *Kommander Amalie* was also in the area, but not expected to participate in the engagement.

To make sure that there was no possible misunderstanding regarding our intentions, the Canadian navy contacted the Spanish navy to say that the Canadian frigates had been authorized to use deadly force against the *Vigia*, *Centinella*, and *Atalaya*. I called my old friend, Ambassador Pardos, to tell him that Canada intended to arrest another Spanish fishing vessel the next morning. Should the Spanish patrol boats intervene, I said, our frigates had orders to open fire on them. I don't believe he thumped his chest this time.

Next I telephoned Canada's ambassador in Madrid, David Wright, using an open telephone line that I hoped was being monitored by the Spanish Intelligence Service. I told David that the Canadian government had decided to arrest another fishing vessel on Easter Saturday unless Spain changed its mind and accepted the deal it had just disowned in Brussels. We expected that the Spanish naval vessels on the Grand Banks would intervene to try to stop the arrest. HMCS *Gatineau* was almost at its action station and would shortly be joined by HMCS *Nipigon*. Cabinet had met, I told him, and had given authority for the navy to use deadly force. In lay terms, the captains of the Canadian warships were expected to open fire, without further recourse to headquarters for instructions, on the Spanish naval vessels to protect the Canadian fisheries patrol boats. David understood that I was also passing a message to the Spanish authorities and made no comment.

Everything that I told the two ambassadors was true. We were heading for a confrontation in which young Canadians and Spaniards would probably die. I wanted to be sure that the Spaniards got the message, so that they could back down in time. They did, but some of us found the Spanish capitulation, when it came, difficult to accept, and were reluctant to take yes for an answer.

The Final Hours

Early on Easter Saturday morning, Deep Throat called to say that the European Union ambassadors had met in an emergency session throughout the night. Spain had come around and a negotiated settlement was now ours for the asking. The European ambassadors would be in touch with Ambassador Roy after they got some sleep.

"But please don't do anything foolish such as arresting another Spanish fishing vessel today," he advised. "Otherwise the endgame being played out in Brussels will disappear and the showdown will be between Canada and Spain alone on the high seas."

The peace camp strongly favoured waiting for a few hours before making the arrest. The war camp disagreed and pushed hard to follow through with plans for early morning action. The prime minister opted to authorize Ambassador Roy to attend a meeting of European Union ambassadors in a final effort to conclude a deal. We would soon see if Deep Throat was right when he said that Spain had been brought on side. Our ambassador's instructions were to accept inconsequential changes if need be, but not to agree to any outrageous demands of the Spaniards for more fish. Happily the Europeans were ready to agree, and Ambassador Roy was soon able to send a draft text to us. We reviewed the text, obtained approval from the prime minister, and told our man in Brussels that the government could accept the final package. Approval, he told us, would come from Madrid within two hours; everyone, he said, even the hard-line Spanish ambassador in Brussels, was now confident that the fish war was over.

But we had not reckoned on the continued obstinacy – there might be a harsher word – of the war camp. A contact in Defence sympathetic to the peace camp telephoned me to say that a radio operator on one of the Canadian frigates had intercepted radio traffic between the Fisheries patrol boats. The war camp, in one final outburst of bad judgement and without consulting anyone else, had sent instructions to the skippers of the civilian fleet to make one last charge through the Spanish fleet. Someone had watched too many bullfighter movies. Deeply regretting my initiative in proposing that an icebreaker be added to Tobin's fleet, I frantically called the prime minister, who countermanded the hare-brained order. Ambassador Roy then telephoned to say that Madrid had acquiesced; the Turbot War was over.

The government's central goal, the saving of the turbot stock, was accomplished even if Spain, bitter and humiliated, would make us pay a price by throwing roadblock after roadblock into Canada's efforts to forge closer ties with Europe for years to come. Brian Tobin emerged as "Captain Canada," his popularity such that he would leave federal politics in short order to be crowned premier of Newfoundland. Bill Rowat would follow Tobin to Newfoundland to apply his considerable management skills to the Labrador Falls hydro-power project, and later would become president of the Railways Association of Canada. Gordon Smith would continue serving his country with distinction until his retirement from the foreign service. Jacques Roy would be named ambassador to France. As for me, I would lick my wounds, re-establish working relations with Jocelyne Bourgon, and focus on the next crisis looming on the horizon – the degenerating situation in the former Yugoslavia.

6

The "Red Cross with Guns" in the Balkans

When Prime Minister Chrétien assumed office, any illusions that Canada could make a difference had long since been dispelled.

The Mess

Prime Minister Chrétien inherited a mess in Bosnia and Croatia that would consume much of his time over the first half of his first mandate. Canada, all too eagerly, had offered to send troops and join reluctant European countries led by Britain and France in a peacekeeping operation in the former Yugoslavia in 1992.[24] Fury with the excesses of the Serbs shown on television every day and a blind assumption that peacekeeping of a traditional sort could bring peace to the Balkans clouded rational thought. Ever since Lester Pearson had won the Nobel Peace Prize in 1957 for proposing the use of peacekeeping troops to separate the warring parties during the 1956 Suez crisis, Canadian governments had prided themselves on participating in every peacekeeping operation that came along, whatever the merits of the mission on offer. Canada thus found itself in over its head trying to carry out a traditional peacekeeping role when all the warring parties were united in only one desire – they all wanted to settle their differences on the battlefield with an attendant disregard for human rights not seen since the Second World War. At times those of us trying to manage Canada's role in the Balkans wondered whether the peacekeepers had become part of the problem rather than the solution – preventing the parties from fighting it out, and thereby prolonging the suffering of the peoples. In our more rational moments, however, we realized that were the peace-keepers to leave, a general massacre of civilians would ensue. Whether we wanted it or not, once in, Canada remained stuck in the Balkan quagmire.

The Crisis Erupts

In 1991, eleven years after the death of long-time president Joseph Broz Tito, the Socialist Republic of Yugoslavia began to crumble. In that year, Slovenia and Croatia declared their independence. Slovenia fought off the troops of the Serb-controlled central government in Belgrade that tried to reimpose control; with no significant Serbian minority to protect, the Serb troops quickly abandoned the alpine province. It was, however, a different story in Croatia, where Serbs constituted 12 per cent of the population. There, Serb soldiers from the rump Yugoslav army entrenched in their garrisons turned their heavy weapons over to the Serb minority and fought alongside them in a brutal campaign of ethnic cleansing, seizing more than 33 per cent of the country, including the Krajina region and the two Slavonian provinces.

In 1992, civil war came to Bosnia. It was the most ethnically mixed of all the provinces of the former Yugoslavia and was the only one where the Muslims, with 44 per cent of the population (to 31 per cent for the Serbs and 17 per cent for the Croats) formed the largest component of the population. Following a referendum on independence boycotted by the Serb minority, war broke out. The Serbs fought to join the lands they controlled to Serbia and the Croatian minority struggled to attach their territories to Croatia. The leftover units of the former Federal Yugoslav army turned over their heavy weapons to the Bosnian Serbs. Special military units sent from Serbia joined in the battle, bested the ragtag Muslim troops of the Bosnian central government and seized the lion's share of the territory of the new state. The Serbs then turned snipers loose on the civilians of Sarajevo and targeted the city with artillery and mortar fire, seeking to crush the will of the people to resist. The city of 400,000 would remain under siege, with brief respites, until September 1995. It became the Guernica[25] of the last decade of the millennium.

"Humanitarian" Intervention

Following a failure of nerve on the part of the European Union, which was reluctant to commit European troops to a mission where their young men and women could get killed, the United Nations sent a large, lightly equipped, and ineffective peacekeeping mission, UNPROFOR, into Croatia and then into Bosnia in 1992. NATO then slowly became drawn in to enforce an embargo on arms shipments to the warring parties by a naval blockade in the Adriatic and by air interdiction over the region. The arms got through anyway. After a slow start, the international community gradually became enmeshed in the crisis, pushed on by a public opinion revolted by televised scenes of wanton shelling of urban areas, butchered civilians of all ages, and emaciated prisoners in concentration camps – terrible images that recalled old American military newsreel scenes of Bergen-Belsen or Dachau. France and the United Kingdom took the lead among the larger powers. The traditional middle-power supporters of peacekeeping operations – the Netherlands and the Scandinavian countries as well as Canada – were there. But NATO's two economic and military heavyweights, Germany and the United States, stood to one side. Germany claimed that its constitution prevented it from deploying troops to the region. The United States, in the words of Secretary of State Baker in 1991: "Did not have a dog in this fight." The world's only remaining superpower was, nevertheless, dragged in against its will. Initially, Washington spoke out against any division of Yugoslavia. It then came out in favour of the central government in Sarajevo, advocating using NATO power against the Serbs and lifting the arms embargo to allow the Muslims to obtain heavy weapons to match those of their Serbian opponents. When

Washington could not obtain the agreement of its allies for this course of action, it resorted to clandestine ways to break the United Nations embargo and get arms to the Muslims.

Ignominy for Canada

By the fall of 1993, when Prime Minister Chrétien assumed office, any illusions that Canada could make a difference had long since been dispelled. There had been heady moments in 1992 when Canadian peacekeepers under the swashbuckling Brigadier-General (later Major-General) Lewis Mackenzie had caught the attention of the world with their bravery and authority in marching into a Sarajevo in flames to seize the airport, thereby providing a bridgehead for the humanitarian and peacekeeping efforts of UNPROFOR. It had been all downhill since that time. True, our troops continued to perform with professionalism and courage. But as the years went by and the ranks of the nations contributing soldiers to the conflicts of the former Yugoslavia continued to swell, Canada became only one of dozens of nations contributing forces to a seemingly hopeless endeavour. Our peacekeeping expertise came to be seen as more appropriate to another era. And our men and women suffered the same loss of face as other contributors, pushed around by strong and weak alike in the war zone.

As Canadian ambassador at NATO at that time, I found myself increasingly on the defensive as I blocked initiative after initiative from the Americans to use NATO air power against the Serbs. It was not that Canada favoured the Serbs; our concern was that bombing would simply expose our troops, who were not well-enough equipped to defend themselves, to Serbian retaliation on the ground. However noble our effort, we gained an undeserved reputation in Washington as a country afraid to take risks. More ignominies were to come. In March 1994, Canada was left on the sidelines when the United States, Germany, Russia, the United Kingdom, and France (later joined by Italy) formed the so-called

Contact Group or inner caucus of major members of the international community charged with hammering out a resolution
of the imbroglio. What rubbed salt in our wounds was the fact
that the United States, Germany, Italy, and Russia did not even
have forces on the ground and yet were key decision-makers.
From this moment on, we became secondary players diplomatically on Balkan affairs.[26]

Role of the Prime Minister
The prime minister did his best to arrest the decline of our
national influence and to ensure that the lives of Canada's young
men and women in the field were not risked unnecessarily. The
first challenge he successfully met at the January 1994 NATO
summit in Brussels. At that time, there was a large contingent
of Canadian peacekeepers in the isolated Muslim enclave of
Srebrenica, surrounded by heavily armed Serb troops. The
Canadians had completed their time in the pocket but the Serbs,
being difficult as always, had not given them permission to
depart. President Clinton, supported by British prime minister
John Major, then sprang a surprise on his new Canadian colleague, proposing that NATO use air power to force the Serbs to
let the Canadians go. Although I was not yet the prime minister's
diplomatic advisor, I was his ambassador to NATO and suspected
that the Americans and British were as interested in making a
symbolic display of air power as they were in helping Canada's
troops get out of Srebrenica. I was also well aware that our officers
on the ground were skilled negotiators. If left alone, I told the
prime minister, they would eventually talk their way through the
Serb lines. The American/British proposal, if accepted by NATO,
would oblige our troops to make a bloody fighting retreat through
narrow mountain passes even if they were supported by air
power, and Canadian soldiers would die for no good reason. The
prime minister accepted my advice and vetoed the initiative when
it came up for discussion in the NATO council. Less than six weeks

later, the Canadians negotiated their way through the Serb lines with no losses. And just in time. As spelled out later in this chapter, the Dutch forces who replaced them would be impotent witnesses and the Dutch nation shamed and traumatized the following year in the face of the slaughter by the Serbs of the Muslim civilians in their care.

A Failed Test of Strength

Canada had dodged a bullet in Brussels but it would not be long before its troops and those of its UNPROFOR partners would be endangered by the ambition of the United Nations mandates. For UNPROFOR, despite absorbing reinforcements raising its force levels to more than forty-four thousand personnel from twenty-three countries, was too lightly equipped even to defend itself. Its mandates were missions impossible: a peacekeeping role when in fact the Muslims, Croats, and Serbs all wanted to resolve their differences by warfare; a humanitarian relief assignment when all convoys were at the mercy of thuggish local warlords; and a protection responsibility for six safe areas or isolated Muslim enclaves within Serb-held territory (Sarajevo, Tuzla, Zepa, Gorazde, Bihac, and Srebrenica) – without sufficient troops or equipment for the purpose.

An early moment of truth came in April 1994. As described in Chapter Two, the United Nations was forced to back down when the Serbs seized hostages, Canadians included, from among the peacekeeping forces, refusing to release them unless NATO stopped bombing its positions. We were left to mull over the consequences of this failed test of strength. It would only be a matter of time, it seemed, before peacekeepers would themselves start to suffer heavy casualties, as they had in Somalia, shortly before. But any effort by governments to pull their forces out of the former Yugoslavia would expose retreating troops to punishing attacks from Muslim and Croatian forces who would feel resentful at being abandoned to the mercy of the Serbs. And withdrawal would lead to accusations of cowardly abdication of responsibility by a world public opinion exposed to daily CNN coverage of the horrors of war in the middle of Europe. A cynical pattern then developed: NATO periodically threatened the Serbs with air power and occasionally engaged in ineffectual bombing when UNPROFOR troops (but not endangered civilians) were directly threatened; the Serbs would back down, temporarily, and then resume their egregious behaviour after the international community calmed down.

By July 1995, no foreign-policy issue, other than the fish dispute with the European Union and the Halifax G7 summit, had taken up more of Prime Minister Chrétien's time. I briefed him regularly and arranged frequent telephone calls to key international players, in particular United Nations Secretary-General Boutros Boutros-Ghali, Prime Minister Major, President Chirac, and President Clinton. With Canada not in the Contact Group, the prime minister sought to maintain our influence by going to the leaders themselves. The stakes for Canada were high with so many troops in theatre and the risk always present that they could suffer large-scale casualties – for which he would be accountable to their families and to the nation.

The Crunch

The civil wars in the former Yugoslavia came to a climax in 1995. Former president Jimmy Carter had negotiated a ceasefire designed to last from December 1994 to April 1995. The Serbs, who by now held 72 per cent of the land, would have been happy to see the war end at this stage. The Bosnian government, however, merely wanted time to prepare for an offensive in the spring of 1995. With a fresh supply of arms obtained clandestinely over the winter months, it launched attacks in May against Serbian positions around the Sarajevo and Bihac areas, but matters did not turn out as expected. The heavily outnumbered Serbs seized the heavy weapons that they had stockpiled under

UNPROFOR supervision the previous fall, and turned the guns against civilian and military targets. This broke the back of the Muslim offensive but provoked pinpoint air attacks from NATO fighter bombers based in Italy and on American aircraft carriers in the Adriatic.

In an all-too-familiar response, the Serbs rounded up UNPRO-FOR peacekeepers from a dozen countries including Canada, the United Kingdom, and France, and chained them to potential target sites. NATO halted its bombing efforts for the time being. The emboldened Serbs then cut off all land routes to Sarajevo, except the perilous Mount Igman route, and turned their attention to the safe areas. On July 12, they swept into Srebrenica, whose thirty-five thousand refugees were ostensibly protected by the Third Dutch Air Mobile Battalion with 450 soldiers equipped with twenty-seven armoured personnel carriers. The Dutch peacekeepers, who had replaced the Canadians in February 1994, allowed themselves to be disarmed and then stood by as eight thousand men and boys were murdered. The Serbs then overran Zepa, a neighbouring safe area, but the men managed to escape through the surrounding hills.

The London Conference
The Srebrenica massacre and the Zepa fiasco marked the low point in the war. A new crisis and new humiliation for the international community appeared on the horizon as Serb forces turned their attention to Gorazde. This time the UNPROFOR peacekeepers in the safe area were the Royal Welch Fusiliers who faced the choice of fighting and being mauled, or stepping to one side and watching the slaughter of the civilians in their care. Either option would constitute a humiliating national setback to the United Kingdom, which prided itself with good reason on the fighting traditions of its armed forces. The British thus issued a call to interested members of the international community to attend a conference in London on July 21 to decide whether

UNPROFOR should pull out of the Balkans or stay and fight – the status quo was no longer an option.

On the eve of the conference, most troop-contributing countries, including Britain and Canada, were seriously considering the first option. The fourth winter of the war was approaching and there was a risk that their troops would get caught in the crossfire of escalating conflict. At NATO headquarters, plans for the deployment of up to sixty thousand NATO soldiers, including more than twenty thousand American combat troops and armour, were ready to protect the retreating UNPROFOR troops from the wrath of the contending parties. But Jacques Chirac, elected president of France in May 1995, favoured staying and fighting, even if that meant joining the war on the side of the Bosnian government. He was enraged that twenty French soldiers had been killed, several deliberately shot by the Serbs while carrying out peace-keeping duties over the years, and his sense of national honour as the president of France was offended by the continuing seizure of French troops as hostages. The president had already forcefully expressed his views to his peers, disrupting the Halifax summit in June by insisting that the participants focus on the carnage in the former Yugoslavia rather than devote all their time to the reform of the Bretton Woods institutions. He had called the head of the French armed forces a coward to his face and castigated the Dutch prime minister for the pitiful showing of his forces in Srebrenica. He now urged UNPROFOR to take on the Serbs with a new Rapid Reaction Force, currently deploying into the area, equipped with armoured fighting vehicles, anti-tank missiles, heavy mortars and artillery.

The Americans, while still unwilling to put their ground forces in harm's way, welcomed the French president's pugnacity, so unlike the hand-wringing passivity that European leaders had displayed since the crisis had begun. Over the past year, Washington had also become more engaged. In addition to winking at the provision of arms from Muslim countries to the

Bosnian government in violation of United Nations Security Council resolutions, it had helped Croatia retrain and re-equip its armed forces using a private security company headed by retired American generals and other guns for hire; and it had become more active diplomatically, assuming de facto leadership of the Contact Group. Congress stepped in at this stage, preparing legislation to force the administration to provide arms directly to the Bosnian government. The problem was that should it succeed, Russia would likely retaliate by opening up an arms pipeline to the Serbs, their Slav cousins, almost literally pouring oil on the fire of conflict. Prime Minister Chrétien raised the matter with President Clinton, who assured him that he would veto the bill. And he eventually did so.

The Canadian team in London included Defence Minister David Collenette; his deputy, Louise Fréchette; Chief of Defence Staff John de Chastelain; Foreign Minister André Ouellet; his deputy, Gordon Smith; and me. The ministers were divided: Collenette favoured staying in Bosnia and Croatia and fighting it out in company with our allies; Ouellet wanted to re-deploy our forces from Bosnia to Croatia to consolidate our military presence and to establish shorter lines of communication in the area should we have to pull out in a hurry. The prime minister was clear in [...]: do not enter into any new commitments, but do [...] consensus for a more muscular approach against the [...] ne develop. He asked me to keep him informed [...] as the meeting proceeded, emphasizing that he [...] p Canada's options open for later discussion and [...] binet.

[...] by Challenger jet on the evening of July 20 and retired early to prepare for the discussions at Lancaster House the next day. Unknown to us, the British met overnight with the Americans and French and then with other members of the Contact Group. They decided to draw a line in the sand around the remaining sanctuaries of Sarajevo, Gorazde, and Bihac. The

Rapid Reaction Force, they decided, backed up by massive NATO bombing of Serb military and strategic targets, would enter into action on the side of the Bosnian government if the Serbs did not back down. The next morning, the British team met separately with delegations from countries not in the inner circle, including ours, to seek our support. I consulted the prime minister to obtain his blessing and he authorized us to join the consensus. Unsurprisingly, when Prime Minister Major circulated his draft agreement, it was quickly approved by the conference participants; whether intended or not, the international community had taken sides.

The moment of greatest risk for the peacekeepers was now at hand. The Serbs eased their military pressure temporarily on the remaining safe areas but the Bosnian government continued its offensives. Everyone knew that it would only be a matter of time before the Serbs used their heavy weapons against civilians once again, precipitating intervention by the Rapid Reaction Force and NATO air power. UNPROFOR commanders urgently moved garrisons and military observers from vulnerable locations. In a diplomatic coup, the British persuaded the Belgrade government to allow them to evacuate their troops from Gorazde across the international border into Serbia proper and out of harm's way. Britain, France, and the Netherlands, the three nations providing the Rapid Reaction Force, redoubled their efforts to move their units into position, taking up stations on Mount Igman, ready to take on the Serbian heavy guns when the shelling of Sarajevo resumed.

In the meantime, at NATO headquarters in Brussels, at the headquarters of the Supreme Allied Commander in Mons, and at Southern Command in Naples, the blueprint to evacuate UNPROFOR was shelved in favour of frantic efforts to dust off and revise long-standing plans, dating back to the days when I was in Brussels in 1993, to punish the Serbs from the air. New rules made it easier for the United Nations and NATO to authorize air strikes; now, the decision to attack would be made by the military commanders in the field. The U.N. secretary-general and his civilian deputy, considered too vulnerable to political pressure from nervous governments in the post–London world, were dropped from the decision-making process. No longer would air power be used only to protect endangered UNPROFOR troops; it would henceforth also be applied to defend the civil populations. Planners also took to heart the harsh lessons learned in applying air power in Bosnia over the past year when pinpoint attacks on selected targets were ineffective. Although this option remained on the table, the new military thinking was that only an all-out air campaign against a broad range of strategic and military targets would get the attention of the Serbs.

A new worry emerged. On July 25, troops of the Republic of Croatia punched through the Serbian lines, cutting off communications between Serb Krajina and the territory controlled by the Bosnian Serbs. The Croatian government, most members of the international community (including Canada) then learned, was in the final stages of preparations to rid its territory of its Serb minority. I called my opposite numbers in Washington, London, Paris, and Bonn. The prime minister called Clinton, Major, Chirac, and Kohl. Our efforts complemented the soundings being made by diplomats from Foreign Affairs and military officers from Defence, since we all knew that in modern-day crises, we all must work together. We asked whether the Croatian drive would lead to generalized war in the Balkans. No one knew. There was general agreement, however, that Croatia was emerging as a major military power, able to stand up and perform creditably if Serbia were to seek to challenge it on the battlefield. And what would happen to the fourteen thousand peacekeepers of the United Nations Confidence Restoration Operation (UNCRO)[27] in Croatia, including more than eight hundred Canadians scattered in isolated observation posts between the Croatian and Serbian lines? Our friends told us that they should be safe if they kept their heads down when the fighting started.

The Final Offensives

The mission of the "Red Cross with Guns," an expression coined by Prime Minister Chrétien to describe the untenable and ambiguous role of United Nations peacekeepers in the former Yugoslavia, now came to a head. Anthony Lake, national security advisor to President Clinton, called me late in the afternoon of August 3 to provide a warning: a full-scale offensive by the armed forces of Croatia against the breakaway republic of Krajina would begin at midnight; the two other Serb-held areas of Croatia, East and West Slavonia, he said, would be attacked later. The region, seized by Croatia's relatively small Serbian minority in the fighting of 1992, made up almost one-third of Croatia, and the government in Zagreb wanted it back. Tony told me that the Pentagon believed the Croatians would take their objectives in a matter of days and then push northwards into the Livno valley in Bosnia, joining up with forces of the Bosnian government in a drive to relieve the safe area of Bihac. The State Department and the CIA, Tony said, differed with the Pentagon on the time it would take for the Croatian army to capture Krajina but all agreed that the days of the self-proclaimed Serb Republic in Croatia were numbered. Tony asked me to ensure that the word was passed to the Canadian military to alert our peacekeepers manning observation posts in the line of advance.

I did not waste time asking Tony how the Americans knew all of this, but immediately alerted National Defence Headquarters, telling them to treat the information as genuine. Colonel Andrew Leslie, since promoted to major-general, grandson of General Andrew McNaughton of Second World War fame, United Nations Chief of Staff and senior Canadian officer at battalion headquarters at Knin in the area of projected attack, told me later that he received the urgent message within minutes of my warning. It was one in the morning local time on August 4, and he issued urgent orders to the Canadian troops to take cover. They in turn passed on the word to the Kenyans and other peace-keepers in the danger zone. Soon, all were hunkered down in their bunkers waiting for the first artillery barrages to begin. The batteries opened up at 0310, the shells passing over the heads of the peacekeepers and into the civilian-populated areas. Using tactics perfected by the German Wehrmacht in the Second World War, the Croatian High Command was just as interested in ter-rorizing the Serb civilian population and forcing them to flee as in destroying military targets. Newly equipped and freshly trained assault troops, 100,000 strong, then cleared out the military opposition. Special police units then moved in, looting, raping and killing civilians, driving them out of the area, and burning their houses to ensure they would never return. Some 180,000 civilians fled into exile in Serbia within a matter of days in the largest ethnic-cleansing operation in Europe since the Second World War. As they crossed the Canadian lines, the Croatian forces rousted the Canadians from their bunkers and moved them out of the area, to try to keep the number of witnesses to their looting and mayhem to a minimum.

But when they tried to do the same at the United Nations headquarters building, Colonel Leslie refused to be bullied, and ordered his troops to fight. They fought back so well that with thirty of their men dead, the attacking Croatians finally with-drew. Leslie and his forces, however, were confined to their base in company with 1,400 civilian Serbs who had sought refuge in their compound from the Croatian Special Police. They were trapped themselves as the standoff went on for five days while the ethnic cleansing in the city continued. Colonel Leslie had no idea how he could take his unwanted civilian guests to safety through the Croatian army lines, but got his chance after the Croats had cleared the town of the bodies of hundreds of massacred civilians.

That was when Croatian president Tudjman arrived with a group of journalists to celebrate the capture of the region; Leslie gambled that the Croatian Special Police would not intervene as long as the media were present. Under the noses of the unhappy Croatians, Canada's senior officer in Knin then moved the refugees by convoy to the no man's land separating Croatian and Serbian fighters and out of harm's way.

The offensive changed the military balance. Within three weeks, the Croatian army had driven Croatia's Serb minority from its national territory. After pulverizing the military opposition in Serb-held Krajina and ethnically cleansing the population, the Croatian army swept into Bosnia, rolling up the Bosnian Serb forces. The stage thus set for the massive use of NATO air power, the Serbs duly provided the occasion for NATO intervention. On August 28, they fired five mortar rounds into Sarajevo, one of which ricocheted off a building into a crowd, killing twenty-eight and wounding eighty civilians. The Muslims had shelled a Serb funeral the previous day and the attack on Sarajevo might have been a retaliatory strike, but no matter. NATO fighter bombers started large-scale air attacks on Serb targets. And French, British, and Dutch artillery and the heavy mortars of the Rapid Reaction Force went into action, systematically destroying the Serb heavy guns around Sarajevo. The decisions taken at London on July 21 were now being translated into sustained military intervention on the side of the Bosnian government. It would only be a matter of time before the Serb forces in Bosnia were defeated. Prolonged bombing, plus the sustained land offensive led by the Croatian army forced them to their knees. By September 20, the land and air routes to Sarajevo were open, and the Serb forces elsewhere defeated.

The Endgame Strategy

Tony Lake spent much of August in Europe, calling on Contact Group governments with an American-designed "Endgame

Strategy," obtaining approval for an imposed political settlement once the dust had settled militarily. Under the American proposal, Bosnia would retain its territorial integrity as the Bosnian government of Bosnia-Herzegovina, divided into two entities – the Federation (for the Muslims and Croats) and the Republica Srpska (for the Serbs). Final arrangements on the sharing of power, return of refugees, and other details were then worked out in talks in Dayton, Ohio, in November with the leaders of Serbia, Croatia, Bosnia, and the key warring factions. A new sixty-thousand-strong force, including divisions of American combat forces under NATO command replaced the discredited UNPROFOR. Canada provided a combat task force of more than a thousand men and women to the Implementation Force (IFOR) that took over on December 20.

Bosnia then faded from public consciousness as IFOR settled into a new long-term commitment. The toll from almost five years of war was horrific: 250,000 dead, 50,000 tortured, 20,000 women raped, 15,000 children killed, and three million refugees. But that was not the end of the story. The Serb minority of Bosnia was no more reconciled to belonging to a state where they constituted a permanent minority than they were when they started their revolt in 1992. Peace in the country would henceforth depend on foreign troops which became in effect, if not in law, an occupying force.

Return to Bosnia

In May 1998, almost four years after my first visit to Bosnia, I returned with the prime minister in circumstances far different from what we experienced in June 1994. This time there was no need to keep the trip a secret for security reasons and to limit the number of journalists in the accompanying party. Our aircraft, it was true, was a bone-shaking Hercules transport from the Canadian Air Force, but that was only because the runway at Sarajevo was too short to take our Airbus. We flew into an airport open to commercial traffic, and transferred to a motorcade waiting in the open on a tarmac no longer vulnerable to fire from the Serb sector of the city – unsurprising since the Serbian population of the city had fled en masse following the signing of the Dayton Peace Accords. Our journey to the city centre was uneventful – no bodyguards hurrying us through sniper alley – and we passed through neighbourhoods slowly returning to life.

Some things, however, remained the same. We called on Alija Izetbegovic, who was now chairman of the collective presidency of the Federation of Bosnia-Herzegovina and representative of the winning side. He was as unsmiling as ever but this time was not wearing his overcoat and the setting was the elegant national museum rather than the shell-marked presidency building. He was accompanied by Kresimir Zubak and Momcilo Krajisnik, the Croat and Serb members of the presidency. There was tension in the air. Izetbegovic expressed satisfaction with the progress his country had achieved since the end of the war. Zubak agreed but Krajisnik launched into a speech emphasizing what divided rather than unified the peoples of the new state: two alphabets, three peoples, and two political entities. The others had heard the Serb line before and remained impassive.

The mood at the Canadian base in Banja Luka, our next destination, was likewise far different from that of four years previously at the camp in Visoko. Our soldiers, wearing battledress and eschewing the blue helmets of the United Nations, were now in the driver's seat, able, with British and American help, to enforce their will on the Serbs. The Chief of Defence Staff, General Maurice Baril, had flown in for the occasion and personally briefed the prime minister over a soldier's meal of baloney and Cheez Whiz sandwiches. Canada would, he said, be in Bosnia for a long, long time – perhaps as long as the thirty years we were in Cyprus – since there was no prospect that the Serbs would ever willingly accept the status quo.

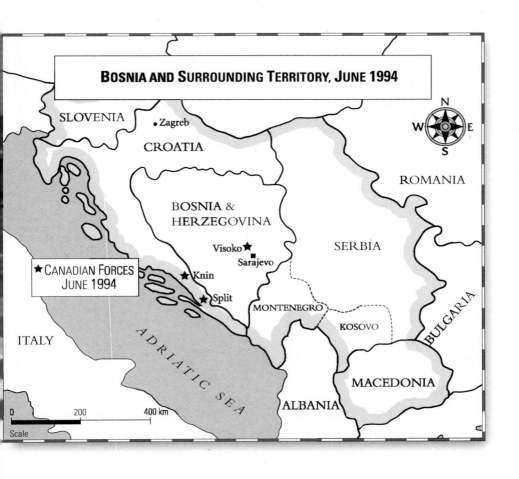

BOSNIA AND SURROUNDING TERRITORY, JUNE 1994

SLOVENIA

• Zagreb

CROATIA

ROMANIA

BOSNIA &
HERZEGOVINA

Visoko ★
■
Sarajevo

SERBIA

★ CANADIAN FORCES
JUNE 1994

★ Knin

★ Split

MONTENEGRO

BULGARIA

KOSOVO

ITALY

A D R I A T I C   S E A

MACEDONIA

ALBANIA

0   200   400 km

Scale

President Clinton (the brightest of the world leaders the
author encountered, although he tried to disguise it) greets
James Bartleman at the White House, April 1997.

In the Oval Office, drinks are served while Messrs.
Gore, Clinton, Chrétien, and Bartleman (among hidden others)
prepare for their discussions.

The Chrétiens are received by the Clintons, the president on crutches.

Official talks at the White House cabinet office. From the left, the Canadians are Art Eggleton, Lloyd Axworthy, Jean Chrétien, Raymond Chrétien, Sergio Marchi, Jane Stewart, and James Bartleman. Thereafter the American side continues with William Daley, Mack McLarty, Charlene Barshefsky, Bill Clinton, Madeleine Albright, and the outspoken Sandy Berger.

The Team Canada trade mission to China, November 1994. The front row from the left shows Canadian premiers Harcourt, Filmon, McKenna, Rae, Trade Minister MacLaren, Prime Minister Chrétien, two translators, and President Jiang Zemin and other Chinese representatives.

Team Canada as tourists, visiting the Forbidden City, led by Mr. and Mrs. Chrétien.

Smiling on this occasion, Premier Li Peng and his wife greet the author.

The affable President Jiang Zemin shares a parting joke with James Bartleman, Jean Chrétien, Jean Pelletier, and Raymond Chan.

Premier Li Peng did not enjoy his 1995 Ottawa visit when, contrary to his wishes, Canadian demonstrators continued to enjoy freedom of speech by staging demonstrations. Here Jean Chrétien tries to argue that the shouting outside comes from people welcoming him. Not everyone is convinced, not even the author, second from right.

With Aline Chrétien in the foreground, a much happier Li Peng (with his interpreter) enjoys meeting Jean Chrétien's former mentor, Pierre Trudeau, an honoured figure in China. Montreal, October 1995.

One of the casualties of the Rwandan genocide, General Roméo
Dallaire, talks in the prime minister's office with Jean Chrétien,
David Collenette, and James Bartleman. The author, not proud
of Canada's role, finds it hard to meet his eye.

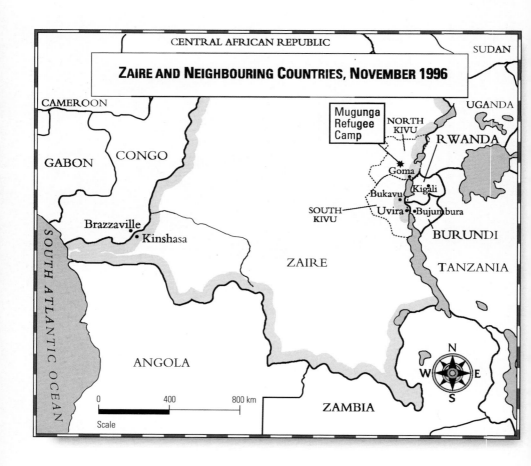

ZAIRE AND NEIGHBOURING COUNTRIES, NOVEMBER 1996

Prime Minister Romani Prodi of Italy made the same point to the prime minister the next day during official talks in Rome. There was, he said, peace but no co-operation in Sarajevo among the three factions in the collective presidency. The money poured into the country for rehabilitation by the international community was being siphoned off by the Bosnian mafia. Refugees were not returning to their homes; those who tried were being beaten or killed. There was little confidence in the future among the people. Significantly, Izetbegovic was building up his army in case of a new war; already he had more 125-millimetre howitzers than the entire Italian army. The moment the international military presence disappeared, Prodi predicted, war would break out again. "We should not have intervened in 1992. Everyone would have been better off if we had simply allowed the warring parties to fight until they established a new geopolitical equilibrium in the former Yugoslavia."

And what were the consequences of the wars in Croatia and Bosnia? All sides lost. Ethnic cleansing returned to Europe for the first time since the Second World War. All parties, the Serbs most dramatically and the Muslims and Croats to a lesser extent, were guilty of atrocities, and all humankind was diminished. An effort, not made in Rwanda in 1994 when the world watched 800,000 die, was made to stop the fighting. But the initial attempts were half-hearted and the fire too hot. It burned the international institutions that sought to extinguish it, setting back the process toward European union, and damaging the United Nations at a time when there were high hopes that it could come into its own in the post–Cold War era.

Few political leaders emerged with their reputations intact: Clinton, Mitterrand, and Kohl, representing three of the most powerful countries in the West, performed indifferently, for different reasons. The real hero in the end was President Chirac who pushed the international community to intervene on the side of the Bosnian government after the Serbs crossed the red line into genocide with the massacre at Srebrenica.

As for Canada, the Canadian Forces were demoralized as an institution and many of those who served there, often reservists removed temporarily from their civilian jobs, came away psychologically damaged. Prime Minister Chrétien stepped into a situation not of his choosing and brought the troops home with as much honour as possible in the circumstances, and without heavy casualties. His finest hour was in January 1994 when he prevented the Americans from using air power to try to free Canadian troops blocked in Srebrenica. As the Dutch troops who replaced the Canadians were to learn to their sorrow, air power alone would not stop a determined adversary on the ground.

No one and no country can, however, turn the clock back. All we can do after the fact is to look at the consequences of our actions and try to do a better job next time. And there will be more next times in the Balkans. I only hope that the Europeans will take ownership of the next crisis in their own backyard and settle it decisively before the flames take hold, if only for the sake of the civilians at risk.

PART THREE

CANADA AND
THE UNITED STATES

7

William Jefferson Clinton

Ambassador Chrétien in Washington, who had received blasts from both the State Department and the White House with threats such as "the next time there's a referendum in Quebec we will support the separatists," wanted the prime minister to pick up the telephone and apologize at once, at the risk of receiving an outraged earful.

Meeting in Naples

In July 1994, Prime Minister Chrétien met with President Bill Clinton in Naples just before the start of the G7 summit. I already knew the city, having spent time there nineteen years before during a posting to NATO headquarters in Brussels. Shortly after our marriage Marie-Jeanne and I had toured the palaces of the rulers of the Kingdom of the Two Sicilies, marvelling at the lives of luxury led by the upper classes amidst the poverty of the mass of people in nineteenth-century Italy. We preferred visiting the ruins of Pompeii and Herculaneum and the modern city itself, with its dynamic crowds overflowing the sidewalks onto the streets, its noisy traffic jams, its itinerant fruit and vegetable sellers, its superb cappuccino coffee, and the scent of hot salty sea air drifting in from the harbour. There was even a magnificent horse-drawn hearse complete with corpse and black-robed mourners that could have driven straight out of Francis Ford Coppola's *The Godfather*.

None of this vitality was to be seen on our arrival this time, as we were whisked from the airport by a motorcycle escort to our small hotel in the city centre, kept isolated from the population by security forces determined to protect Italy's distinguished guests. Official motorcades dominated the streets. They flashed by, sirens wailing, carrying prime ministers, presidents, and foreign ministers to individual meetings before the official meetings began. I counted the vehicles in the American motorcade – twenty-five cars and trucks including a pickup at the rear with Secret Service agents manning a heavy machine gun mounted on the open box at the back.

After settling in, we joined the parade, making for the hotel housing the American delegation, where Bill Clinton was "at home" receiving visitors. The president shook hands with everyone in our group and led the prime minister to two armchairs on a raised dais at one end of the room. The leaders, with American and Canadian flags behind, faced the accompanying entourages rather than each other. Those Canadians and Americans lucky enough to be included were neatly arranged in two rows facing each other in order of seniority. They may have been ideal for the purposes of a photo opportunity and impressing country cousins, but the seating arrangements made it impossible for the two leaders to hold a serious discussion. Perhaps it did not matter.

Prime Minister and President

Prime Minister Chrétien was no stranger to things American. The United States was the part of the world outside of Canada that he knew the best. He grew up listening to stories of life in New Hampshire from his father, Wellie, who sold insurance for *L'Association Canado-Americaine* and often travelled to the largest city, Manchester, to attend board meetings. As finance minister, he jousted with American financiers unhappy with Canadian banking laws and rubbed shoulders with the American secretary to the Treasury at G7 meetings. As minister of Trade and Commerce, he was intimately involved in promoting trade and encouraging investment with the United States. His greatest triumph was the deal he helped broker that saw Canadair, an ailing Canadian aircraft manufacturer, acquire the rights to develop the first Challenger passenger jets from its venerable and much larger American counterpart, the Learjet Corporation; as a result Canada's aircraft manufacturing sector would be transformed. As a personal passion, he devoured American political biographies, especially those of his hero, Harry Truman, like him a little guy from a small town who had achieved great political success. And as soon as he was sworn into office, the new prime minister took personal charge of Canada's relations with its giant neighbour to the south, appointing a trusted professional diplomat as ambassador to Washington and setting out to cultivate a close working relationship with his American counterpart.

The two leaders had hit it off when they first met at the November 1993 Seattle APEC summit, shortly after the prime minister's election victory. Chrétien put his cards on the table at that time, explaining that one of his campaign planks had been to promote a close but not chummy relationship between the leaders of Canada and the United States. Clinton welcomed this straight talk and found he had much in common with Canada's new leader – although perhaps not as much as he believed. Both were small-town boys, populist champions of the common people who, against the odds, had risen to the highest offices of their countries. The president, however, was from a dysfunctional family and the prime minister from a closely-knit, high-achieving one. Clinton was a lady's man and a charmer, in contrast to the prime minister, who was devoted to his wife and an upholder of family values. The American president was a policy wonk, perhaps the brightest leader I saw in action in over thirty-five years in the foreign service, able, at the drop of a hat, to discuss authoritatively the most arcane detail of international monetary policy, the origins of the Balkan crisis, and obscure labour market problems in Mexico, although he hid his intellectual dominance over his peers under an "Aw shucks, I'm just a country boy" demeanour. The prime minister was more pragmatic than blue sky, and possessed far more common sense than his American partner.

The two leaders faced similar domestic and international challenges. Their countries were in the midst of a continent-wide economic recession, and unemployment on both sides of the border was at record levels. To cope, Bill Clinton and Jean Chrétien, although left-of-centre in personal political orientation, shifted their economic policies rightwards to deal with deficits and national debts. Clinton, it soon transpired, was an admirer of Canada's social safety net, especially our medicare program – a model he was eventually to try to introduce into the United States. Both saw the centre of world economic gravity shifting eastwards to the Asia-Pacific region. They were anxious to exploit the burgeoning markets of the so-called Asian tigers (South Korea, Taiwan, Singapore, and Hong Kong) and the economic miracle of the countries grouped together in the Association of Southeast Asian Nations (ASEAN). Both saw China as the big prize; it was in the process of dropping its central planning model for a capitalist approach while keeping political control through the Communist Party.

Like almost all of their contemporaries, both men assumed, however naively, that the threat of catastrophic war was over. Europe, the traditional centre of foreign-policy interest during the Cold War when security interests trumped all others, was of lesser priority to both now that the Soviet Union and the Warsaw Pact had disappeared. The two North Americans were inclined to take the Europeans at their word when they said that they wished to assume a greater responsibility for the security in their own backyard. At the time there was no pressure from the United States on Canada to increase its defence spending as there had been during the Cold War, and as there would be under George W. Bush. In fact, during this period in the mid-1990s, the shoe was on the other foot. Canada had troops on the ground in Bosnia and Croatia that had become virtual hostages to the warring factions. The United States did not. Canada was thus able to point a finger at the United States and reproach it for not doing its fair share for European security. But after the debacle in Somalia some months earlier, when American forces trying to be peacekeepers were slaughtered and their corpses defiled, the United States had no intention of following Canada's lead.

The Seattle APEC summit had taken place as negotiators from both countries were putting the finishing touches on NAFTA, which essentially extended the terms and conditions of the 1989 Free Trade Agreement between Canada and the United States to Mexico. The prime minister, who had expressed reservations about NAFTA during the election campaign, sought American concessions on anti-dumping, energy, water, and subsidies as a condition for Canada's adherence. Although both the Democrats and the Liberals were divided on the merits of NAFTA, their leaders were in spirit free-traders. It did not take long after the summit for the prime minister to find a face-saving formula that allowed him to recommend acceptance to his Cabinet and permit the agreement to come into force on January 1, 1994.

Dodging the Vice President
Although the Chrétien-Clinton relationship had got off to a good start, the prime minister had to sidestep an attempt by the administration early in the life of his government to make Vice President Al Gore the point man for everyday dealings with Canada's leader. Some weeks before the Naples summit, the White House proposed that Gore pay an official visit to Ottawa. The prime minister agreed and set aside July 18 and 19 for the distinguished visitor. American ambassador James Blanchard then proposed that he host an official dinner for the vice president and prime minister on the first evening. The prime minister, he suggested, could offer reciprocal hospitality to Gore the following day. But the ambassador's suggestion posed a dilemma for Chrétien. The president had already delegated to Gore lead

responsibility for deepening American ties with Russia and South Africa.[28] If the prime minister accepted Blanchard's invitation, he could well find that in the future it would be Gore rather than Clinton who picked up the telephone when Canada's leader called to discuss Canada–United States problems. On the other hand, were he to decline to attend the dinner, he would offend Blanchard. The prime minister, as he always would when faced with choices between personal and national interests, turned down the Blanchard invitation. While not wishing to have as intimate a relationship with the president as his predecessor, he could not afford to accept the vice president as his equal.

It was left to me to call in Blanchard to convey the bad news. The ambassador was deeply disappointed and furious at the same time, telling me that we Canadians had no idea how influential Gore was in the formation of American foreign policy. He then telephoned me later in the day to say the White House had cancelled Gore's engagements for July 18 and would limit the vice president's visit to July 19 only. Fortunately, Blanchard, a former Michigan governor, confidant of Clinton, and one of the most effective American ambassadors to Canada in recent memory, quickly got over his irritation, and Gore never mentioned the matter during his visit. The only jarring note occurred when Fisheries Minister Brian Tobin breached protocol at the luncheon table at the prime minister's residence by starting an argument with the vice president on American fishing practices off Canada's west coast. Gore, who was as well briefed on the issues as Tobin, took him on in a sharp exchange that left everyone embarrassed.

State Visits
Having established that there could be no substitute for leader-to-leader contacts, Chrétien and Clinton stayed in touch thereafter by regular telephone calls[29] supplemented by more formal meetings at the plethora of summit talks they were obliged to attend each year. Just as important, they began to meet on the fairway

for regular rounds of golf. A friendship[30] developed between the Chrétiens and the Clintons that was strengthened by the obligatory official visits that each paid to Washington and Ottawa.

The Clintons made the first move, flying into Ottawa in late February 1995 for a twenty-four-hour stay, preceded by a contingent of more than a thousand Secret Service agents. There was a black-tie gala state dinner at the Museum of Civilization in Hull, late-night drinks at 24 Sussex Drive for the leaders and their spouses, as well as two sessions of talks focusing on bilateral trade disputes, the conflict in Bosnia, and the forthcoming G7 summit in Halifax. En route to the airport, the Clintons and the Chrétiens stopped for some skating, a snack of "Beaver Tail" pastries, unique to Canada (which caught the president's attention),[31] and an intimate lunch at Dow's Lake on the Rideau Canal. In the case of this visit, as in the prime minister's return visit two years later, the public demonstrations of friendship between the two leaders and their spouses, rather than the substance of the issues addressed, were the messages.

In early April 1997, it was Prime Minister Chrétien's turn. The White House pulled out all the stops to make the Canadians feel welcome. Although the prime minister was a head of government and not a head of state,[32] the president decreed that as many of the trappings of a state visit as possible be provided. When he went to pay his respects to the grave of President John F. Kennedy at Arlington National Cemetery, the honour guard was several thousand strong, or more than all the troops Canada had serving overseas at that time in peacekeeping missions in Bosnia and the Middle East. Accommodations were at Blair House, the presidential guest house. Each bedroom was furnished with beds and commodes from the estates of previous presidents. My bed, the charming chatelaine told me, was the very one in which President Eisenhower had died. That was too much information. I spent the night with one eye open, expecting Ike's ghost to pay a visit to see who was profaning the place where he had breathed his last.

The formal part of the program started with an intimate session to break the ice between the two leaders in the Oval Office. Clinton and Chrétien then moved next door to the cabinet office (unchanged, I noticed, since I had last seen it in 1977 when I accompanied a NATO delegation to visit President Ford). There were at least twenty items, ranging from Pacific salmon, anti-personnel mines, and climate change on the agenda. Foreign Affairs Minister Lloyd Axworthy, Environment Minister Sergio Marchi, Trade Minister Art Eggleton, and Revenue Minister Jane Stewart backed up the prime minister. Vice President Al Gore, Secretary of State Madeleine Albright, Secretary of Commerce William Daley, and Acting Trade Representative Charlene Barshefsky were on Clinton's side of the table. The press conference afterwards in the Rose Garden had its hilarious moment when an American correspondent indignantly demanded that the prime minister comment on an alleged flow of illicit drugs from Canada. Thinking she had said trucks rather than drugs, Prime Minister Chrétien initially told the astonished press corps that this type of traffic was just "more trade." The president, with an injury to his knee which prevented him from playing golf, and preoccupied with yet another Middle Eastern crisis, was courteous but grumpy, at least initially. Then again perhaps America's leader had more than matters of state on his mind. For in April 1997, Monica Lewinsky, transferred to the Pentagon after her internship one year earlier, was still sneaking back to the White House for quiet sexual encounters with Bill Clinton.

The president did not remain ill-tempered for long. The dinner at the White House was elegant and welcoming. Famous Canadian cultural icons such as Yousef Karsh, Howie Mandell, and Diana Krall were there, along with Washington's movers and shakers. According to the wine-stained menu that I quietly stuffed into my pocket at the end of the meal, we ate Maple-Cured Salmon with Fiddlehead Ferns, Herb-Crusted Lamb with Artichokes, and Raspberry and Chocolate Truffle served on the

"Ronald Reagan State China Service." The after-dinner entertainment in the East Room was by mezzo-soprano Denyce
Graves. I had to pinch myself to be sure I was not dreaming. What
was someone whose first home in the village of his youth had
been a tent near the dump doing as a guest in the White House?

A Joke Backfires

There was not, however, always harmony at the top. The White
House was not amused by the prime minister's candid comments
on the American political system at the Madrid summit of July
1997. At that gathering, leaders agreed to expand NATO's membership to take in three former members of the Warsaw Pact –
Poland, the Czech Republic, and Hungary. It was a time of rejoic-
ing. The prime minister had been a long-standing advocate of
enlarging NATO to take in the countries of Central and Eastern
Europe held captive by the former Soviet Union throughout the
Cold War. At the NATO summit of January 1994, President
Clinton had proposed that these former communist-controlled
countries be accorded a status equivalent to partial membership
only in a structure called "Partnership for Peace." Canada's prime
minister was the only NATO leader to take to the floor to argue
passionately that the alliance should immediately admit to its
ranks the newly liberated countries of Central and Eastern
Europe. If that were not possible (and it was not), then "Partnership for Peace" should be regarded as a step on the way to full
membership rather than the end of a process. We must not, he
said, repeat the mistake of the West in the 1930s and 1940s when
these countries were left in a power vacuum at the mercy of
Hitler, and then of Stalin.

In the coming years, the prime minister continued to champion the cause of enlargement, meeting regularly with the Central
and Eastern European leaders to encourage them and to help
them plan strategy. At the OSCE summit in Budapest in December
1994, he met with every prime minister or president from central

Europe with aspirations to join NATO to offer them Canada's support. He did the same at the next OSCE summit in Lisbon in December 1996. NATO membership topped the agendas during visits to Ottawa of Polish president Lech Walesa in September 1994, Prime Minister Václav Klaus of the Czech Republic in February 1997, Foreign Minister László Kovács of Hungary in July 1995, and Prime Minister Janez Drnovsek of Slovenia in May 1996. Drnovsek, the astute Slovenian leader who managed to extricate his country from the former Yugoslavia in 1992 with a minimum of bloodshed, became a close friend of the prime minister, telephoning him frequently for advice on the campaign he was waging to join NATO. The prime minister remained the only alliance leader offering the Central Europeans unconditional support during these years, helping keep alive their hopes as the debates were waged on whether to take in new members. Our own Foreign Affairs establishment, not wishing to provoke Russia and uneasy that Canada was so far out in front of its allies, was initially aghast at the position the prime minister espoused, but soon came on side and enthusiastically supported his cause.

Prime Minister Chrétien was thus well placed to broker a deal in Madrid in July 1997 when differences between France and the United States threatened to block all progress. France wanted the immediate entry of Hungary, Poland, the Czech Republic, Romania, and Slovenia, as did Canada. The United States wanted only Hungary, Poland, and the Czech Republic. In separate discussions at the official dinner the evening before the meeting, Spanish prime minister José Maria Aznar and President Chirac confided their fears of deadlock to Chrétien, who promised to do his best to help find a solution. The next day, after dispensing with the services of foreign minister and diplomatic advisor, the prime minister did just that, coming up with a formula that bridged the differences between the presidents of France and the United States. Hungary, Poland, and the Czech Republic would be admitted in the first wave of expansion. Romania and Slovenia would arrive in a second wave. And the door would be left open for the Baltic countries to join later.

So far so good. But then disaster struck. An open microphone picked up the prime minister making jokes about the American political system. The power of the president, he was caught saying, was circumscribed in the United States under its division of powers; Congress and the Judiciary had as much power as the White House. Trade-offs had to be made to get votes which, in other countries would be seen as criminal vote-buying, and so on. What he said was unexceptional. What offended the White House was his obvious glee in relating these insights to his peers, Chancellor Kohl of Germany, Prime Minister Dehaene of Belgium, and Prime Minister Aznar of Spain among others – who joined in the hilarity while waiting for the notoriously tardy American president to join them for the closing press conference. The administration was also furious that CNN carried the joking and chortling live to the United States and across the world, and repeated the clips time and again in the course of the day. The president's handlers had scripted a plan in which Clinton would appear before the world's press surrounded by an admiring group of acolytes – the leaders of the lesser members of NATO, the grand and historic American-dominated regional security organization – to announce the momentous summit decision to expand the alliance to take in new members. That scenario had been blown apart and the White House was as mad as hell.

The Canadian delegation was blissfully unaware of all this as we departed immediately after the press conference for the airport in two motorcades: the Chrétiens in one to fly to Portugal for a few days' holiday, and the rest of us in another to return to Ottawa in the government Airbus. We were, in fact, feeling rather satisfied with ourselves. Clinton and Chirac had both thanked the prime minister for saving the summit. Prime Minister Chrétien had left the conference centre with their words of appreciation ringing in his ears. His advisor, for his part, basked in reflected glory.

Imagine my surprise, therefore, somewhere over the Atlantic, when I took an angry telephone call from Sandy Vershbow, a member of the National Security Council. Sandy, whom I knew well from service together on another posting, was calling from Warsaw, President Clinton's destination after Madrid. The president had hurried to the former Warsaw Pact country to announce the results of the summit inviting Poland to be a member of NATO – and of course to accept the gratitude of the Polish nation. When called forward to the cockpit to take a message so urgent that it could not wait until our aircraft landed in Ottawa, I was preparing myself to accept with modesty the expected praise for the accomplishments of the prime minister. Instead, I received a brusque question with no qualifying explanation.

"Well," my erstwhile friend demanded, "what are you going to do about it?"

"About what?" I innocently asked, only to be given a lesson on the iniquity of Canadian political leaders, with language such as "betrayal" and "to think of what we have done for you in the past" – and on and on and on. I finally realized, on recovering from my shock, that I was supposed to apologize on behalf of the prime minister to permit a White House spokesperson to announce to the press that "a senior member of Canadian prime minister Chrétien's staff humbly regretted the errors of his boss's ways" to provide some sort of answer to the ridicule coming from the media. I had no intention of doing this, of course. I was not that stupid; I also wanted to keep my job. By the time the Airbus arrived in Ottawa, I had thought of a strategy to deal with the American fury: advise the prime minister to wait a few days for Clinton to cool down and then call to apologize. Ambassador Chrétien in Washington, who had received blasts from both the State Department and the White House with threats such as "the next time there's a referendum in Quebec we will support the separatists," wanted the prime minister to pick up the telephone and apologize at once, at the risk of receiving an outraged earful. This approach – a "lancing the boil strategy" – I thought to be too high risk. Their personal relations might never recover. The prime minister agreed with my approach and put off his call for three days. When he telephoned, the president could not have been more gracious.

"We all do these things. . . . Why Jean, I remember the time I spoke on an open mike and inadvertently offended people. . . . Don't you worry, my friend," and so on.

Clinton may have forgiven the prime minister, but his staff had not. They decided that someone would have to pay a price and I was the designated victim. Sandy Berger, who had replaced the courteous Tony Lake as national security advisor, telephoned to provide his "personal views." The White House then informed the media that the official reaction of the American government had been conveyed to the advisor to the prime minister. The story died, but what Berger said about the prime minister was so outrageous that our personal relations never recovered. I did not tell the prime minister. I did not want to give Berger the satisfaction of having his remarks passed on.

Pacific Salmon

Not all Canada–United States disputes resulted from simple misunderstandings – sometimes the Americans were bullies. After returning from the NATO summit in Madrid in July, I had to forgo my annual holidays, just as I had each summer over the previous three years, to help coordinate the federal government's response to American overfishing of salmon in the Pacific Northwest. Under the terms of the Pacific Salmon Treaty of 1985, "each Party shall conduct its fisheries and its salmon enhancement programs so as to . . . provide for each party to receive benefits equivalent to the production of salmon originating in its waters. . . fish shares would approximate the numbers of salmon originating in their respective waters." Simply put, Canada and the United States were supposed to divide the catch equitably.

In 1992, however, the fishing agreements negotiated to implement the treaty expired, and the Americans found excuses to avoid
concluding new ones. Most commercial fishing was done in
waters off southern and northern British Columbia. In the south,
Canadian fishermen held the advantage, since the fish passed
through Canadian territorial waters en route to their spawning
grounds upstream on the Fraser River. In the more lucrative
northern zone, however, the Americans held the upper hand. The
coast along the Alaska panhandle was sovereign American territory and American fishermen reigned supreme, harvesting enormous quantities of salmon returning from the ocean to the streams
where they had been born to spawn. Canadian fishermen were
bitter because most of the fish the Americans harvested in their
territorial waters came from the headwaters of rivers originating
in Canada. Rubbing salt in Canadian wounds, the Americans
boasted that their catches were so good because Canada was
doing such a good job of enforcing conservation measures and
stocking their portions of these rivers with hatchlings, or baby
fish, that eventually ended up in American nets.

Every year, the prime minister would telephone President
Clinton to ask him to intervene to make the United States negotiate in good faith to resolve the impasse. The president, barely
suppressing his boredom, would plead that his hands were tied.
The local states and Indian tribes, he said, decided policy on West
Coast fishing and he could not overrule them, even to enforce
an international treaty. In fact, as both he and the prime minister
well knew, he did not want to alienate the senators and members
of Congress from the Pacific Northwest by being too sympathetic to Canada. Each year, therefore, after much bluster, we
would come up with a face-saving formula to mask Canada's
inability to get them to play fair, usually getting the Americans
to agree to the appointment of a team of high-priced and high-
profile negotiators to recommend solutions, always to come into
effect sometime in the future.

Nineteen ninety-seven had been particularly difficult. Frustrated fishermen had blockaded the Alaskan ferry *Malaspina* with their fishing boats in the port of Prince Rupert and someone, later identified as a dual Canadian-American citizen, burned an American flag. Washington warned the Canadian embassy that such behaviour would not be tolerated. A senior member of the White House called me to express outrage and to warn that the United States was not Europe. Should Canada try to push it around as it had Spain off the Grand Banks of Newfoundland, we would be in for a great surprise. He demanded that the government order the police to move immediately to free the ferry. I listened politely but, of course did nothing to interfere in the police's handling of the incident. Eventually, in good Canadian style, the RCMP negotiated a peaceful end to the blockade. And once again the United States and Canada announced the establishment of another high-priced team to come up with another solution that everyone knew would be ignored when fishing season came along the following year. An agreement generally satisfactory to both sides would not be signed until June 1999.

Anti-personnel Mines

Clinton also blew his top when pressed beyond his limits over anti-personnel mines by the prime minister in September 1997. Earlier, I have described how the prime minister, after his meeting with the president of the International Committee of the Red Cross in May 1994, had made the ban on the production and use of anti-personnel mines a Canadian foreign-policy priority. His initial move was to raise the issue at the June 1994 Naples summit, the first leader of the G7 to adopt the cause. His colleagues heard him out but were not interested: the mines issue was an idea whose time had not yet come. The prime minister carried on with his missionary work, lobbying presidents and prime ministers and encouraging Foreign Minister Ouellet to commit Foreign Affairs to the struggle. Throughout 1995 and early 1996, world leaders gradually began to show interest, stimulated by the growing support among their publics for a ban. But even those who were personally sympathetic found themselves faced with reluctant military establishments who argued that removing anti-personnel mines from their arsenals would endanger their troops and put them at a disadvantage in fighting wars.

In January 1996, Lloyd Axworthy replaced André Ouellet as foreign minister and enthusiastically adopted the cause, making it the centrepiece of his human security agenda. The prime minister continued his efforts with world leaders. In summit meetings in May and June, he persuaded the leaders of the Commonwealth Caribbean, and European Union to issue political declarations favouring a ban. In September, he dealt once and for all with foot-dragging from Canada's own defence establishment by ordering Canada's military to destroy immediately one-third of Canada's anti-personnel mine stocks. The other two-thirds would be disposed of "in the context of successful negotiations." And in what would be the turning point in the campaign, he accepted Lloyd Axworthy's recommendation that Canada issue a challenge to delegates at an international meeting in Ottawa to return to Canada's capital to sign a final treaty before the end of 1997.

Nobody and no country, Canada and the United States included, anticipated the wave of popular support that followed. More than one thousand non-governmental organizations in the Mine Action Group swung into action pressuring governments in a massive public relations campaign. The prime minister and his foreign minister lobbied relentlessly. The prime minister alone would eventually raise the matter in private meetings with more than one hundred world leaders at various G7, G8, APEC, Commonwealth, and Francophonie summits, with official visitors to Canada, and during his official travels abroad. One after another, the recalcitrant countries, including France and the United Kingdom, fell into line. The big holdout was the United

States. Ostensibly the Americans were on side. Clinton in May 1996 announced American support for an international agreement to ban anti-personnel mines. At the same time, however, he said that American negotiators had red lines that they would not cross. The first and most important was that the treaty not apply to Korea, where American and North Korean troops had been confronting each other for over forty years across a heavily mined so-called demilitarized zone. The second was that anti-personnel mines used in conjunction with anti-tank mines be exempt from the ban. And the third was that a nine-year period be allowed to phase in the treaty.

The negotiations to finalize the draft treaty opened on September 1 in Oslo, Norway. The Americans arrived with a senior delegation and worked hard, but achieved nothing. By September 15, President Clinton was most unhappy. The conference was scheduled to wind up on September 16 but none of the American conditions had been accepted. Princess Diana, a great champion of the cause, had been killed just the day before the conference opened, imbuing the movement with a saintly aura and attracting massive interest from the world press, which played up the isolation of the United States in company with the likes of Iran, Iraq, China, Cuba, and Russia. Making matters worse, the president personally supported a treaty and even kept an inert mine on his desk as a symbol of his commitment. In an act of desperation, therefore, he intervened personally with world leaders to see if language could be found that would meet the concerns of his military without undermining the substance of the treaty. His interlocutor of choice was Jean Chrétien.

I had returned home close to midnight in the evening of September 15 after accompanying Mrs. Chrétien to the funeral of Mother Teresa in Calcutta. No sooner was I in the door than the telephone rang. It was the PMO switchboard: President Clinton wanted to speak to the prime minister urgently. Assuming the president wanted to discuss mines, I called Foreign Affairs

Undersecretary Don Campbell for a quick update on the Oslo negotiations. Don told me that he and Axworthy had been responding to appeals all evening from their opposite numbers in Washington to help them bridge their differences with the rest of the international community. The call from the president, he told me, was an indication that the situation was desperate for the Americans. The call I then put through would be the first of four or five that would take place throughout the night as the two leaders sought a formula that would allow the Americans to join the consensus.[33] The prime minister, while unwilling to compromise the substance of the treaty, did his best to be helpful, waking up Ralph Lysyshyn, Canada's negotiator in Oslo to try out ideas, discussing options with President Chirac, and calling President Mandela to enlist his support to give the Americans more time to solve their internal problems. In the end, President Clinton could not persuade the Joint Chiefs of Staff to agree, and was forced to tell the prime minister that he had failed.

Chrétien, however, would not take no for an answer, telling Clinton that he could not understand why the leader of the most powerful nation on earth could not overrule his generals. And surely the country that had put a man on the moon could overcome the technical obstacles to accepting the draft treaty? The failure of the administration to come on side, he added, would isolate Washington on an issue of critical importance to humanity at the end of the twentieth century. The prime minister, of course, adopted a high moral tone. After all, we Canadians have always felt that it was our duty – even our birthright – to point out to our American cousins how they could better organize their affairs and those of humanity. And he was following in the noble tradition of Canadian leaders such as prime ministers Diefenbaker, Pearson, and Trudeau, who consistently gave excellent, if unsolicited, advice on the big foreign-policy issues of their day to their presidential contemporaries – even if their wise counsel merely infuriated their good American friends, leading one famous former secretary of state in the 1960s to call Canada the "Stern Daughter of the Voice of God."[34]

In this instance, however, it was the American president who had sought the help of his Canadian counterpart. Nevertheless, faced with a persistent Canadian leader who continued to press him not to give up the fight when he had already done so, the president fought back. No one, he said, had the right to question the good will of the United States! And his country would not, he said, be the skunk at the garden party when the treaty was signed! That, unfortunately, was the way things played out.

In December 1997, United States delegates were forced to look on, as representatives 2,400 strong from 122 signatory and thirty-five observer countries plus a roomful of non-governmental organizations celebrated the signature of the convention in the Conference Centre at the old Ottawa Union Station. There were many heroes: the mine action groups who kept up public pressure; Cornelio Sommaruga, head of the International Committee of the Red Cross, who had brought the prime minister on side in April 1994; Prime Minister Chrétien, who provided the strategic direction to his foreign ministers and personally lobbied so many heads of state and government; André Ouellet, who kept the issue on the front burner in Foreign Affairs throughout 1994 and 1995; Lloyd Axworthy, who challenged the world to come to Ottawa to sign the treaty; and the exceptional foreign-service officers – Jill Sinclair and Ralph Lysyshyn – who came up with the ideas and did the work behind the scenes.

Climate Change

The two leaders had somewhat better luck in coordinating the positions of their countries on climate change. I was no expert on the subject, but my daughter, Anne-Pascale, a university student spending her summers assisting a professor of geography doing fieldwork on the effect of climate change on permafrost in the Yukon, had been doing her best over the years to sensitize me to the danger. She told me that the average temperatures on the earth's surface had been increasing dramatically and ocean levels had been rising for more than a century because of growing levels of carbon dioxide and other gases in the atmosphere. At the Rio Earth summit of 1992, the major developed countries and the former communist governments of Central and Eastern Europe had agreed, as a consequence, to reduce their greenhouse gas emissions to 1990 levels by the year 2000. Developing countries were not bound to make reductions.

I looked into the matter and learned that the Rio targets had been too optimistic. No one, other than a handful of European states, had been able to meet them. And these Europeans had done so more by good luck than by good planning. The British had benefited from the conversion of homes and industry from coal to gas discovered in the North Sea, the Germans from the industrial collapse of the former East Germany, and the Russians from the implosion of their economy with the disappearance of the Soviet Union. Neither the United States nor Canada, however, had made an effort to meet their Rio commitments. In Canada alone, carbon-dioxide levels were expected to be 12 per cent over 1990 levels by 2000. The United States record was no better.

A review conference to look at what had been accomplished in the interim and to set new targets for the next decade was scheduled for November and December 1997 in Kyoto, Japan. Within the tidily organized world of the Canadian bureaucracy, however, neither I nor the members of my secretariat had anything to do with the file. Rather, the PCO economic secretariat was responsible for working with Environment Canada, other interested government departments, and the relevant cabinet committee to oversee Canadian policy. But nothing had been accomplished by the time of the Denver G7 and the New York environmental summits in June 1997, when climate change was on the agenda. John Major, Helmut Kohl, and Jacques Chirac rubbed the noses of their North American partners in the dirt of their poor performance since 1992. They noted that the European Union had set for itself a new goal of 15 per cent below 1990 levels by 2012 and appealed to Canada and the United States to accept the European goal as their own. Embarrassed, Bill Clinton and Jean Chrétien resisted the pressure, saying it was premature to spell out their national positions six months ahead of Kyoto. Both swore, however, that they would have credible positions to put into play in the fall.

Fast-forward from June 1997 to the prime minister's official visit to Russia in the fall. At midnight local time October 21 in St. Petersburg, the telephone rang in my hotel room. It was the PMO's switchboard in Ottawa. The operator told me that President Clinton, unaware that his Canadian counterpart was out of Canada and in a different time zone, wanted to speak to him. I knew that the prime minister had just returned from dinner, was thus awake, and would want to take the call. There were three possible things, I thought, on the president's mind: anti-personnel mines, the Asian financial crisis, and climate change. I quickly prepared myself to brief him on all three and knocked on the prime minister's door. He was already familiar with the first two items, so I focused on climate change.

As I handed him the relevant briefing card, I told him that Canada still did not have a position on Kyoto. Environment Canada and the PCO economic secretariat had not been able to find common ground with a divided Cabinet, a hostile business sector, and a reluctant group of western premiers. In the circumstances, their advice to the prime minister was to say nothing should any foreign leader ask about Canada's position. They had also prepared a list of a dozen reasons why it would be difficult if not impossible for Canada to do anything. The prime minister stopped me as I started to rhyme off reasons for inaction, threw the card away in disgust, and exploded.

"Leaders have responsibilities to future generations. That is what I am going to tell Clinton should he raise the matter. I will even say that Canada will come up with targets that will be more ambitious than those of the United States. Perhaps that will help the president to get his various constituencies on side. The bottom line is, however, that Canada and the United States should never get too far out in front of the other."

In the call that came in ten minutes later, Clinton told Chrétien that he was worried. The lobby against making any meaningful moves to prevent climate change was so strong in the United States that it would be difficult obtain any consensus to move before Kyoto. What was Canada going to do? The prime minister said that a final Canadian position had not yet been determined and then repeated to the president what he had told me.

On my return to Ottawa, with the support of Jack Stagg, head of the PCO economic secretariat, I took over the international coordination of the file, assigning an excellent economic analyst, Barbara Martin, to work with me in preparing a strategy for the use of the prime minister. The key points, incorporating the prime minister's comments in St. Petersburg and a dose of instinct, were as follows: The European position of 15 per cent reductions below 1990 levels by 2012 was unrealistic; that of the United States, although not yet spelled out, was likely to be too cautious. Canada should work to bridge the gap, adopting a position in-between, pushing both the Europeans and the Americans off their extreme approaches. It would also not be long before developing countries would be producing more greenhouse gases than developed ones; a way had to be found to oblige them to make reductions. Time, however, was running out. There were now less than two months before Kyoto and the chances that the international community would be able to achieve a consensus on new targets were no better than 50 per cent. By good fortune, however, the Commonwealth, Francophonie, and APEC summits were scheduled for the fall of 1997 and the leaders of Japan and China would be paying official visits to Ottawa. Should he so wish, the prime minister was well placed to assist Japan, the host state, in bridging differences between the key players and ensuring that Kyoto was a success.

The prime minister so wished and gave his approval to the proposed strategy. There was an immediate impact in Ottawa. Warring bureaucrats and disputing ministers got the message that the global dimensions of the issue were so pressing that they out-weighed the domestic ones, and that they should start preparing an advanced position for Canada to adopt at Kyoto. Prime Minister Chrétien then added climate change to anti-personnel mines and the Asian financial crisis as key themes for discussion in the more than one hundred private meetings he held with world leaders in the fall. And the results? It is impossible to say. His private meetings supplemented by telephone discussions with President Clinton and major European leaders may have played a role in drawing the Americans and Europeans together. His bilateral sessions with leaders of developing countries were the first time many of them debated the issues with a leader of a G7 country. He even managed a coup of sorts by including the issue on the agenda of the Vancouver APEC summit, forcing the leaders of major developing countries to confront the consequences of not accepting to limit their emissions, even if they still balked at making commitments.

For my part, I remained in close touch with Environment Minister Christine Stewart and Canada's negotiator in Kyoto, Paul Heinbecker, a senior assistant deputy minister at Foreign Affairs, to keep them up to date on the prime minister's media-tion efforts and to pass on his comments on their activities. In the end, Vice President Gore, who joined the American delega-tion as chief negotiator at Kyoto at the last minute, went over-board in proposing dramatic reductions under 1990 levels by 2012. The Gore initiative led to a deal at Kyoto but it was soon seen in the United States as a cynical election manoeuvre by a presiden-tial candidate anxious to appeal at any cost to the American envi-ronmental lobby. When Congress rejected the deal, I felt that

Canada had been left holding the bag – committed to a 6 per cent reduction target, while the United States, its closest trading partner, remained unconstrained.

The prime minister did not share my pessimism. We had, he told me, protected our industrial base by linking our acceptance to obtaining concessions to an international emissions trading regime, to securing credits for our vast forests that soak up carbon dioxide, and to a so-called clean development mechanism that would allow us to obtain credits for investments in emission-reduction projects in developing countries. In any case, Canada would have the last laugh. When the predictions of the scientists came true, the United States would be forced to make drastic reductions in its emissions to help save itself and the planet. By that time, Canada would have adapted to the new energy-efficient world. Sometimes, he said, leaders had to make leaps of faith.

Pol Pot

The latter part of the 1990s was also one of those rare times when the United States needed Canada's help on global issues as much as Canada needed that of the United States. To be sure, the prime minister only said yes when American proposals made sense and served Canada's interest. On other occasions, the answer was no. For example, in June 1997, a senior official in Foreign Affairs called to ask that I pass to the prime minister a proposal from Secretary of State Madeleine Albright that Canada accept the Cambodian mass murderer, Pol Pot, and place him on trial in Canada for human rights abuses under a newly passed Canadian law. I was astonished. It was as if Hitler had been found alive, and Canada was being asked to put him on trial for war crimes.

A little history: In April 1975, the Khmer Rouge, led by Pol Pot, seized control of Cambodia, turned the calendar back to Year Zero, and embarked on a process of genocidal "purifica-tion." In 1979, Vietnam invaded Cambodia to end a slaughter of Vietnamese nationals, seized the capital, Phnom Penh, installed a puppet regime, and drove the Khmer Rouge into sanctuaries along the border with Thailand. At the time, I felt relief that the genocide had ended, but soon found that my views did not reflect official Canadian policy. In those Cold War years, the Soviet Union was the enemy and an ally of Vietnam. China was hostile to the Soviet Union and an ally of Pol Pot and the Khmer Rouge. Canada thus supported the United States and regional Southeast Asian countries in backing Pol Pot's claim to continue representing his country in the United Nations. I asked a colleague who was Canada's representative on a pro–Pol Pot international committee. "How can Canada support a leader who turned his capital into a ghost town, who spread anti-personnel mines indiscriminately, who oversaw the massive torturing of prisoners, and who killed millions of his own people in a savage social engineering experiment?"

"Jim," he said, "you just don't understand power politics!"

A decade and half later, the old debate over who would represent Cambodia in the United Nations had long been forgotten. Vietnam had pulled out of Cambodia at the end of the Cold War and Pol Pot's Khmer Rouge remained a fringe force hunkered down in its remote jungle hide-outs. Democratic elections had been held under United Nations auspices and life was gradually returning to normal. Pol Pot, however, although sick and shorn of his power, was still a disruptive presence in Cambodia. Hence the appeal from Madeleine Albright, who argued that the peace process would be facilitated by his removal from the country. Determined to do my best to ensure that Canada did not put itself in another morally ambiguous position, I called a top international lawyer in Foreign Affairs who told me that the Canadian legislation in question was untested. There was a good chance, he said, that once accepted on Canadian soil, Pol Pot would be acquitted for lack of due process or on some technicality. Canada would then have to face the nightmare prospect of one of the world's most brutal dictators being nursed back to health, cocooned in our generous medicare system, and living to a ripe old age in downtown Toronto or Vancouver, with Canada the laughing stock of the international community. I explained the situation to the prime minister, who rejected the proposal out of hand. Pol Pot would die unmourned in his jungle refuge within the year.

Haiti

The prime minister's response to appeals from the president for help with Haiti was more nuanced. In June 1994, President Clinton made his first approach, telephoning Prime Minister Chrétien to ask Canada to send military forces to join an American-led invasion force being pulled together to expel the Haitian dictator of the day, General Raul Cédras. Washington intended to return to power the legitimately elected president, Jean-Bertrand Aristide, who had been forced from office in a military coup in 1991. True, Aristide had often engaged in anti-American tirades after his election as president in 1990, and his followers had a penchant for applying necklaces of burning tires around the heads of his domestic opponents. Washington, however, was gambling that his return would restore political stability in the Caribbean's most impoverished nation, lead to long-term economic growth, and staunch the exodus of desperate people fleeing on all manner of rickety boats and rafts for Miami. Secretary of State Warren Christopher kept up the pressure, telephoning Foreign Minister André Ouellet to lobby for Canada to send troops, arguing correctly that the cause was just and that the United States, in a departure from past practice, would seek a mandate from the United Nations Security Council before it went into action. Ouellet, mindful that going in with the Americans would be popular with the large Haitian-Canadian community in his Montreal constituency of Papineau–St-Denis, agreed, and passed on his opinion to the prime minister, adding that Canada would gain political credit with our powerful neighbour to the south should we give them a hand.

I was familiar with Haitian issues, having been responsible for the management of relations with the poverty-stricken francophone Caribbean state in the early 1980s when I was Foreign Affairs director for the Caribbean and Central America. At that time, I visited Port au Prince to look into rumours that millions in Canadian aid money were being siphoned off by corrupt Haitian officials. It was a fascinating, surrealistic return to the Haiti of Graham Green's classic novel *The Comedians*. The *tonton macoutes*, popularly known as the bogeymen, the sinister militia responsible for murdering some forty thousand people to keep the Duvaliers in power, were still omnipresent, wearing their trademark dark sunglasses. From my bedroom at the residence of the Canadian ambassador, I could hear the pounding of voodoo drums late into the night. Jean-Claude (Baby Doc) Duvalier, the playboy son of the infamous dictator François (Papa Doc) Duvalier, who had ruled the country for over a generation with an iron fist, was still in power. In the fashionable restaurants, the local elite dined on *pâté de foie gras* flown in from France and washed down with the finest of imported champagnes – and this in a country where the overwhelming mass of the people lived in a poverty so profound and abject that even the Cubans refused to foment revolution there for fear that they would find themselves having to prop up economically an unsustainable state in the Caribbean.[35]

The staff at the Canadian embassy gave me a warm welcome. Some had special talents. One officer had become a master of the local Creole dialect, giving him access to segments of Haitian society not frequented by most expatriates, including the world of the *tonton macoutes*. They were, he naively confided to me, actually nice guys who sometimes had to do nasty things. Another officer, despite a lack of any medical training, worked part-time in the emergency ward of the local hospital assisting a local doctor carrying out medical procedures. My initial doubts about his capabilities were dispelled, however, when I broke my foot and needed his help; he set my broken bones very competently, and encased them in a temporary cast. The aid officers, but not the conscientious ambassador, were certain that there could be no corruption in their well-run program. The possibility did not exist. When I asked others in the expatriate community whether Haitian government officials had their hands in the Canadian aid till, they laughed. Corruption in the Canadian aid program was an open secret. The ambassador ordered a full audit of the program, which in the end, confirmed everyone's worst fears.

On how to respond to the American appeals, my view (in hindsight overly dogmatic) was that Canada should stick to peacekeeping operations rather than become involved in invasions, no matter how just they might be. As an old Latin American and Caribbean hand, I was mindful of the unhappy history of American relations with the countries of the region. In the nineteenth century, under the Monroe Doctrine, Washington told the world that Latin America fell within its regional sphere of interest. In wars with Mexico, it carved out for itself huge territories for new states. In the Spanish-American War of 1898, it took Cuba and went on to dominate successive Cuban governments until the arrival on the scene of Fidel Castro. Teddy Roosevelt seized territory from Colombia to build the Panama Canal and instituted a policy of "speaking quietly and carrying a big stick." The American military and CIA regularly overthrew governments in support of American business and political interests throughout the twentieth century. The people of Latin America and the Caribbean had long memories and resented the long American history of intervention. I knew that many leading countries of the region, including Mexico, Colombia, and Uruguay, had their doubts on the wisdom of the proposed American-led intervention. Not for the first time, Canada's leader would be faced with one valid principle: helping to remove a

vicious dictator from power or refusing to participate in the invasion of a sovereign country.

At the delegation briefing prior to his meeting with President
Clinton at the June 1994 Naples G7 meeting, the prime minister
listened as Ouellet and I reviewed Canada's options. After a
period of reflection, he opted for a compromise: declining the
American appeal to participate in the invasion stage but agreeing
to contribute troops to the follow-up peacekeeping phase.[36] In
the end, with the blessing of a United Nations Security Council
resolution, an American-led multinational force (MNF) with
21,000 troops from nineteen countries, but not including Canada,
occupied Haiti peacefully in October of 1994, using the threat
of the use of force to chase Cédras from power. In March 1995,
the MNF was replaced by a 6,050 strong peacekeeping force, the
United Nations Mission in Haiti (UNMIH), led by an American
general and overwhelmingly American in composition but this
time including a Canadian contingent.

By 1996, however, the American administration was concerned at the growth in anti-American sentiment in Haiti and
wanted to remove its troops before they wore out their welcome.
Tony Lake thus woke me up in Mumbai, the former Bombay,
during the Team Canada mission to South Asia in January 1996
to pass on an urgent request from the president. Would Canada
be prepared to replace the United States as leading nation in
UNMIH when its mandate expired in March, to allow the
Americans to pull out with dignity? The mission would continue
to be a classic peacekeeping operation and the United States was
confident that the United Nations Security Council would pass
the necessary resolution.

This time the prime minister was happy to oblige. It was, he
told me, in Canada's interest to help maintain stability in the
Caribbean's most impoverished nation, to support a fellow
member of the Francophonie, and to respond to the wishes of the
tens of thousands of new Canadians in Quebec who claimed

Haiti as their homeland. In short order, Canada supplied a force commander, Brigadier-General Pierre Daigle and sufficient troops to give the Americans the cover to pull out. The administration's moral debt to Canada, however, would be as short-lived as our peacekeeping presence in the Caribbean nation. Canada would remove its troops before stability was fully restored, make a valiant but ultimately ineffective effort to train a police force, and provide amounts of aid too modest to make an impact. In fact, no one other than Fidel Castro, who sent dozens of doctors to work in shanty towns and isolated villages, and Latin American drug lords, who took advantage of Haiti's deepening culture of corruption to use it as a drug transhipment centre, would pay any attention to the impoverished failed state in the coming years.

Then in 2004, Haiti was once more in turmoil and in the news. This time Canada joined the United States and France in forcing the same Jean-Bertrand Aristide from the office of president that he won in controversial elections in November 2000. Jean-Bertrand Aristide was no more corrupt in 2004 than he had been in 1994. He had, however, fallen out of favour with Washington and Paris.

The Israeli–Palestinian Conflict

And sometimes, the White House just wanted Canada's moral support. Such was the case in March 1996 when a contact in the National Security Council called me. Could I ask the prime minister if he would be prepared to leave for Sharm el Sheikh, a resort town in Egypt on the Red Sea, to attend a summit meeting on the Israeli–Palestinian conflict? Less than five months had passed since the assassination of Yitzhak Rabin, he said, and the peace process that the former Israeli prime minister had championed was in deep trouble. In the previous three weeks, Palestinian suicide bombers had killed themselves, together with five dozen Israelis. The American president, representative of the world's only superpower, my American colleague informed me, was alone among the leaders of the world in having real influence in the Middle East. President Clinton was hopeful that if key leaders from North America, Europe, and the Middle East were to join him and Egyptian president Hosni Mubarak, who would co-chair the meeting, in holding what in essence would be a giant rally for peace in the desert, frightened Israelis and Palestinians would be reassured, the dynamic toward conflict changed, and the peace process saved.

My recommendation to the prime minister was that he should go. In so doing he would be showing solidarity to the American president. And, I said, who could tell? Perhaps the pep rally in the desert would do some good. I did not tell him how deeply pessimistic I was about the prospects. Having spent almost five years in the late 1980s and early 1990s as Canada's ambassador to Israel with responsibility for managing relations with the West Bank and Gaza, I was as well-informed as anyone in Canada about the issues. But I recognized that I was also a "burnt-out case," having seen so much suffering, bigotry, hatred, and so many failed peace initiatives that it was not possible for me to believe that outsiders could in any way change the tortured course of Middle Eastern history. Canada, I knew, had important interests in the Middle East, homeland to so many Jewish and Arabic Canadians, but its influence there was limited. I thus did not propose making the Middle East a personal priority for Canada's leader during my years with him. Canada's foreign and trade ministers, I thought, should manage the time-consuming, complex, and ultimately frustrating file. There were, I thought, far more rewarding foreign-policy areas for the prime minister's attention in these days before 9/11 changed the dynamics of world history and once again propelled the region into the centre of global foreign-policy concern.

I had no desire to return to the Middle East in March 1996. My family and I had actually visited Sharm el Sheikh on holiday seven years earlier at a time when Marie-Jeanne and I had badly needed a respite from the pressure-cooker atmosphere of the period. In those days, to prepare myself for the difficult day ahead, I used to walk in the mornings along the cliff overlooking the Mediterranean behind our house in the Israeli community of Herzliya Petuah. One morning, my dog pawed at what I thought was an animal bone. Curious as to its origin, I brought it home to Marie-Jeanne, a former medical student, who identified it as a human femur. I then went exploring, discovering the bones of long-dead people protruding at odd angles from the earth or lying scattered negligently among the wild grasses, weeds, and garbage. Our residence, I discovered, was located behind an old cemetery, bereft of grave markers and abandoned by Palestinians fleeing their homes in the 1948 war of Israeli independence. What hope, I wondered, was there for Arab-Israeli reconciliation when the local Israeli community had no idea that this cemetery even existed; and when, somewhere in a refugee camp in South Lebanon or Gaza, old men and women dreamed of this spot and kept alive the impossible hopes of the young that they would reclaim their ancestral lands someday?

With our two children, we fled Tel Aviv late one afternoon in March 1988, passing through roadblocks manned by the Israeli army around Jerusalem and through groups of stone-throwing Palestinian kids in the West Bank – the intifada of the late 1980s was coming to a head. Descending to the Dead Sea, we travelled all night through the Negev to avoid the glare of the desert sun, driving under stars so bright we could have dispensed with headlights. The next day, we crossed into Egypt, past vigilant Israeli border police and Egyptian customs and immigration officials, to continue along the Gulf of Aqaba on a road built by the Israeli army during a past occupation. After skirting copper mines last worked in the time of King Solomon, and Mount Sinai, sacred to all three warring Middle Eastern monotheistic religions as the place where Moses received the Ten Commandments, we reached Sharm el Sheikh, a place I thought I would never see again.

The Sharm el Sheikh of 1996, I saw, had not changed. Brutal heat still rose in waves, shimmering off sand and sea. The luxury hotel still looked like an artificial appendage set down haphazardly along an otherwise abandoned coastline to attract well-heeled European tourists anxious to escape northern winters. This time the guests were the dozens of world leaders and their entourages who were busy networking, in between long-winded speechifying sessions on the need to keep the peace process alive. I exchanged a few words with Prime Minister Shimon Peres and Foreign Minister Barak, key contacts during my years in Israel for whom I had enormous respect. They were deathly worried that the pendulum was swinging in favour of conflict, and they were right. The stirring words of the world leaders at Sharm el Sheikh would be no match for the extremists on both sides, for whom history and religion divided rather than united. Sharm el Sheikh also defined the limits of American power in the Middle East in the 1990s, a lesson to which George W. Bush might have paid attention before invading Iraq in 2003. President Clinton could not, however, be faulted for making a last-ditch effort to save the peace process and Canada could not do less than show solidarity with him in his ultimately fruitless effort. And Prime Minister Chrétien's 1996 trip into the heat of the desert would constitute his only Middle Eastern foray (other than his attendance at Rabin's funeral) in the years I was with him. His official visits to Israel, Egypt, Lebanon, and Syria would be in the future, when he would take counsel from a more objective and less emotional diplomatic advisor.

The Quebec Referendum

Even if personal relations between the leaders of Canada and the United States are excellent, it is a rare occasion indeed when an American president has the authority and is willing to step in to help his Canadian counterpart with a difficult file. President Clinton did so, however, in the run-up to the referendum of

October 30, 1995, perhaps saving Canada as we know it in the process. At first the president did not need to intervene. Bolstered by opinion polls that showed that a majority of Quebeckers continued to oppose sovereignty, even after the victory of the Parti Québécois in the provincial elections of September 1994, the prime minister remained confident throughout 1994 and most of 1995 that the sovereignty option would be rejected.

I am in no position to comment on the policies he adopted to counter the separatists at home. Internationally, however, I was a witness to his actions to ensure that they gained no international support for their cause. He first of all reminded Foreign Affairs, which had grown lax over the years in allowing Quebec and other provinces more scope to deal directly with foreign governments, that the federal government had the exclusive authority to represent Canada abroad. In all countries, with the exception of France, where Ottawa had conceded to Quebec the right some years earlier to have direct contacts, Canadian embassy officials would henceforth make all appointments for and accompany all travelling provincial ministers and premiers on their official calls; in this way, separatist lobbying for international support would be curtailed. He also told dozens of world leaders that international law allowed breakaway regions or provinces to become independent states only in conditions of repressive colonialism. Canada, however, was a democracy and Quebec was not a colony. And francophones, including the then governor general, the prime minister, and the head of the public service, were represented at the highest levels of Canada's power structure. The implied message was that Canada would consider the recognition by any country of a unilateral declaration of independence by Quebec to constitute an unfriendly act. His appeal was received sympathetically. Many of the leaders governed countries with minorities or regions which would have been tempted to follow the example of Quebec should it succeed in its bid for independence. The result, they all agreed, would be international chaos.

The president was then dragged into the debate. Lucien Bouchard, leader of the official Opposition Bloc Québécois managed to wangle a meeting with President Clinton during his February 1995 visit to Ottawa, arguing that it was his right as leader of Her Majesty's official Opposition to make courtesy calls on official visitors to Canada. The prime minister agreed, but insisted that Canada's ambassador to Washington sit in on the discussion. The president listened politely to the separatist leader's case for a sovereign Quebec and then left to deliver a speech to Parliament endorsing Canadian national unity. In October 1995, the president spoke out again in favour of Canadian unity, just when the momentum for separation seemed to be unstoppable. No one will ever know to what extent Clinton's efforts influenced the referendum outcome. He was, however, personally popular and respected in Quebec. And in a virtually deadlocked situation where the sovereigntist option was rejected by a bare majority, his support for a united Canada may well have made the difference.[37]

The Good Years
Despite differences, mishaps, and misunderstandings, the Chrétien-Clinton years were good ones for Canadian-American relations. Canada's public, which was a keen judge of such matters, seems to have concluded that the personal relations between prime minister and president were neither too close nor too distant. Prosperity in both countries accompanied an explosion in trade as trade barriers fell. No Walter Gordons or John Turners emerged to try to rally a national movement against the surging flow of goods and services through new North-South continental corridors. Canada was drawn intimately into the American economic and cultural empire; and the century-old East-West trade pattern fostered by the National Policy of Canada's founding fathers was abandoned without any growth in popular pressure for Canada to take the ultimate step and become the fifty-first state. To be sure, trade disputes continued to crop up, on issues as diverse as

durum wheat, beer, and split-run magazines. With the exception of the conflict over softwood lumber, however, which proved to be as difficult to resolve as that over Pacific salmon, Canada won and settled its fair share of the cases it took to the newly established dispute settlement tribunals. And only a fraction of the enormous volume of transactions was affected – perhaps because some 40 per cent of trade was actually between American-owned corporations in both countries, and it was as much in the American interest as the Canadian to have a smoothly functioning NAFTA.

Good chemistry between the leaders, combined with a recognition that the two North American partners shared much in common, helped ensure this success. However, as the prime minister pointed out to his European counterparts during the July 1997 open-microphone incident in Madrid, the president was but one player in the American power structure. Opposed by the Pentagon, he could not deliver the goods on anti-personnel mines; confronted by influential Pacific Coast congressmen and congresswomen, he was unwilling to intervene on Pacific salmon. On the other hand, President Clinton helped us when it really mattered, speaking out in favour of a united Canada in the run-up to the referendum. The prime minister likewise did not roll over and say yes every time the American president asked him for a favour. He said no when the Americans proposed bombing the Serbs around Srebrenica in Bosnia in January 1994 when our troops would have been endangered, and rejected repeated requests during the summer of the same year to help invade Haiti, even when the cause was just. However, as the next chapter shows, we should also have said no when the White House, promising, but later withdrawing, its support, quietly asked us to lead an international rescue mission in aid of hundreds of thousands of Hutu refugees in peril in Eastern Zaire in November 1996.

8

Canada and the United States to the Rescue in Africa

On Thursday, November 7, the United States made its move. . . .
The Americans offered to place their military forces under
Canadian command if we would lead the international mission.

The Myth

In 1995, Canada had been prepared to fight Spain in support of a
direct national interest – saving the fish stock. In 1996, we were
once again ready to use force to achieve a foreign-policy goal, but
this time in circumstances where neither economic nor security
interests were at stake. This time Canada would seek to save civilians caught between warring parties in a remote area of Africa.

The Zaire story has been told many times. It is used as a case
study in university political-science classes on how mistaken it is
for a middle power to attempt to fight above its weight in seeking
to solve problems that even the major countries of the world
would hesitate to tackle. Non-governmental organizations and
humanitarian agencies alike use our experience as a benchmark
on what a country should not do if it seeks to mount a humanitarian rescue mission. *Saturday Night* magazine and the award-
winning television documentary program *the fifth estate* savaged
the carcass of what they claimed was a failed enterprise.

The myth on which they base their case runs as follows: Prime
Minister and Mrs. Chrétien are spending the rainy weekend of
November 9 and 10 at their retreat at Harrington Lake, close to
Ottawa. Not able to play golf and unable to concentrate on the

novel he is reading, the prime minister turns on the television to be confronted with dramatic scenes of suffering endured by refugees in Zaire's two most easterly provinces, North and South Kivu. The refugees, caught between warring Tutsi rebels and members of a Hutu militia force responsible for the genocide in Rwanda in 1994, are described as Rwandan Hutus who fled their country after losing out in a civil war that had pitted English-speaking Tutsis against French-speaking Hutus. At this moment, the prime minister's telephone rings. Raymond Chrétien, Canada's ambassador to the United States, on a special mission on behalf of the United Nations to bring peace to Eastern Zaire, is on the line from Kampala airport in Uganda. He urges the prime minister to take the lead in organizing an international military force to put troops on the ground to save the refugees.

The commentary continues with an aroused prime minister calling more than a dozen world leaders on the Saturday and Sunday and persuading all, including those from the United States, France, and the United Kingdom, to put military contingents under a Canadian general and proceed. A grateful United Nations Security Council then votes unanimously in favour of a resolution authorizing a mission under Canada's leadership. Before the force can be deployed, some 750,000 refugees return home to Rwanda, the *raison d'être* for the mission evaporates, and the coalition falls apart. Canada tries in vain to keep the mission alive to save some 500,000 refugees marooned in Eastern Zaire, but is unsuccessful and tells the United Nations that it is giving up. The refugees left behind are massacred. There are recriminations all around, with the media blaming the humanitarian organizations, the humanitarian organizations blaming the international community, and everyone blaming Canada.

My Story
I was the public servant most intimately associated with the crisis, and my account is different. I am not an African specialist and

did not have a posting in Africa until I was later assigned as High Commissioner to South Africa in 1998. I did, however, know something about Rwanda and its history. As a junior protocol officer arranging the Ottawa programs of visiting heads of state and government coming as official guests to help celebrate Canada's centenary in 1967, I organized the schedule and pre-pared the briefing material for Rwanda's first post-independence president, Grégoire Kayibanda, when he paid an official visit to Canada. I remember that I was unable to interest any francophone cabinet minister in meeting with the president; his country was, it seemed, too unimportant. Justice Minister Pierre Trudeau and Forestry Minister Maurice Sauvé could not be bothered when I sought to involve them. The president's only official call in Ottawa was on Prime Minister Pearson. The encounter was awkward. The president was so shy that he was uncertain whether to offer his right or left hand when he greeted Canada's leader. The prime minister sought to put him at ease by dispensing with the services of his interpreter, and launching into an ani-mated explanation of the significance of 1967 for Canada and Canadians. I doubt if Rwanda's leader understood a word of Lester Pearson's fractured French. And Kayibanda's diffident demeanour belied the fierce leader who, several years earlier, had led the Hutu uprising that dispossessed the Tutsi ethnic minority of Rwanda of its lands, at a cost of more than 10,000 lives.

Fast-forward to 1977. My wife Marie-Jeanne was born in the Belgian Congo, lived for the first ten years of her life in a small Congolese town where her father was a medical doctor, and had Africa in her blood, figuratively speaking. We spent our honey-moon in Kenya and Tanzania in 1976 and enjoyed it so much that we returned to Africa on holiday the next year, this time to Rwanda. I was nervous, given the violent history of tribal conflict in the country but our visit proceeded without incident. There were no tourists and few white people to be seen either in the capital, Kigali, or at Gisenyi on the shores of Lake Kivu, where

we spent most of our time. From Gisenyi we could see the
Zairean city of Goma, with which I was to become all too familiar in November 1996, and the smoke rising from a volcano some
kilometres away that would become the site of the huge and
insalubrious Mulenga refugee camp. Everyone was exceedingly
courteous and kind. It would have been unthinkable that these
same people and their children a generation later would participate in one of the greatest crimes against humanity of the twentieth century.

As a result of these fleeting contacts, I paid more than passing
attention to developments in Rwanda and its sister republic
Burundi from the time I encountered Grégoire Kayibanda in
1967 until I joined the prime minister's team in March 1994. The
news was always bad. President Kayibanda was overthrown in a
coup d'état by the National Guard Commander Major General
Juvénal Habyarimana in July 1973; the new leader then remained
in power until his death in April 1994, sustained by the support
of the Hutu army and rigged elections. A Tutsi army, drawn from
the refugee Tutsi community in Uganda, invaded Rwanda in
1990 and was repelled with the assistance of French and Belgian
troops. Diplomatic efforts to reconcile Hutus and Tutsis, led by
the Organization of African Unity, were ineffectual. The Security
Council authorized first an observer mission (the United Nations
Observer Mission Uganda-Rwanda – UNOMUR) and later a
peacekeeping force (United Nations Assistance Mission in
Rwanda – UNAMIR) with Brigadier-General Roméo Dallaire of
Canada as its first commander.

Meanwhile, neighbouring Burundi was in constant turmoil.
The ethnic mix in both countries was about the same: 90 per
cent Hutu and 10 per cent Tutsi. In Burundi, however, the Tutsi
minority never lost control of the armed forces or the government to the Hutus. The Burundian Hutus, as a result, waged
unrelenting guerrilla warfare against their Tutsi masters, provok-
ing massive reprisals and the flight of Hutus from their villages,

leading to the creation of refugee camps throughout Burundi and neighbouring countries.

Rwandan Genocide

Then occurred one of the most horrific episodes of twentieth-century history. I had just returned on April 7, 1994, from the prime minister's official visit to Mexico to my office on Sparks Street when news agencies began reporting that the aircraft carrying presidents Habyarimana and Ntaryamira of Rwanda and Burundi had been shot down on its final approach to Kigali airport. The next day, we learned that a slaughter of Tutsis had started in Rwanda, but that the situation in Burundi remained no worse than it was before. Even though inured to reports of the suffering of Rwanda, I was shocked by the brutality of what followed. A Hutu militia, called the Interhamwe or "those who attack together," set up secretly in 1993 for the specific purpose of killing Tutsis, murdered the Rwandan prime minister, the president of the Supreme Court, and various cabinet ministers. A mass murder of Tutsis began that was to go on for three interminable months, fully covered in the international press, until from 800,000 to 1 million people, largely Tutsis but including moderate Hutus, had been slaughtered.

It was thus in the spring of 1994, and not on a rainy weekend in November 1996, that the prime minister first became exposed to the tragic situation in the Great Lakes area of Africa. He followed subsequent developments and authorized the redeployment of two Hercules transport aircraft and forty-five aircrew in the week of April 9 from their base in northern Italy, where they were supporting U.N. operations in Bosnia, to Nairobi to assist in the evacuation of civilian and military personnel from Rwanda. More than six thousand people were removed from Kigali before the operation came to an end. Almost the entire time, the Canadian aircraft were the only ones providing an air link between the outside world and Rwanda. The courageous performance of their aircrews (confirmed to me years later by Ghanian general Henry Anyidoho, who was Dallaire's chief of staff in Kigali) who landed their aircraft time and time again in the face of hostile artillery and small-arms fire at Kigali airport, is one of the few positive chapters in a generally sordid story.

It was by this time June 1994, and the leaders of the most powerful economic powers in the world, the G7, were holding their annual summit meeting in Naples. I sat in as the prime minister met privately with Prime Minister Berlusconi of Italy before the beginning of the official meetings. (Protocol demands that leaders must meet privately before the official meetings, so that they can greet one another as friends at the public event.) Everything about the Italian leader was smooth. He was one of Italy's wealthiest people and had made good use of his ownership of a television and newspaper empire to win the recent elections. He accepted every proposal Prime Minister Chrétien put to him on all subjects, but I doubted that he would keep his word. Berlusconi lamented the fate of the Tutsis in Rwanda, musing aloud about the need for the world "to do something" to stop the genocide. Chrétien suggested that an international military force be sent, saying Canada already had two aircraft operating into Kigali and a distinguished general on the ground with the United Nations. Berlusconi quickly changed the subject. The leaders of the seven most powerful economic countries on the planet all studiously avoided the issue during their summit.

During this period, I followed the attempts of General Dallaire to bring an end to the massacres; but neither I nor anyone I knew had any knowledge of his desperate efforts before the beginning of the genocide to obtain authority from the United Nations to conduct searches for weapons to head off the planned killings. Nor were we aware how dangerous and isolated his position was. We regarded him as a genuine hero then, and even more so later when the facts surrounding his role came out.[38] I remember meeting him outside the prime minister's office in the

Centre Block in August 1995 and escorting him in to receive the prime minister's and the nation's thanks after he completed his mission. A true soldier, he made no complaint at the time regarding the disgraceful way the United Nations had behaved, and successfully hid the inner trauma consuming him. I remember thinking, however, that it was not only the United Nations that had let him down. His own country could have done more. And in that regard I was as culpable as anyone in the Canadian power structure. After all, I was the trusted diplomatic advisor to the prime minister and other than recommending the dispatch of a couple of cargo aircraft to help out, I had sat on my hands. I found it difficult to look into Dallaire's eyes.

France, with a long experience in fighting wars in Africa and cynically used to intervening militarily to prop up its friends in francophone Africa, then went into action. After obtaining the blessing of the U.N. Security Council, it dispatched a large military force in Operation Turquoise to seize the western part of Rwanda. Its ostensible goal was to put an end to the genocide, but its real aim was to save its traditional allies and long-standing customers for arms purchases, the Hutu militants and their families, from the revenge of the Tutsi. For a well-trained Tutsi army had swept out of its strongholds in northern Rwanda and from a fortified camp near Kigali to save the surviving remnants of the Tutsi civilian population and seize control of the country. The French army then provided protection to the hundreds of thousands of Hutus, including the main body of Interhamwe militia and Rwandan army units involved in the genocide, who fled the country to seek refuge on the western side of Lake Kivu in Eastern Zaire.

By early July, the genocide was over. The U.N. Security Council called for contributions for a new peacekeeping force to be called UNAMIR2. Canada's contribution, largely communications, medical, and engineering troops, began to deploy into Kigali on July 18. Ottawa also authorized the replacement of Roméo

Dallaire, promoted in the interim to Major-General, by Major-General Guy Tousignant, another Canadian. The signals unit remained until January 1995, replaced by transport and logistic units, which stayed until early 1996.

Into the Limelight

Canada's record in attempting to help in the crisis up to 1996 had been barely noticeable. It was scant solace that other members of the international community had behaved with even greater indifference, or that some had blood on their hands through selling arms to the Hutu over the years. The stage was set, however, for Canada to walk out briefly into the limelight. It was a role available for any country that wanted to assume it; the region was of little interest to the so-called developed world. No security advantage was to be gained by forging alliances with any of the warring states or factions in Africa. The international business community, interested in investing abroad only where high and safe returns could be achieved, knew that no money was to be made here. Not just the Great Lakes region of Africa, but all of sub-Saharan Africa, with the exception of South Africa and Nigeria, were of marginal importance internationally.

The problem for the leaders of the developed world went beyond one of disinterest. Frankly, it was also reluctance and even fear of becoming involved in what was perceived to be the hopeless future of Africa. The international donor community, including the World Bank, had come to the conclusion that forty years of aid to African countries had largely been a failure.[39] Vast areas of Africa were wastelands where the writ of government had long ceased to apply. Zaire, Angola, Burundi, and the Republic of the Congo were failed states wracked by civil war. In many countries, life expectancies were falling, banditry was endemic, ethnic or tribal conflict was prevalent, and HIV/AIDS and ever more virulent varieties of malaria were ravaging the populations. Much of sub-Saharan Africa, including Eastern Zaire, had been abandoned to the angels and devils.

Angels and Devils

The angels were the humanitarian organizations such as the United Nations High Commissioner for Refugees (UNHCR), Doctors Without Borders, and Oxfam that moved in to fill the vacuum created by the collapse of local government and the absence of involvement by the international community. They assumed responsibility for feeding and caring for massive numbers of displaced people uprooted in the events of 1994 in Eastern Zaire and elsewhere. The devils were the arms merchants who found ways to keep supplying weapons to all sides in the ongoing conflicts in Africa, including to the Interhamwe in the camps of Eastern Zaire. They were also the unscrupulous carpetbaggers who flocked to the region to bribe local leaders in order to obtain lucrative diamond and gold concessions. Included in this category were the ambitious leaders of Rwanda, Angola, Zimbabwe, and Uganda who foresaw the implosion of Zaire, the region's largest state, and wanted a piece of it for their countries, for themselves, for their families, and for their business associates.

In this environment of evil and suffering, it was not surprising that the angels made mistakes attributable to hubris and inexperience. Their biggest error was in giving exaggerated estimates of the number of refugees in the camps in Eastern Zaire in order to be sure that there were reserves of food, medicine, and other supplies for the refugees. The figure used by the UNHCR was 1.2 million. Doctors Without Borders said that there were 950,000. The Interhamwe took charge of distributing supplies provided by the humanitarian agencies, appropriated the (considerable) surplus to buy arms and supplies for themselves, and thus strengthened their hold on the camps used as bases to attack the Tutsis who now governed Rwanda.

The Crises of 1996

The situation spiralled out of control. In March, Interhamwe members and former soldiers of the defeated Hutu government based in the Eastern Zairean refugee camps, assisted by corrupt members of Zaire's army, attacked a community of Tutsis living in the Masisi area of North Kivu (west of Goma). Many Tutsis were killed. The survivors fled, with approximately eight thousand seeking refuge among their compatriots in neighbouring Rwanda. In August, the same unholy coalition of Interhamwe and Zairean army units turned their attention to another Tutsi community, the Banyamulenge, living on the Mulenge plateau west of Uvira in South Kivu. This time the Tutsis were ready, trained and armed in the interim by the Rwandan Tutsi army, and they drove off their attackers. In retaliation, the Zairean military commissioner of South Kivu on September 9 ordered the expulsion of the entire Tutsi population of Eastern Zaire, even though these people had lived in the region for roughly 150 years.

The military commissioner's decision constituted an enormous, stupid failure of judgement and set in train the events which led to the destruction of Zairean government authority in North and South Kivu and to the eventual overthrow of Mobutu. The Banyamulenge Tutsis, with nothing to lose now that they had been declared unwanted in their country of birth, went on the offensive, pursuing their attackers down onto the plains, defeating Zairean government and Hutu Interhamwe forces alike in the area of Uvira. This precipitated a flight of Hutu refugees from their camps in this region to North Kivu. The Rwandan army of battle-hardened, well-trained, and competently led Tutsi war veterans then intervened, claiming that Zairean forces had fired across the border. Bukavu, Uvira, and Goma fell to the Banyamulenge by November 6, at which time they declared a three-week ceasefire. The armed forces of Zaire had totally collapsed by this time.

Meanwhile, from about mid–October, the attention of the international community had focused on the plight of the refugees caught in the crossfire in Eastern Zaire. Inexperienced officials from humanitarian organizations provided inaccurate reports to the media and to United Nations headquarters, making a bad situation appear even worse.[40] According to these so–called experts, cholera had broken out in the camps and people were dying of hunger. The U.N. secretary–general, fed the same inaccurate reports, issued a statement claiming that heavy fighting was continuing, that 1.2 million refugees had been displaced and that people were dying of hunger and cholera. He then withdrew all humanitarian personnel from Eastern Zaire "for their own safety," indirectly creating a blackout on reliable information on developments in the area.

Canada's Role

Throughout this period, Canada had but one lonely officer in Kinshasa and one diplomat isolated in Kigali who did not have the capacity to provide Ottawa with up–to–date reports. The Americans and the British, who normally fill the gaps in information–gathering for Canada in places like Zaire and Rwanda, had weak political sections in their embassies and were thus of little assistance. We and our closest allies, therefore, found ourselves relying on reports from the humanitarian agencies and the media, neither of which now had representatives in Eastern Zaire and who allowed their imaginations to run wild. Prime Minister Chrétien (together with his diplomatic advisor) and leaders around the world thus developed a sense of impending tragedy, heightened by their guilty knowledge that the international community had stood by just two years earlier during one of the worst genocides since the Second World War. Anxious that Canada do whatever it could to help, the prime minister authorized the temporary release of Ambassador Raymond Chrétien from his duties in Washington to serve as special envoy of the United Nations secretary-general Boutros Boutros-Ghali. The ambassador then departed for Africa on November 5 on a mission with three goals: to arrange a ceasefire if at all possible among the warring parties; to ascertain the feasibility of convening a conference of regional countries to bring about a long-term peace to the area; and to report back to the secretary-general on whether or not he should appoint a permanent high representative for the Great Lakes area of Africa.

Ambassador Chrétien's mission would prove to be important in mobilizing world opinion in favour of action to relieve the plight of civilians in Eastern Zaire and in providing the United Nations and the Canadian government with information on the attitudes of African leaders. But the story that he persuaded the prime minister to volunteer Canada to lead a quixotic military operation into the heart of Africa, by a telephone call on a rainy Remembrance Day weekend, is not backed up by the facts. When the ambassador departed for Africa, the secretary-general had already called for the creation of a military mission to proceed to Eastern Zaire to allow the humanitarian agencies to distribute supplies and to establish secure corridors to permit Hutu refugees to return to Rwanda if they wished, free of Interhamwe coercion. Likewise, by this time, the prime minister had given instructions that Canada contribute to the mission, if one was authorized by the United Nations Security Council. Foreign Affairs and Defence differed on the nature of the contribution, but Defence reluctantly agreed that it could make available transport aircraft and a field hospital,[41] just as it did during the 1994 and 1995 phases of the crisis.

In my daily updates, I told the prime minister that African leaders meeting in Nairobi on November 5 had endorsed the call for an international military force of the nature proposed by the secretary-general. European ministers meeting in Brussels on November 7 had done the same. Germany and France had taken the lead in the Security Council to put a force in the field and had offers from a variety of European countries to contribute military forces. However, as of November 6, the United States had not indicated whether it would help, and without the participation of American military forces on the ground, the initiative would go nowhere. The situation then changed dramatically for Canada.

An Offer Too Good to Refuse

On Thursday, November 7, the United States made its move. In surprising back-channel calls to me from the president's national security advisor, Tony Lake, and from Peter Tarnoff, State Department undersecretary for political affairs, to Gordon Smith, Foreign Affairs Undersecretary, the Americans offered to place their military forces under Canadian command if we would lead the international mission. I should have questioned Tony more closely. It was unheard of for the United States to put its military forces under the command of a general from another country. At the time, I considered the telephone call as an indication that the United States was not prepared to support the French-sponsored resolution being debated in the United Nations. The United States, I assumed, neither wanted to commit its troops to an operation under French command nor to assume the command itself.

This I found unsurprising. There was little love lost between France and the United States on international security matters, and it was no secret that Washington considered that Paris was too closely identified with the discredited government of Mobutu in Zaire and the former Hutu government of Rwanda to be a credible leader. Likewise, having suffered the ignominy of seeing elite Ranger and Delta Force troops massacred in Mogadishu three years earlier during the failed Somalia operation, the United States was unwilling to lead a major military operation in Africa once again, especially when Congress and the American public opinion would have been opposed. I took Tony's approach, however, as an indication that under the right circumstances, the

United States was prepared to participate in a military operation in Eastern Zaire.

I asked myself two questions. Why was the United States so interested in saving refugees in Eastern Zaire? And, why ask Canada rather than the United Kingdom or some other more militarily capable ally to take the lead? On the first point, although I never discussed the matter with Tony, I suspected that he and the president were so ashamed of the failure of the United States to halt the genocide of 1994, that they were prepared to go to extraordinary measures to prevent a repetition of the massacres. And on the second, perhaps the Americans had turned to us because, lacking a colonial past, we would be more credible with the countries of Africa than France, or for that matter the United States, in providing military leadership? Perhaps the Pentagon was comfortable working with the Canadian Armed Forces and trusted us? Perhaps the United States expected that Canada would allow it to lead the operation from behind the scenes, calculating that Congress would be less hostile to American participation if a close ally like Canada provided the leadership? Perhaps the Pentagon thought that with Canada out in front, the United States would find it easier to terminate their participation on a set date and pull their troops out, leaving it to Ottawa to decide whether there should be a follow-on international presence in the area after the initial objectives had been accomplished? Most likely, however, it was simply because the Clinton foreign-policy team worked well with us, trusted us, and wanted our help. And when Tony Lake and Peter Tarnoff made their unusual calls, they probably did not suspect how limited Canada's military resources actually were.

I immediately convened a meeting of Gordon Smith, Louise Fréchette, deputy minister of Defence, and Vice-Admiral Larry Murray, Acting Chief of Defence Staff. We would constitute the core of the informal task force that would manage the crisis. (Lieutenant-General Maurice Baril, commander of the army and former military advisor to the U.N. secretary-general in the Department of Peacekeeping Operations, would soon join the group.) The initial reaction from Louise and Larry to the approaches from the Americans was disbelief. They said that virtually all of Canada's ground troops were already committed to peacekeeping operations. At the most, a thousand soldiers might be scraped together; certainly not enough to give Canada the credibility to take the lead, even supported by the Americans, in such a major operation. A secretary then interrupted us to tell me the prime minister was on the line. Excusing myself, I took the call in the next room. Prime Minister Chrétien wanted the latest news. I briefed him. His instant reaction was that regardless of the American motivation, it would be irresponsible of Canada not to say yes. Before providing a definitive answer, however, he wanted to consult Boutros Boutros-Ghali, potential troop-contributing countries, his Cabinet colleagues, and the leader of the Opposition. Louise and Larry went white when I told them we were probably going to accept the American proposal.

My team in the PCO then went to work throughout Friday, November 8, setting up telephone calls to some twenty world leaders. I then called Tony to brief him on the prime minister's response. He seemed relieved that Canada had picked up the ball dropped by the major powers in the United Nations Security Council debate.

On Saturday, November 9, the prearranged telephone calls started to come in. The leaders of the United Kingdom, Belgium, Senegal, and Ivory Coast said that they would support a force led by Canada. The United Kingdom and Senegal pledged troops. The British added that they would consider putting a brigade group of five thousand in the field. Belgium, as the former colonial power in Rwanda, and still in shock from the murder of ten of its soldiers by the Interhamwe in 1994, said that it would provide transport aircraft and other assistance to help Senegal field a battalion but would not put troops back into the area. The Ivory

Coast prime minister said that he needed all the troops he could muster to deal with a secessionist movement at home and thus would be forced to limit his help to non-military support. And Boutros Boutros-Ghali publicly endorsed the prime minister's initiative, saying that there was no other way forward.

On Sunday, November 10, the presidents of France and Kenya pledged sizable contingents, as did the prime ministers of the Netherlands and Italy. In the coming days, the presidents of Tanzania, Cameroon, Argentina, Brazil, Chile, and the prime ministers of Japan, Spain, and Ireland promised their support. Those who could not provide troops said that they would finance African contingents. All urged Canada to persevere since we held the key to American participation and were acceptable to all parties in the conflict. We were eventually to have offers of between 12,000 and 16,000 troops, pledges for more than 100 million dollars and the moral backing of Canada's closest friends internationally. And this did not even include American military support, which the Pentagon assured us via military channels would be provided.

The Cabinet met on Monday, Remembrance Day, and formally took the decision that Canada would lead the mission provided certain caveats were met, including a commitment by the United States to follow through with its undertaking to back us up and put forces on the ground in Eastern Zaire under our command. I then called Tony who expressed appreciation and said that he expected confirmation from the president to proceed as we had discussed. Tony's reaction was a surprise since his overture and that of Tarnoff to Gordon Smith the previous week had not been conditional on returning to the president to obtain new authority to entrust the mission to Canada. Since we had put together a force, there could be no turning back by us. The next day, Prime Minister Chrétien, accompanied by Defence Minister Doug Young and Foreign Affairs Minister Lloyd Axworthy, told the press that Canada was prepared to command a mission provided the following conditions were met: the Security Council provide authorization; the mandate be limited to humanitarian assistance; the countries in the region accept Canada's leadership; a force of from six to ten thousand disciplined troops be available; a mix of American, European, African, and other troops be available; there be clear command and control arrangements under a Canadian general; and the mission be limited in time to four to six months.

The Americans Get Cold Feet

As I was watching the prime minister's press briefing on the television in my Sparks Street office, the telephone rang. An agitated Tony Lake was on the line. He said that he had just chaired a meeting of the "principals" (the secretary of state, the secretary of defence, the chairman of the Joint Chiefs of Staff, the director of the CIA, and the national security advisor) who served as the top crisis managers in the American system. There had been last-minute problems, he said, in particular with the proposed command structure. He would not be able to get the president to sign off on our understanding until he managed to forge a consensus. He was prepared to come to Ottawa with a team to discuss matters, but that could take a day or two.

I was disheartened, and suspicious. Expectations, I told him, had been raised that a force led by Canada backed up by the United States would shortly be en route to Eastern Zaire. We could not waste time while he put together a team to come to Ottawa. I would depart immediately for Washington with the members of the task force to sort matters out. I then called the prime minister as soon as he had finished his press conference to tell him the bad news. The Americans seemed to be having second thoughts. I was departing for Washington immediately to try to put the train back on the tracks. An unhappy prime minister told me not to hesitate to seek guidance from him even if the negotiations proceeded into the night.

A Lesson in Great Power Politics

At this point, some background on my relations with Tony Lake is relevant. The national security advisor to the president occupies one of the most powerful positions in the American government, roughly similar in influence to that of secretary of state. While in no way exercising similar influence, as diplomatic advisor to the prime minister, I was Tony's point of contact in the Canadian government just as he was mine in Washington. I had called on Tony in Washington soon after I joined the PCO, and he in turn came to Ottawa to see me, visiting our modest cottage in the Gatineau Hills for a swim and family barbecue in July 1995. I had been planning to visit him again in Washington in the summer of 1996. On August 30, the day I was to depart for Washington, Tony called to say that he and Strobe Talbot, the most senior official at that time in the State Department, had to leave on an emergency mission to Haiti. Members of President René Préval's Presidential Guard had been caught using murders and beatings to discourage troublesome members of the opposition. Tony's task was to persuade the president to fire his bodyguards and let a State Department security squad train a new team. Since Canadian peacekeepers were responsible for the physical protection of the president's palace (two companies of Canadian soldiers manned machine-gun posts at the entrances), perhaps I could fly down with the American team and lend a hand with the persuading?

Officials in Foreign Affairs provided me with a quick briefing on the general situation in Haiti, explaining that Jean-Bertrand Aristide, whose term as president had expired some time before, was pulling the strings of government from behind the scenes as he bided his time to run for president again. Canadian Intelligence sources, for their part, confirmed that President Préval's bodyguards, goons who actually owed their allegiance to Aristide, were indeed violating the rights of prisoners and engaging in other nasty activities. The situation was murky indeed but I had met

President Préval when he had paid an official visit to Canada some months earlier and thought I might play a useful role. The prime minister told me that Canada could not accept the violation of human rights by a government we were supporting through the provision of peacekeepers and a large aid program. He told me to go with the Americans and help out if I could.

Gordon Smith joined us. The small American air force jet departing Washington was crammed with senior State Department and CIA officials as well as heavyweight General John Sheehan, NATO's Supreme Allied Commander Atlantic and American Commander of South Atlantic Command. Once aloft, a meeting was held with officers crowding around Tony, sitting on the floor, and even squeezed into the door to the washroom. I listened in fascination as the strategy for the session with President Préval was mapped out. The president had already been "invited" to come alone to the residence of the American ambassador in Port au Prince. Various roles were assigned to members of the visiting American team. One official was to be the bad cop, reading the riot act to the president. Another was to be the good cop making the point that the United States was obliged "to speak frankly and with a heavy heart" saying that if extrajudicial violence against political opponents continued, Congress would surely cut off aid. Since no one on the visiting American team was bilingual, Gordon and I were asked to ensure that the messages passed in English and translated by the American ambassador, acting as interpreter, got through to the unilingual French-speaking president.

The president was waiting for us when we arrived at the American residence, not knowing why he had been summoned to appear at such short notice by the American superpower. Gordon and I did our bit in ensuring the president understood what was wanted. Afterwards, however, I found it hard to forget the puzzled expression in his soft eyes when confronted with Canadians aiding Americans in applying pressure on the leader of a minor country. To my surprise, the strategy worked. The president, after asking for time to consult his colleagues, agreed to dismiss his unsavoury bodyguards. A forty-person-strong State Department team of security experts arrived within a week to clear the bad apples from the Presidential Guard and to retrain those worth keeping.

Poetic Justice

Now just four months later, I was on my way back to Washington with a glum team of senior civil and military officials to try to salvage the Eastern Zaire rescue mission. John Higgenbotham, Canadian chargé d'affaires, met our private flight at Dulles airport in Washington and accompanied us to the back entrance of the White House. After a lengthy wait at the guard post, a visibly uneasy Tony Lake came out to meet us and escort us to the under-ground Situation Room of the National Security Council where the big crises affecting the security of the United States were managed. From the furtive looks on the faces of our American colleagues, we guessed that they had left us to cool our heels outside while they frantically worked out a strategy to present to their betrayed friends. After a round of hand-shaking, Tony gave the floor to Peter Tarnoff of the State Department. Tarnoff stopped smiling, screwed his face into a tough, uncompromising scowl and began lecturing us with a high-pitched northeastern American accent that matched the buttoned-down Ivy League attitude he had adopted for the occasion.

"You Canadians," he said patronizingly, "have done a good job in assembling a coalition. The principals, however, have come to the conclusion that the job is too big for you to handle. We have, accordingly, reconsidered our proposal; the United States rather than Canada, will now lead the mission. Canada, however, will have its chance 'to play leader.' Exactly thirty days after the beginning of the operation, American troops will be withdrawn, leaving the command to Canada. And please understand that our troops will pull out, no matter what the conditions on the ground are at that time. It will be up to you guys to decide on the nature of the follow-on force, should you decide to have one." He smirked and stopped talking.

Then it was Tony's turn, and his role was the good cop. Looking pained and solicitous, he sadly noted that "things have not turned out exactly as foreseen. The United States, however, really appreciates the efforts the Canadian prime minister has made. You Canadians should not worry since his efforts to put together a force will not be in vain. We will now command it and ensure that it carries out its proper role for thirty days. As Peter said, Canada will have its turn at the controls when we pull out."

It was Haiti all over again, but this time it was the Canadians who were being softened up by the superpower! Poetic justice was being meted out to me by the gods for having participated in the comedy in Port-au-Prince the previous summer! I decided to stop the meeting before any members of the stunned and enraged Canadian party could comment. I headed for the door followed by Tony, who earnestly told me as I hurried up the steps out of the bunker that we all should be relieved that a formula had been found for the United States to participate. I said that I needed to consult Prime Minister Chrétien immediately and Tony ushered me into his private office. As I dialled the PMO switchboard in Ottawa, I glanced down at Tony's desk. There in black and white was a memorandum to the American national security advisor from a member of his staff outlining the strategy the Americans intended to use that evening to deal with their earnest Canadian cousins. I looked away, not quite ready to read a friend's mail, even if we were being double-crossed in a neighbouring room. A cheerless prime minister then came on the line. The operator had summoned him from the table at the residence of the Japanese ambassador where he was the guest of honour; he knew that whenever I called him, it was always with bad news. He did not take my message well, shouting into the receiver so loudly that I had to hold the telephone a foot away from my ear. I undertook to do what I could to put matters right, and to call him back.

I then repeated to Tony the exact words of the prime minister, and I swear that he blushed. I added that my advice to the prime minister had been to call the president, if the officials involved could not come to an arrangement. We Canadians were as disturbed as any member of the international community at developments in Eastern Zaire and had been prepared to participate under the leadership of the United States or any other credible big power in a mission. Better than anyone else, we were aware of our limited military capability. We had, moreover, acted responsibly in responding favourably to the American request that we take the lead, backed up by American military might. We would now look ridiculous in the eyes of the nations the prime minister had contacted if we went along with the change in scenario. Canada would also be most reluctant to help the United States out of jams in the future if the matter were not resolved to our satisfaction.

Tony, a thoroughly decent person, seemed embarrassed at the antics in the Situation Room, and did not want the prime minister to telephone the president, who would not be happy with the way his officials had been handling the file. "Give me time to find a solution," he asked.

The Operational Plan

He then led our brave but somewhat overwhelmed band of Canadians to a large office and told us to wait. Two long hours later, a smiling Tony came to fetch us. Everyone in the bunker was now a good cop. Of course, Canada could take the lead. Of course, American military forces would be placed under the operational control of General Baril. Why not send out for pizza or Chinese food? What was our preference? (We picked pizza, and it was delivered in fifteen minutes piping hot to our underground bunker. The pizza delivery boy, I admiringly noted, made it through White House security much faster than we Canadians some hours earlier!)

The Americans then told us that, by the way, in return for giving us the command, there would be a few changes in the plan. The United States would cut back on its commitment of military forces to reduce the risk to its personnel. Instead of sending four or five thousand ground troops to the theatre, the number would now be limited to 1,500 personnel, plus airlift and other support elements outside of Eastern Zaire. Instead of taking control of the airports at Goma and Bukavu and deploying troops to help form a protective corridor from the Rwandan border to the refugee camps, American forces would protect only the several hundred metres of road from the Rwandan bordertown of Gisenyi to the airport at Goma; France, if it wanted, could take over the Bukavu airport. Moreover, the United States opposed allowing the troops to use force to accomplish their mission. (The new commander, we realized, would have no more authority than General Dallaire had had in the spring of 1994 to stop another massacre.) Were fighting to break out between any of the rival forces in the area, or a slaughter of civilians to start, the force commander would not be authorized to use his soldiers to intervene. And should the Interhamwe forces in the camps prevent refugees from departing for Rwanda, the multinational force would not be authorized to rescue them. Our American friends also insisted that the geographic scope of mission operations be limited to a zone fifty kilometres from the Rwandan border. The United States firmly intended to pull its troops out by March 31, 1997. A follow-on mission could take over at that time if necessary. The United States also insisted that the political direction for the mission be provided by a steering group composed of representatives from countries contributing troops and financial and material resources.

If Tony had said that the Americans intended to keep their forces out of harm's way when he telephoned to me on November 7 to seek our help, I doubt that the prime minister would have seriously considered his proposal. At this stage, however, with thousands apparently dying in Eastern Zaire and with Canada already committed to leading the mission, we had no choice but to carry on. We reasoned that even if the American forces cowered at the airport at Goma, their presence would guarantee the participation of the coalition the prime minister had put together. The presence of even one American soldier on the ground in the danger zone would provide a guarantee to coalition members that the United States cavalry would ride to our rescue if we had to leave in a hurry. Perhaps naively, we also reckoned that if a slaughter of civilians were to start, we could shame the Americans into agreeing to allow the force to intervene.

In the ensuing discussions, I was uncertain how many on the American side were aware of the nature of the arrangement that we had entered into with Tony Lake and Peter Tarnoff, and of how it had all started. The Americans present at first behaved as if they were now responding to a purely Canadian initiative. They asked us detailed questions on local conditions, for which we had no answer, and on our concept of military operations, on which the thinking of Canada's military planners was preliminary. Having exposed our ignorance, they then distributed a pile of draft documents providing answers to their own questions. We gritted our teeth and worked on the basis of the American texts to reach agreement on the basic issues, discovering in the process that our friends did not really know much more than we did. Their main sources of information were the humanitarian agencies and the international press. It was a dialogue of the ignorant.

We then hammered out a mission statement which read as follows: "When directed, a multinational force deploys to and conducts operations in the Great Lakes Area of Eastern Zaire to facilitate the delivery of humanitarian aid by civilian relief organizations to alleviate the immediate suffering of refugees and displaced persons and to facilitate the voluntary repatriation of refugees and the voluntary return of displaced persons."

Tony proposed that he and I meet in New York on Thursday, November 14, to draft a resolution for Security Council approval incorporating these principles. I telephoned the prime minister around midnight to get approval; Tony disappeared into the private quarters of the White House to obtain the blessing of the president. Our team then departed for the airport to board our waiting Canadian Forces aircraft for home. This was just the first of our lessons on the perils of trying to play in the same league as a superpower.

Euphoria

The deal we struck with the Americans remained intact for just three glorious days. On Wednesday, November 13, President Clinton appeared on national television to say: "Following consultations with Canadian officials last night, we reached general agreement with Canada on the mission definition, command and control arrangements, duration of the mission, and other key issues. We will work through the details in the next day or two." He added that the United States welcomed Canada's offer to lead the mission but that the final decision on United States participation would depend on the findings of an American military assessment team sent to the region on November 12. The Canadian media went wild. For once it seemed that the United States was following Canada's lead on a major international event rather than the other way around. Story after story appeared focusing on the so-called conversion of the prime minister, like Saint Paul on the road to Damascus, on a rainy Remembrance Day weekend in November to the cause of rescuing civilians caught in the war in Eastern Zaire. The media raised the prime minister so high up on a pedestal that the fall from grace, when it inevitably came, was all the harder.

On Thursday, November 14, the prime minister authorized a special Challenger flight to New York to take Gordon Smith, Lieutenant-General Baril, and me to the Canadian mission to the United Nations. Tony Lake met me at our delegation and we quickly hammered out a draft text acceptable to both Canada and the United States based on our discussions in Washington two days earlier. Robert Fowler, Canada's ambassador to the United Nations, then hosted a working lunch in the boardroom to which he had invited the ambassadors of the countries that had pledged contributions of troops or money in the prime minister's marathon telephone calls the previous weekend. The wind was in our sails. Reports from Rwanda, fed by the fears and imaginations of humanitarian representatives who no longer had access to the camps in Eastern Zaire, lent a crisis atmosphere to the discussions. The heads of the main United Nations humanitarian organizations provided their latest and gloomiest assessment of developments in the war-affected areas (later proven to be wrong) and urged Canada to move quickly to get a mission into Eastern Zaire. They wanted their fieldworkers to return to the camps under military escort as soon as possible. It did not take long for agreement to be reached on the concept of operations, command structure and other relevant details as already worked out between Canada and the United States. Gordon Smith and Lieutenant-General Baril then met with the press, hundreds of whom turned up to cover what had become the leading story internationally – at least for the time being.

Mission Accomplished?
When I returned to my office in Ottawa at the end of the day, feeling rather satisfied with myself, my staff handed me a report prepared by the intelligence service of a country (not the United States) close to Canada. It said that if Canada succeeded in gaining Security Council support to lead a mission into Eastern Zaire, Banyamulenge Tutsi rebels supported by Rwandan troops would

pre-empt any such deployment by attacking the Hutu Inter-hamwe forces guarding the camps and herding the refugees home to Rwanda. In other words, Rwanda and its ethnic allies would remove the problem for the United Nations by expelling the refugees from Eastern Zaire. The Rwandans, according to the report, had designs on Eastern Zaire and did not want an inter-national force entering the area that would hand back control to the Government of Zaire when its mission was over.

And that is exactly what happened. As I watched the debate in the Security Council on November 15 move ponderously to approve the resolution establishing the mission on one television channel, another channel was reporting that the Interhamwe had been driven from the camps by Banyamulenge rebels. Soon, all news channels began to show a tidal wave, forty kilometres long, of well-fed, healthy refugees moving towards the Rwandan border. More than 750,000 crossed peacefully in the next several weeks, soon to be joined by large numbers from camps in Tanzania.

I called the prime minister to say that the problem was being solved without the need to deploy the mission. Canada's initia-tive to mobilize an international rescue mission had forced the Rwandans to intervene and solve a humanitarian problem that affected their own nationals. Tony Lake telephoned to say that the changes in facts on the ground meant that the terms of the mission had to be rethought. But that was easier said than done. The unique strength of the coalition was its diversity. Never before had countries from every continent united so rapidly in support of a cause that affected human values rather than national interests. Offers to provide contributions continued to arrive from countries as diverse as San Marino, Israel, and New Zealand. Even though the United States (and the United Kingdom) was having second thoughts, the other players, in particular the humanitarian agencies, were not. They pointed out that hundreds of thousands of refugees remained unaccounted for, and insisted that we press on. The prime minister shared their view, saying that we could not receive authorization from the Security Council to mount a mission one day and abandon it the next.

A New Task-Force Leader

Up to this point, I had been completely absorbed in the management of the crisis, working eighteen-hour days. The deputy ministers of Defence, Foreign Affairs, and the acting Chief of the Defence Staff were doing the same. The prime minister and his ministers of Defence and Foreign Affairs, Doug Young and Lloyd Axworthy, were devoting most of their time to the matter. This could not continue, at least as far as the prime minister and his diplomatic advisor were concerned. We were scheduled to depart in less than one week to attend an APEC summit at Subic Bay in the Philippines following which we were to travel to Shanghai to complete the final negotiations for the sale of two CANDU (Canada Deuterium Uranium) nuclear reactors to China. After China, we were to go on to Japan to make an official visit and then travel to the other end of the world to attend a summit of the OSCE in Lisbon, Portugal. We would leave on November 21 and not be back to Ottawa before early December.

The clerk, Jocelyne Bourgon, then thankfully took matters in hand, establishing a proper crisis management task force, headed by Jim Judd, pulled away from his job as assistant deputy minister of Finance, and Ralph Lysyshyn, seconded in temporarily from his duties as director-general of Defence Relations in Foreign Affairs. Both had worked for me previously and I had full confidence in them. They in turn were backed up by the best military and foreign-service officers Defence and Foreign Affairs could provide. Since the prime minister wished to maintain direct involvement, it was decided that he would telephone his two ministers at 0700 each morning local time abroad (the middle of the night in Ottawa). Jim Judd would call me fifteen minutes ahead to allow me to prepare the prime minister. In this way the prime minister maintained "hands-on" control and we all worked our way into complete exhaustion.

The Death of a Thousand Cuts

The initiative then died the death of a thousand cuts with Canada eventually telling its increasingly fractious allies at a meeting in New York on December 13 that there was no longer any need for a mission. Before that happened, however, raging battles went on behind the scenes and in public within and without the diverse coalition we had cobbled together, feeding the public perception that the Canadian initiative had been doomed and badly managed from the outset. The military establishments in all countries, including the United States, our ostensible sponsor, were fearful of becoming embroiled in the turmoil of interstate war, ethnic conflict, and civil war that was roiling Eastern Zaire and looked for excuses not to proceed with the commitments of their political leaderships. Foreign ministries, not having the direct responsibility for the safety and management of troops in the field, favoured stretching the mandate given by the Security Council to seek out refugees fleeing westwards into the jungles of Zaire and to escort them back to Rwanda. The humanitarian agencies were on the defensive since they were now subject to strong criticism from the media for their misleading briefings in the weeks leading up to the return of the refugees to Rwanda. They could not explain why, contrary to their reports, the refugees who flooded back were in such excellent physical shape. They had not been starving and had not suffered from a massive cholera outbreak. The Rwandan authorities had not, despite the predictions of humanitarian agencies, engaged in massive killings of the returning Hutus to avenge the genocide of 1994.

Several agencies urged Canada to deploy the mission to provide them with security as they returned to the zone. Others said that they did not want outside military forces around as they carried out their duties. They also quarrelled over how many refugees had originally been at risk and how many were left in the area – the remaining critical question – with some saying that 500,000 were missing and others 250,000. Discussion then broke out among the countries most directly concerned. Although President Mobutu had told Ambassador Chrétien early in the exercise that his country could accept the deployment of the mission in its eastern provinces, his government became increasingly uncooperative. The Rwandans flatly said that the mission was no longer needed now that the bulk of the refugees had returned home. And while officially silent on the use of its territory as a base for the mission military headquarters, the Rwandan government refused to negotiate a Status of Forces agreement with the advance Canadian military team and made every effort to make it unwelcome. And now that the immediate crisis was over, leaders from the surrounding African countries were no longer interested in the dispatch of a rescue force. While we Canadians, as good boy scouts, continued to focus on the fate of the Hutu refugees who had fled into the Zairean jungles, the prime minister's regional counterparts probably foresaw the looming collapse of Zaire and were positioning themselves to feast on the spoils. With crocodile tears, therefore, they complained that Canada was not consulting them adequately and found fault with virtually every proposal we advanced to keep the mission alive. President Mandela joined the chorus, testily telling Chrétien on the telephone that should the operation get off the ground, an African rather than a Canadian should head the force. He offered no South African forces, however, and made no mention of the fact that South African arms merchants had been major suppliers to the former Hutu government and to the Interhamwe.

France and Belgium adopted positions diametrically opposed to those of the United States and the United Kingdom. They made no secret of their fear that the two anglophone countries favoured the Tutsi leadership of Rwanda since it was English-speaking. They spoke darkly of an anglophone cultural offensive into the heart of francophone Africa and pushed hard for Canada to carry on with the mission despite the return of so many refugees to Rwanda. American and British ministers made public statements saying that they no longer saw the need for a mission but their diplomats and military staff officers attended all planning sessions, freely criticizing Canadian proposals to begin air drops of food to isolated pockets of refugees or to run humanitarian food convoys from the airport at Entebbe, Uganda, overland to Eastern Zaire as a means of overcoming Rwanda's reluctance to allow the use of its territory. British negotiators nastily asked how many thousands of Canadian soldiers Canada intended to put into the field to realize these ambitions, aware that we had few troops available and could not do much without American military support. By that time we were too embarrassed to admit to the British that Canada had taken the lead to save the refugees at the request of the Americans, who were now abandoning us.

In Canada, Defence Minister Doug Young urged the government to bring the initiative to a close. Lloyd Axworthy, under pressure from European foreign ministers led by France whom he met at a NATO foreign ministers meeting in Brussels, disagreed. Lieutenant-General Baril, the force commander-designate, settled the matter by making a detailed reconnaissance of the area and recommending that the mission come to an end. The goal of facilitating the delivery of humanitarian aid had been largely met by the voluntary return of most of the refugees. There were no reliable estimates of those who had not returned, but they had fled deep into the jungles and did not want to be repatriated. The humanitarian agencies had regained access to the area and did not need a multinational force to protect them.

I supported ending the operation. We had known from the beginning that we could lead only if the Americans were willing to back us, and their support had disappeared. The purpose of the

Security Council resolution had been fulfilled, however messily: those refugees who so desired had returned home. The clerk and I met with Ministers Young and Axworthy on December 12 to review Lieutenant-General Baril's report; the two ministers strongly disagreed with each other on the way ahead, with the former arguing to end and the latter to continue the mission. The prime minister made the final call, reluctantly accepting Baril's conclusions and giving instructions for the windup of the mission. The 352 Canadian Forces personnel deployed into the field were back in Canada by early January 1997.

Not True

Thus, the story that Canada tried to punch above its weight in Eastern Zaire in November 1996 is simply not true; we were acting in close collaboration with the most powerful country on the planet. Canada reacted responsibly to back-channel requests from the White House and the State Department to help the United States find an acceptable way of committing its military forces to a potentially perilous operation in Africa. We were, however, left holding the bag and bore the blame for allegedly forsaking hundreds of thousands of Hutu refugees. It is not fair, however, to say that refugees were abandoned. The terms of reference of the rescue mission did not include forcing refugees to return to Rwanda. By precipitating the Rwandan government attack on the camps before the mission could be deployed, however, it led to a return to Rwanda of all refugees who wanted to go back. Those who feared judgement in their homeland for genocide and other crimes fled into the jungles escorted by their Interhamwe escorts. Some fifty thousand refugees crossed the Congo River to add to the Republic of the Congo's turbulent tribal mix. Others are reported to have made it to the Central African Republic. An unknown number were later massacred by Rwandan soldiers on their way to Kinshasa to overthrow Mobutu. Later on, Interhamwe forces were drawn into the fighting on the

side of the new government against Rwanda. They appear destined to roam Africa in a state of self-imposed exile indefinitely,
as punishment for their horrific crimes in the spring and summer
of 1994, afraid to go home, but unwanted except as soldiers in
their places of refuge.

There was, however, an even greater tragedy than the flight
into exile and death of the Hutu refugees and their Interhamwe
protectors in November and December 1996. For when the
rescue force did not deploy, the Tutsi army was left free to occupy
Eastern Zaire, to assemble a motley collection of anti-Mobutu
Zairean fighters and to march on Kinshasa. The Tutsis then
installed Laurent Kabila, an obscure Zairean rebel, as president of
Zaire. Kabila, whose chief claim to fame up to then had been an
unsatisfactory collaboration with the famous Che Guevara in a
failed rebellion decades earlier,[42] renamed the country the
Democratic Republic of the Congo and turned against his Tutsi
friends. In the ensuing turmoil, "the widest interstate war in
modern African history," in the words of Amnesty International,
broke out. The armed forces of Rwanda, Namibia, Chad, Angola,
Zimbabwe, and Uganda allied themselves with competing
Congolese factions and joined the bloody fight for diamonds,
precious metals, and spheres of influence. More than a million
would die, towns and cities would be destroyed, entire regions
would be depopulated, the vestiges of civilization would disappear in vast areas, children and youth would be turned into hired
killers, and even cannibalism would reappear in the eastern part
of the country. The Western press would largely ignore the story,
even though the number killed would exceed by far those massacred in the Rwandan genocide of 1994.

And finally, it is worth reflecting on the response that more
than a dozen heads of state and government gave to Canada on
the weekend of November 11, 1996. With no prior notification,
they committed troops and financing solely on the word of
Canada's leader that their help was needed. President Fernando

Henrique Cardoso of Brazil, who could have been speaking for the others, told Canada's prime minister: "Just tell me where to send our peacekeepers and they will be on their way." His answer was an eloquent testimony to the credibility Canada had earned internationally in the latter half of the twentieth century. I hope, however, that we remember November and December 1996 the next time our American friends make us an offer too good to be true.

PART FOUR

NEW FRONTIERS

9

Embracing Our Pacific Destiny

*Visits to the area by Canadian leaders had . . . been infrequent
compared with those made by presidents or prime ministers from
Germany, France, the United Kingdom, and Australia.*

The Importance of the Pacific Region

Next to the United States, no other part of the world received as
much sustained attention from the prime minister as the Asia-
Pacific region. The reasons were compelling. For decades, the
average growth rates throughout much of the area had been twice
those of North America. The region would shortly account for
50 per cent of global production, 40 per cent of consumption,
and 60 per cent of world population. Already, Canada exported
more to Asia than to all of Europe – East and West – plus Africa
and the Middle East combined. And Japan alone imported more
from Canada than all four European G7 countries together. There
were also political and cultural reasons. Nowhere else were the
prospects as promising for developing markets to help offset our
growing dependency on trade with the United States. By 1994,
most immigrants to Canada – some 120,000 out of a total of
220,000 annually – came from Asia-Pacific countries, in particular from Hong Kong, China, India, and the Philippines. They
had already changed the face of our large urban centres, not just
Vancouver but the Greater Toronto Area, Montreal, and
Winnipeg, and naturally maintained close family and business ties
to their countries of origin.

Canada had been busily cultivating closer relations with the vast region for over a quarter century. Diplomatic missions had been opened in potential new markets and the private sector was encouraged to become involved through the creation of the Asia-Pacific Foundation and other organizations. Visits to the area by Canadian leaders had, however, been infrequent compared with those made by presidents or prime ministers from Germany, France, the United Kingdom, and Australia. In some cases, more than a decade had elapsed since a senior Canadian minister had visited countries as important as Australia, India, Pakistan, and Indonesia. In turn, relatively few leaders, or even senior ministers, from the region had been received in Canada. The absence of prime ministerial engagement would have been noticed in the status-conscious hierarchical political establishments in the area. The attention of the prime minister himself was required if we were to make our mark in the Asia-Pacific.

Team Canada was the prime minister's chosen instrument to compensate for generations of political neglect. Between 1994 and 1998, three missions would be launched into the Asia-Pacific. The goal was political – to use a "mother of all trade missions" approach to blast awareness of the world outside North America into the consciousness of Canadians, and to expose Asians to Canada. For these expeditions were modern-day voyages of discovery by five hundred or more business people, presidents of at least fifty universities, premiers from most provinces and territories, and a representative sample of mayors. Before he left on his first mission to China, however, the prime minister had to deal with Japan's newly elected prime minister, Tomiichi Murayama, at the July 1994 Naples G7 summit.

An Unhappy Japanese Prime Minister
Prime Minister Chrétien was looking forward to meeting Japan's new prime minister. Tradition dictated that newly elected leaders make courtesy calls on those with more seniority before the

beginning of formal talks. And Murayama was the junior leader in Naples, having just taken office as a result of a deal in which he led his small socialist party into a coalition with the much larger Liberal Democratic Party. He had become prime minister but the Liberal Democrats had kept key portfolios, including trade and economic development, for themselves. Murayama thus came to the small luxury hotel where the Canadian delegation was staying, held his talks, and left. We Canadians thought the meeting had been a great success. The session had gone on much longer than expected and had ended with many smiles and much bowing. So we were astonished to learn later that the Japanese considered the meeting a failure so damaging that it produced a frostiness in Canada–Japan relations.

I have often wondered what made the Japanese so mad. Could it have been that little incident in which the new leader of Japan was forced to walk up four flights of stairs in the dark to meet with his Canadian opposite number when the power suddenly failed? After all, it was not our fault that the hotel's antiquated electrical system could not accommodate the load from fax machines and other electronic paraphernalia in our delegation office. Could Murayama have taken offence at the fact that there was only one solitary candle at the meeting, illuminating the faces of the two leaders from below, casting spectral shadows on the ceiling and making them look like characters from an old black-and-white silent movie? Had not our Japanese friends specifically asked for an intimate setting? Our logistics people had done their best, going shopping for candles locally only to find all stores in Naples closed for the summit; we had to make do with the one provided by the hotel management.

Was it because the prime minister ignored the earnest message received prior to the meeting from members of the Japanese delegation not to engage in substantive discourse with the new leader and to reserve any serious messages for the leader of the Liberal Democratic Party, Ryutaro Hashimoto, waiting in the wings for exactly such a purpose in Naples? The prime minister liked Murayama and it was natural that he would want to keep him engaged in a discussion that went well beyond the scheduled time, even if his minders, cooling their heels in the dark hallway outside, were not amused. Or could it have been related in some way to Murayama's subsequent illness at the summit itself? Could one blame the prime minister's normally astute communications director, Peter Donolo, who could not conceal his mirth when he repeated to the international press the precise explanation from his Japanese opposite number that Murayama was suffering from an attack of "soft poo"? Peter had a reputation for *bon mots* to uphold and the temptation was just too great for him, even if inadvertent offence was given.

From Canada's perspective, we had no desire to downgrade relations with our long-standing friend and ally. So we were baffled when the Canadian ambassador in Tokyo, Don Campbell, reported that a leading Japanese newspaper had run a story to say that the Japanese considered Canada–Japan relations seriously damaged. Campbell, who had been informed by the Canadian delegation in Naples that the candlelight meeting and talks had gone well, was puzzled. He thought that the newspaper had confused Canada with some other country, but it had not. By this time, Canada's tilt towards China was in full swing and the Japanese embassy in Ottawa would have reported the glowing infatuation in Canada with all things Chinese, and total silence about Japan. The Japanese may have thought that Canada was abandoning them because their economy was in a deep and long-lasting recession and the prospects for spectacular growth in trade with Canada were not good. The planned Team Canada mission before the end of the year to China would not have improved matters.

It was, however, in Tokyo's interest to maintain close ties with the Canadians, even if we were too dense to realize we seemed to be neglecting our best friend in Asia. To make up lost ground,

Japan invited the Canadian prime minister to make a "first-class" official visit to Tokyo. The distinction, we were told by our Japanese friends, was important. "First-class" guests were entitled to an audience, however brief, with the emperor, and an official lunch and black-tie dinner with the most succulent of foods and wines. Recipients of "second-class" visits, from countries held in less esteem, of course, were not received by the emperor and got only a working lunch or dinner with more officials than ministers in attendance, and presumably wines and foods of secondary quality. The prime minister accepted the invitation and the "first-class" visit that would heal all old injuries was set for the first week of November 1995.

In mid-1995, however, the Government of Quebec decided to hold its referendum on sovereignty on October 30. So confident of victory was the federalist side, that at first no thought was given to the possibility that the vote would be close, or that it might even be lost. Then Lucien Bouchard arrived on the scene at the last minute, making the victory of the Yes forces a real possibility. In these circumstances, a visit to Japan immediately after the referendum was out of the question. The prime minister would have to be available in Canada in the first week of November to deal with the aftermath of the challenge to Canada's survival.

I called in Japan's ambassador in Ottawa to give him the bad news. He did not take it well. Neither did his authorities. It was inconceivable, they intimated, that Canada, a model among nations, the winner year after year of the United Nations's prize for top spot as the best place to live, would ever break up. We were, they hinted, just looking for an excuse to put off visiting their country. Did we not realize that a call on the emperor had already been scheduled? And "first-class" banquets arranged? The win by the Yes side on October 30, however narrow it proved to be, confirmed their view that the Canadians had simply been looking for an excuse not to go to Japan. And then, to add insult to injury, the prime minister went off to Israel to attend the funeral of assassinated Prime Minister Yitzhak Rabin, an event which in the Japanese view did not compare to visiting Japan, in the very week he had been scheduled to make his official visit.

The Japanese informed us that the prime minister was now entitled only to a "second-class" visit. I am not sure, however, that the Canadian side noticed. When the visit took place in November 1996, we were too busy planning our next Team Canada mission to South Korea, the Philippines, and Thailand. Perhaps that was why Prime Minister Hashimoto drank too much at the "second-class" official dinner that he hosted in Tokyo, was in a foul mood, and took his frustrations out on his conscientious ambassador to Ottawa in mean personal attacks as the rest of us looked at our plates in embarrassment.

Team Canada to China – and on to Indonesia and Vietnam
The prime minister had better luck in his quest to establish a new relationship with China, Asia's rising economic superpower. Staff from Foreign Affairs, the PMO, and my PCO team worked non-stop from May, when they were told to begin the planning, until November 1994, when the visit began, putting together the largest trade mission in Canadian history. Their achievement was all the more remarkable in that they also had to cope with official visits to Canada at the same time of the presidents of Argentina, Poland, Tanzania, Benin, and Ukraine plus the prime ministers of Jamaica, Belgium, Thailand, and Rwanda. So much for my advice to the prime minister in May 1994 that he should restrict official visits to Canada to six per year!

On November 4, the first Team Canada left Vancouver with nine premiers (Quebec did not participate in the initial mission, but did in subsequent ones), two territorial leaders, two mayors, a huge business contingent, and a large group of media. At Vancouver International airport, the send-off was festive (champagne and orange juice) but no one was particularly interested in the drinks. They were there to do business. Small knots of people were scattered here and there exchanging business cards and discussing wares and business plans. The business contingent and press stuffed themselves into the economy seats on the lower level of the Canadian International Airlines 747 to begin the long flight. Downstairs, they were soon making merry. Upstairs in business class, nerves were fraying among the officials and elected leaders who were worried that the mission might not meet the high expectations generated by media hype. I had told the prime minister that if we were lucky, a billion dollars in deals might be concluded. The press had caught word of the estimate and would be certain to report that the mission had been a failure if anything less was achieved. Trade Minister Roy MacLaren took out his frustration on me.

"Listen, Jim, some idiot has listed in the briefing book the wrong Canadian battalion as being captured in Hong Kong in 1941! This is intolerable! What sloppy work!"

There was no doubt that he thought I was the idiot in question. The point he made was an important one, but he had come to the wrong address. I suggested that the member of his staff who wrote the brief should make the corrections. It was then the turn of Saskatchewan premier Roy Romanow.

"Bartleman, I am told that you have notionally included a large Saskatchewan potash contract as a probable sale in your internal calculations. How can you be so reckless! We are not sure to get the deal! How unprofessional!"

Once we were safely arrived, and after a day of sightseeing and photo opportunities on the Great Wall, Prime Minister Chrétien and Premier Li Peng met without the premiers for preliminary talks. After the polite opening remarks expected of a visiting dignitary, the prime minister made two points. First, Hong Kong was scheduled to go from British to Chinese rule on July 1, 1997. The many hundreds of thousands of Canadians with relatives there were anxious about its future. Canada hoped that the handover would be accomplished peacefully and that the fundamental rights and freedoms of the people would be safeguarded. Second, China's economy was booming and needed goods and services readily available in Canada. The signature of a record number of deals between Team Canada business people and their Chinese counterparts would launch a new relationship. And by the way, he could vouch for the two Canadian-designed nuclear power stations Atomic Energy of Canada Limited was seeking to sell to China. He had even personally monitored the preparation of the position Canada had adopted in its negotiations with China and hoped China would sign a memorandum of understanding during the Team Canada visit.

Premier Li listened intently, eventually saying that he could reassure the prime minister that the Hong Kong handover would take place peacefully and the rights of the people safeguarded under China's one country–two systems formula. On the second point, he said that he was worried. He had taken personal charge of the nuclear file. He was a nuclear engineer by training, had visited Canadian-built power plants in South Korea, and had been impressed by their technology, safety, and efficiency. Then, dropping a bombshell, he said that the Chinese leadership was concerned that if China–United States relations were to deteriorate for whatever reason in the coming years, the United States might force Canada to renege on its commitment to complete the plants. "We are simply not certain that you are sufficiently independent of the United States to be a reliable supplier to us of such strategically important products."

Prime Minister Chrétien was startled, not expecting that Canada's ties to the United States would complicate Canada's trade relations with China. He assured the premier that Canada, while a close friend of the United States, pursued an independent foreign policy. If Canada made a commitment to provide nuclear power plants, then Canada would deliver on it. And "as prime minister of Canada, I give you my word that if you undertake to purchase these reactors, we will fulfill our part of the contract." Without smiling, Premier Li accepted Jean Chrétien's assurances, and said that China would buy our reactors.

Despite Premier Romanow's worries, we got the potash contract. In fact, sixty-five contracts and memorandums of understanding worth $8.6 billion were signed. Just as important as the deals were the contacts established between Canadian and Chinese politicians and between Canadian business people and their Chinese equivalents. Our Chinese hosts threw a monster official dinner at the Great Hall of the People and as a mark of esteem for their new Canadian friends, served North China delicacies such as sea slugs, snakes, and parts of animals I never knew existed. I would have preferred the more familiar, and to my taste more delectable, Cantonese cuisine available in Chinese restaurants across Canada. There were dozens of toasts to Canada-China friendship with fiery Mai-Tai liqueur. The dinner became a happening as guests and hosts left their tables to mix, with much backslapping, picture taking, and conversations so animated that the interpreters found it hard to keep up.

The accompanying Canadian media contingent, for its part, was interested in only one thing: human rights. The prime minister, despite being a champion of the underdog at home, was never comfortable discussing human rights abroad. He nevertheless found ways to criticize Chinese practices without jeopardizing the deals – or mentioning human rights. President Jiang Zemin smiled but made no comment as the prime minister urged him to introduce Canadian-style elections. With Premier Li Peng, Chrétien did not refer directly to human rights per se but said Canada wanted to help China make improvements in "democratic governance and the rule of law," an expression the Canadian embassy said was the acceptable code for communicating human rights concerns to the Chinese government. I was not certain, however, that Li Peng was in on the secret. The premier looked puzzled as the prime minister spoke, and then frowned as his meaning gradually penetrated. There was no dialogue, however, and the discussion quickly moved on to the more agreeable topic of trade and business deals.

The Canadian premiers and their staffs bonded with the prime minister and the rest of us. In Shanghai, Ontario premier Bob Rae led the group in a singsong at a late-night restaurant, pounding out tune after tune on the piano. Jean Pelletier pulled me out of the delegation office to join the others, saying that I could not spend all my time with my nose in briefing books. The prime minister did not need to discuss federal-provincial relations with this group of premiers to know that they accepted him – in this early honeymoon period in any case – as Canada's undisputed leader, representing both national and provincial interests abroad.

Team Canada then carried on to Hong Kong to attend Remembrance Day ceremonies at the Sai Wan Military Cemetery where hundreds of forgotten Canadian soldiers were buried. A delegation of veterans flown out by the Department of Veterans Affairs stood stoically in the late morning sun, tears in their eyes as they contemplated bitterly the hand fate had dealt them: sent to Hong Kong by a Canadian government that should have known better, just in time to be overwhelmed by Japanese forces; enduring interminable years working as slave labour contrary to the rules of war in Japanese prisoner-of-war camps; and subject to indifferent treatment by the Canadian government and public alike after their liberation in 1945. It was a hot humid day and a number of the old warriors were on their last legs, afflicted with cancers and heart disease. An accompanying military doctor kept a compassionate eye on them as they navigated the steep hillside graveyard.

Team Canada concluded, the premiers dispersed to pursue separate programs and to make their own way back to Canada. The prime minister's delegation boarded the Airbus to attend the annual APEC summit meeting in Jakarta, witnessing President Suharto, then at the peak of his domestic power and international influence, throwing his weight behind the drive for a Pacific Free Trade zone by 2010. It was then on to Hanoi on an exploratory trade mission. During the planning phase for the trip to Asia, we had considered stopping off in either Kazakhstan or Vietnam to drum up business. I argued in favour of Vietnam, saying the communist country was following the example of China in introducing market capitalist practices and could become an important market for Canadian business. There was also every reason to believe a prime-ministerial visit would be well-received. Canada had not participated in the Vietnam War, had been a member of the International Control Commission for decades, had just appointed its first resident ambassador, had acquired a new chancery, and had become a significant aid donor. Canada was also a senior member of APEC, and Vietnam wanted our support to join. Both countries were members of the Francophonie and tens of thousands of Vietnamese now made Canada their home, sending healthy remittances in Canadian currency to their relatives, helping sustain the local economy.

Minister MacLaren, who had preceded us to Hanoi with a business delegation, was at the airport to greet us, together with Ambassador Christine Desloges. The drive into the city was a return to old television pictures of Vietnam during the 1950s, 1960s, and early 1970s when the communists chased first the French and then the Americans from their homeland. The two-lane heavily potholed road was crowded with bicycle, scooter, and truck traffic. There were few cars to be seen. Peasants in black pyjama outfits and wide-brimmed hats, following practices unchanged for hundreds of years, tended to their rice fields with wooden plows and water buffalo. Big billboards advertising Japanese tractors, appliances, and vehicles were incongruous intrusions of globalization into the age-old scene. As we entered the city, a member of the Canadian embassy pointed out the site of the "Hanoi Hilton," the notorious prison built by the French in 1901 where so many American prisoners of war, including John

McCain (later to become a famous senator and presidential candidate), were held in brutal captivity for so many years.

In November 1994, there was only one decent hotel, the Metropole, in the city. But we could not stay there. As honoured official guests of the state, it was the Government Guest House for us. In my room, an unshaded forty-watt bulb attached to a rudimentary fixture hanging by a wire from the ceiling provided dim lighting, and a strong smell of human waste wafted out from the doorless toilet. Fortunately, the PMO advance team, which had arrived several days before us, had thoroughly sprayed the beds of all delegation members to kill the resident fleas and bedbugs. There were also beautiful Vietnamese girls in traditional slit dresses to greet us when we called on the government leaders, bargains to be had in the local shops, delicious Vietnamese cuisine, toasts to Canadian-Vietnamese friendship at official events, but few business deals. I would return to Vietnam three more times in the coming years; once to a Francophonie summit and twice on secret missions to successfully negotiate the release of a Canadian rotting in a local prison. On these occasions, I was not an official guest and could stay in the Metropole.

A Furious Chinese Premier

For several frantic days in October 1995, it seemed that the prime minister's efforts to develop privileged relations between Canada and China would go up in smoke. Chinese premier Li Peng was scheduled to make the first visit to Canada by a senior Chinese leader since the 1989 massacres in Beijing. There would be private talks in Ottawa with Prime Minister Chrétien, followed by a general meeting involving ministers and senior officials. In the afternoon, the premier would depart for Montreal in his own aircraft for the highlight of the visit: a reunion with the Team Canada premiers gathered to welcome him at a gala dinner, as well as a sentimental meeting with Pierre Trudeau, who had been prime minister when Canada established diplomatic relations with China. The premier would depart after the festivities for Dorval airport to continue his world tour.

But Premier Li, we discovered, wanted to be difficult. Less than two days before his scheduled arrival in Ottawa, a grim-faced member of the People's Liberation Army, accompanied by the Chinese ambassador to Canada, came to my office to lay down the law. The uniformed officer snapped out his message:

"I am here to tell you that if Premier Li sees so much as a single anti-China demonstrator, he will cancel his official visit to Canada and return home. Canada will suffer the consequences."

Premier Li Peng, also known as "the butcher of Tiananmen" for his role in the brutal suppression of the pro-democracy movement in China in 1989, was in Mexico on the foreign tour that would take him to Canada and had taken umbrage when confronted by demonstrators in Mexico City. Determined to accept no further affronts to his country and to his personal dignity, he had sent ahead the army officer, a member of his personal retinue, to ensure that there would be no demonstrators on the streets of Canada during his visit. The body language of the emissary and the disquiet in the eyes of the ambassador indicated that this was no bluff. My instinct was to tell them that if the premier could not abide demonstrators, then he should skip Canada. Sometime earlier, the ambassador of another friendly dictatorship had come to my office to ask in all seriousness that I give orders for the arrest of people planning a protest march against her regime. It had given me great pleasure to give her a lesson on the functioning of Canadian democracy and to show her the door.

In this case, however, Premier Li was coming in response to the Team Canada mission to his country the previous November. With almost nine billion dollars' worth of deals signed in Beijing, the imagination of Canada's premiers, the business establishment, and the academic world had been captured by China and all things Chinese. Should the premier leave in a fit of pique, our opening to China would be seriously set back. As a citizen and as a public servant, I knew that there was no question that we would agree to the Chinese demand that we ban demonstrators. But a subtle form of diplomacy was required to convince the Chinese premier to come – and, after arriving, not to cut short his visit.

Foreign Minister Ouellet invited me to his office to help devise a plan to save the visit. It would, we decided, be guile against intransigence. We decided to enmesh the premier in the program in Ottawa to make it too difficult for him to turn around and leave when he eventually – and inevitably – encountered the reality of Canadian street democracy. To lure him into our trap, we moved the scheduled talks from the cabinet room in the Centre Block of Parliament – with its banks of windows open to the parliamentary lawn that was all too likely to be filled with chanting demonstrators – to rooms buried deep in the heart of the fortress-like Pearson Building on Sussex Drive. The demonstrators would be free to do their thing, but we bet that the premier would not walk out when the sounds of the crowd filtered their way through the walls.

Twenty-four hours later, a smiling Premier Li descended the stairs from his aircraft, which was drawn up outside the tightly controlled hangar dedicated to the arrivals and departures of official visitors at Ottawa airport. The crowd assembled in the hangar gave him a rousing welcome – unsurprisingly, since they were all staff and families from the Chinese embassy. A little girl handed over the obligatory bouquet of flowers, the leaders delivered their mandatory speeches, the customary national anthems were played, the standard smartly dressed guard of honour was inspected, and the motorcade formed up routinely. But in a departure from usual practice, the RCMP escort officers took the back roads into Ottawa. The first rendezvous our distinguished guest had with the Canadian public was thus with an enthusiastic group of foreign-service employees in the lobby of the Pearson Building – commandeered to leave their offices and applaud. Had the premier known, he would surely have approved – "rent-a-crowds" were the way dictatorships greeted visitors the world over. We, however, were stooping only temporarily, and to conquer – inviting him into the Pearson Building under false pretences to expose him to the face of Canadian democracy in the form of assembled ranks of protestors when he emerged.

A protocol officer escorted the two first ministers, accompanied only by their ambassadors and advisors, to a small, windowless room in the interior of the building for the first meeting. It was, in fact, a meeting before a meeting, to allow the leaders to become comfortable with each other before the beginning of official talks. All went well until the prime minister delicately tried to discuss demonstrators and democracies. Li Peng's affable smile turned into a scowl. By this time, the coalition of anti–Li Peng groups was, as expected, marching down Sussex Drive towards the Pearson Building. A distant roar could be heard in our inner sanctum but the prime minister said that the noise must be from crowds cheering for Canada's distinguished guest. The premier replaced scowl with smile as the waiting protocol officer escorted us to a large conference room as far from the street as possible, where ministers and senior officials waited patiently. The meeting was over in short order – there were few substantive items on the agenda other than trade matters – and it was time to depart.

Emerging from the elevator on the ground floor, the premier walked through the rows of applauding foreign-service employees. Their acclamations were more than offset, however, by the howls of the banner-waving crowd outside, held back by Ottawa's finest. The RCMP and Chinese security officers decided not to risk trying to leave from the front entrance, where the crowd was concentrated, and led a by now deeply unhappy guest to the back exit in the basement. There, a group of public servant smokers was to be found, puffing furtively as always on the cigarettes banned from the working and public areas of the building.

This hardened group of outcasts was not about to applaud anyone, not even the head of government of a country of great importance to Canada, and they looked on with tight smiles as the premier was hustled into his car. The media and demonstrators, however, were lying in wait as the RCMP driver gunned his car out the door. Several were knocked to one side by the accelerating vehicle but no one was seriously hurt. Some said afterwards that it looked like John Dillinger escaping a bank robbery with the FBI on his tail.

The big question now was whether the premier would cancel the Montreal portion of the trip. The Canadian interpreter assigned to the premier and sitting forgotten in the front seat of the Canadian-supplied limousine that took him to his aircraft – who debriefed me later – was an invisible witness as the premier raged against the villainy of Canadians and considered whether he should carry out his threat to abandon his mission. I hitched a ride to Montreal with Peter Donolo, crossing my fingers and hoping that the premier would decide to carry on with his program. Arriving at the hotel, I was given good and bad news. The good was that the premier had arrived; the bad was that he had been jostled by a group of "Free Tibet" protestors who had breached the lackadaisical Montreal police lines, forcing him to run the gauntlet from his car to the front door. Our gamble, nevertheless, seemed to be paying off. Now that he was in Montreal – in the same hotel as the cluster of admiring premiers and business people who had visited China the previous fall – it would be harder for him to bolt for the airport.

There was one last dramatic act to be played in the farce. Prime Minister and Mrs. Chrétien went to fetch Premier Li and his wife at their suite to take them up to the gala dinner. I followed as they took the escalators, located on an outside wall alongside huge windows, to the banquet floor. At the top, Canada's smiling premiers awaited. Outside, and clearly visible to the prime minister's distinguished guests on the escalator, which seemed to be moving at a snail's pace, was a veritable wide-screen Imax view of papier mâché tanks, imitation Statues of Liberty, huge banners painted with Chinese characters, and thousands of people screaming imprecations at Canada's honoured guest. Premier Li, glum at the beginning of the ride, was red-faced and furious by the end.

"I am departing immediately! Never have I or my country been so humiliated!"

"You have it all wrong," the prime minister quickly explained. "They are mad at *me*. They do this all the time – not to worry."

Premier Li had no ready answer. But his face, and the visit, were saved.

Fortunately, it was not Li Peng but the affable President Jiang Zemin who was the prime minister's main contact in developing his links with China's leadership. It was Jiang whom the prime minister met at the annual APEC meetings, Jiang who hosted the Team Canada mission to China in 1994, and Jiang who paid an official visit to Canada in 1998. With his ready smile, his greater understanding of the West, and his willingness to conduct a dialogue on human rights, his was the more humane face of China to the world. Prime Minister Chrétien sought a constructive and practical way to engage the Chinese. He encouraged CIDA to become more involved in projects such as training judges, promoting the rights of women, and assisting the National People's Congress in the codification of laws to reduce the arbitrary nature of China's legal system. When Qiao Shi, chairman of the National People's Congress, and Foreign Minister Qian Qichen called on him during their visits to Canada in 1996, he thus was able to discuss human rights with them in a practical, non-confrontational manner.

The prime minister even coined a name for the approach he adopted. It was the so-called Shediac doctrine, a concept he pulled together when unexpectedly questioned by a reporter on our position on human rights in China, when he was in Shediac, New Brunswick: "China is a huge country and Canada is a small one. Canada does not have the power to force a change in China's human rights behaviour. Change will, however, come to China as it becomes exposed to the main currents of the outside globalized world through trade and the Internet. Engagement rather than an attempt at isolating China is the long-term key to the eventual humane treatment of the population." In the years I was with the prime minister, however, China's human rights record remained the principal obstacle to the development of closer political relations. I became all too familiar with hectoring visits from the Chinese ambassador threatening Canada with unspecified consequences if we dared support resolutions in the United Nations Human Rights Commission critical of China, or received at official levels Chinese or Tibetan human-rights activists. Most of the time, but regrettably not all of the time, I ignored his complaints.

Team Canada to India, Pakistan, Indonesia, and Malaysia

With one successful Team Canada project concluded, a second mission left in January 1996 with high expectations, not to mention seven premiers, two territorial leaders, a handful of university presidents, a smattering of mayors, a gaggle of press, and over three hundred business people. The first stop was Mumbai, the Bombay of history, India's fastest-growing, most dynamic city, with an aggressive globally minded entrepreneurial class. In the seventeenth century, no more than ten thousand people, largely fisherfolk, lived on the seven islands on the Arabian Sea that would eventually be joined together by landfill to form the modern city. The British then turned it into their principal gateway to the subcontinent. Minorities seeking religious freedom and an outlet for their business energies, such as the Parsis and Gujaratis, arrived in due course. And a flood of poor villagers poured in, seeking a better life.

Motorcycle outriders escorted our motorcade through the dust and haze of the heavy afternoon traffic. The world we entered — surrealistic, polluted, ugly, overpopulated, and throbbing with life — could not have been farther from the orderly, antiseptic, snow-covered Canada that we left less than twenty-four hours before. According to our *Lonely Plant* guide, 50 per cent of the population of Mumbai lived without water or electricity, just breathing the air was equal to smoking twenty cigarettes a day, and oxygen bars were opening to provide those who could afford it some relief for their lungs. Incongruously, land prices at choice locations were now higher than those in downtown Tokyo. The city fathers, against all reason, reputedly had aspirations for their city to become the largest in the world. The sidewalks overflowed with shoppers, loiterers, beggars, and tiny stalls offering all manner of goods. I was reminded of Bangladesh when I opened Canada's first diplomatic mission in that war-battered country in the early 1970s.

We departed Mumbai for New Delhi after a speech from the prime minister, contract-signing ceremonies, courtesy calls on local dignitaries, and a meeting with young Canadians on a Canada World Youth exchange program. From the aircraft window, the ground below was obscured by a massive black cloud of pollution. After an hour of circling, the pilot found a hole in the filth and came down to land at New Delhi airport. The city I knew more than two decades previously, when I was a visitor from Dhaka, had disappeared. Traffic at that time was light, the air was crystal clear, and trees were filled with gloriously coloured birds. Now, one hundred metres was the maximum we could see through the daytime gloom and in the background there was an ever-present rumble of traffic from hundreds of thousands of poorly maintained vehicles.

The visit was an ostensible success, involving the signature of an impressive list of business deals, a visit to a Canadian development project in a slum area, and a guided tour of the Taj Mahal in nearby Agra. Business people rushed from one place to another to conclude deals and to pose at photo opportunities. The hospitality from the government was warm, but not overly so. Our communications experts lauded the number and the value of the contracts, the lines of credit, and the memorandums of understanding signed.

But there was no breakthrough in Canadian-Indian relations as there was in Beijing with China. Clearly, the Indians had not yet forgiven us for turning our back on them a generation earlier after they improperly used a CANDU reactor provided by Canada to make nuclear weapons. More than two billion dollars in aid provided to India since independence had likewise bought no goodwill. The Indian government was also suspicious of all this talk of globalization, uncomfortable with the concept of the market economy itself, and wary of the enthusiasm their business community was showing for doing away with a lifetime of government controls. I was surprised to note that they appeared more curious than pleased that there were so many Canadians of Indian origin on the mission. India, they were signalling to us, was an ancient civilization that had seen foreign invaders come and go – and Team Canada, they seemed to be saying, was just another invading group. The refrain from Kipling's poem – "here lies the man who thought he could hurry the East" – repeated itself like a broken record in my mind.

I was also disappointed. One of the highlights of my life was a visit I made to Agra in 1973 en route to take up a new posting in Europe after my assignment to Bangladesh. The Taj Mahal I saw then, I saw alone at dawn. The light off the marble towers was incandescent and the mood in the park subdued. I thought I would never again see anything as beautiful. Those memories I now discovered, had been replaced by another – a horde of good-natured Team Canada participants, protocol officers, guides, and souvenir vendors milling around in the hot sun taking in just another tourist attraction.

Mother Teresa

I would return to India one last time in the service of the prime minister, in far different circumstances eighteen months later, when I accompanied Mrs. Chrétien as she represented Canada at the funeral of Mother Teresa. The news of Mother Teresa's passing had arrived in September 1997 at the height of the public hysteria over the death of Princess Diana. What irony! One young, a divorcee, touched by scandal, and secular; the other old, a living saint, Nobel Peace Prize laureate, and the embodiment of deeply conservative religious values. Both were, however, dedicated to the poor and marginalized. And both were victims of depression and feelings of inadequacy at low points in their lives that they overcame to become role models for millions.

The funeral was in Calcutta, but it was a city far different to the one I knew as a young diplomat coming here on business or holiday. The local authorities had cleared the refuse and human wrecks from the side of the road coming in from the airport; now advertising billboards honouring Mother Teresa – and selling Indian automobiles, baby food, and electronic goods – decorated the route. An indoor sports stadium seating twelve thousand had been fitted up for the funeral service. The majority of the official guests were ladies in black mourning – as if the wives of world leaders had conspired to make the event an all-woman happening. Hillary Rodham Clinton, Bernadette Chirac, and Sonia Gandhi joined Mrs. Chrétien, classically elegant as always, in the places of honour.

At one point as the distinguished guests stood chatting, the British High Commissioner bore down on the group in his role as the modern day representative of the Raj. "Make way! Make way for the Duchess of Kent! Make way for the Duchess of Kent!", he proclaimed, but no one paid him heed, and the duchess had to fend for herself.

The funeral began when soldiers in a death march without drum rolls entered, carrying Mother Teresa on an open bier – a person whose soul had departed and whose flesh was all too mortal. There was a smell of decay, incense, mosquito repellent, and sweat, and I found it hard to keep my eyes off the hands on her chest – large, full, work-scarred, and clutching a rosary. The service began: hymns, sacraments, speeches, wreath-laying, popularity contests, flashbulbs, jostling press, and bemused looks on the faces of the phalanx of assembled bishops, archbishops, and cardinals as they listened to the eulogies from representatives of other faiths – Hindu, Parsi, Muslim, Buddhist, and Protestant. Individuals whose lives she had touched – a leper, a former criminal, a handicapped person – came forward with offerings that included a painting of the Sacred Heart of Jesus and flowers. The official guests approached the bier for a final farewell. The cortège then departed, led by altar boys with crucifixes and candles, followed by a guard of honour in full-dress uniforms and turbans, moving with an air of destiny like a squad of mechanical soldiers. A crowd of Sisters of Charity, clergy, and representatives of the poor and sick followed.

India thus honoured a foreign-born nun of the tradition and spirit of Saint Francis of Assisi with military honours and pomp remote from her lifestyle. It was a ceremony appropriated by the state for the purposes of the state, by the church for the purposes of the church, and by the mourners for the purposes of the mourners. And yet, in the Indian context, there was no sense of inappropriateness. All of us, myself included, wanted to pay tribute to her, were conscious that we were saying farewell to one of the giants of the twentieth century, and shared a desire to be present as history was made.

Pakistan: Trying to Help Ahmed Said Khadr

The media contingent were in a bad mood as Team Canada flew into Pakistan. Some had disregarded the advice of the accompanying doctor not to drink the tap water in India and had contracted "Delhi Belly," the fierce local diarrhea familiar to travellers to the subcontinent. Others were tired of covering good news stories about happy businesspeople concluding deals and describing colourful tourist outings by the prime minister, the premiers, and their spouses. All hungered for a good juicy scandal to enliven their reporting. And in Islamabad they found one. A Canadian citizen of Egyptian origin, Ahmed Said Khadr, was being held in jail on suspicion of involvement in the recent bombing of the local Egyptian embassy that had killed more than a dozen people. Khadr's wife, Maha Khadr, a Canadian citizen of Palestinian origin, visited the press room. With her children in tow, she complained about the lack of help she was obtaining from Canada's diplomats for her husband, who, she alleged, was being tortured in prison.

At the press briefing, the journalists peppered High Commissioner Marie-Andrée Beauchemin with questions. "Have you or any member of your staff been to see Khadr in prison? Has he been tortured?" Beauchemin said that, actually, no one had been to see him, and no, she really had no idea whether he was being tortured.

The reporters were outraged, or at least they said they were. What lack of sensitivity! What incompetence! They then managed to interview Ahmed Said Khadr himself in the prison hospital, where he was on a hunger strike. He solemnly proclaimed that he had had nothing to do with the bombing of the Egyptian embassy and, yes indeed, although he had been tortured, no one from the Canadian High Commission had come to his assistance. The reporters were filled with a potent mixture of self-righteous indignation and delight. They had the scandal they had been searching for, complete with photogenic wife, cute children, and brave Canadian husband suffering in a prison hospital.

The prime minister then met with the wife to hear her side of the story. There was nothing extraordinary in the prime minister's gesture. He made it a practice to meet with Canadian citizens during his foreign travels. In New Delhi, for example, he met with the wife of a Canadian citizen of Indian origin who had disappeared during a crackdown on the Khalistan Liberation Movement some time before, and was believed to have been killed and dumped into a well by the Indian security service. The Indian president, with whom Prime Minister Chrétien discussed the matter, acknowledged that the individual had probably been killed by rogue elements in the Indian security service. His government, he said, was conducting an investigation. And on the same day that the prime minister met the Khadrs, he also set aside time to meet twelve-year-old Craig Kielburger from Thornhill, Ontario, who was just starting his campaign against the use of child labour in the Third World. Craig would grow up to establish "Kids Can Free the Children," an organization that raised funds to build more than three hundred schools and to provide millions of dollars in medical supplies to poor families in the Third World.

The prime minister thus listened attentively to Mrs. Khadr, offering her tea and sympathy, but made no comment on the merits of the case against her husband. He would, he said, do what he could to ensure that her husband was treated fairly under Pakistani law. The accompanying brood of well-behaved children, several of whom were no older than Craig Kielburger, but whose choice of future could not be more different, shyly accepted candies before they left. The prime minister then raised the case of Ahmed Said Khadr with Prime Minister Bhutto, asking only that he be accorded the rights due to him under Pakistani law. Bhutto heard him out but said nothing. Several weeks later, the Pakistani authorities freed the husband and that was the end of the matter.

Or so we thought. The young Khadr boys with impeccable manners, who accompanied their mother to call on Prime Minister Chrétien that day in January 1996, grew up as playmates to the children of al-Qaeda leader Osama bin Laden, attended

al-Qaeda terrorist training camps, and became fierce militants for his cause. Five years later, al-Qaeda terrorists wreaked their destruction on New York. Six years later, the United States was in control of Afghanistan, after swiftly driving from power the Taliban, who were sheltering Osama bin Laden. Seven years later, family patriarch Ahmed Said Khadr was killed in an anti-terrorist operation by Pakistani troops. His widow, who had sought the prime minister's help in 1996 to protect the human rights of her husband, appeared on television to denounce Western democracy and all that it stood for. One son, Abdul Karim, returned to Canada to recover from a bullet to his spine sustained in the battle that killed his father. Another, Omar, was in detention in Guantanamo Bay, Cuba, as an "enemy combatant." A third, Abdullah, was in hiding in Pakistan. The fourth, Abdurahman, a self-confessed fighter who became an informant for the CIA after his capture in Afghanistan, was back in Canada telling his story to anyone who would listen. And the media, which screamed bloody murder at the failure of Canada to do more for Ahmed Said Khadr in January 1996, would complain loudly in 2004 that Prime Minister Chrétien had done too much for him.

Prime Minister Benazir Bhutto

Superficially at least, the official visit of Team Canada to Pakistan could not have gone better. Prime Minister Benazir Bhutto was at her charming best, displaying brilliance in blending a Radcliffe education with feudal custom as she welcomed the Canadians at her luxurious white stone residence. We were vaguely aware that Asif Ali Zardari, her husband, who stood laughing beside her as she received her guests, was reputed to be extremely corrupt, as were many of the country's upper class, the hundred families that ran the country and who lived in gross luxury alongside the abject poverty of the mass of the population. And none of the hand-shaking Canadians knew at the time that Pakistan was in the final stages of developing nuclear weapons, and for the past decade had been secretly and recklessly selling the technology to Iran, Libya, and North Korea. Benazir Bhutto herself, it would later transpire, may have authorized the transfer of nuclear-weapons technology to North Korea in exchange for missiles.

Certainly the Pakistani prime minister did not lack the authoritarian touch. Learning that Team Canada had just signed deals worth several billion dollars with Indian companies, she decreed that Pakistan should do at least as well as its rivals. On the spot, she ordered the heads of state corporations to sign contracts, lines of credit, and memorandums of understanding to an equal amount with the visiting Canadians.

There would, however, be no breakthrough to Pakistan as a result of Team Canada 1996. Before the year was over, the military would stage a coup and the prime minister would flee the country. Her husband would end up in jail for drug smuggling, murder, and other crimes. And the majority of the deals concluded with Team Canada, shaky to start with, would collapse. A year later, in exile and wanted by the law in her own country, she visited Ottawa to lunch with Prime Minister Chrétien and try to explain away the criminal charges that she and her husband were facing. When the conversation happened to turn to the Pakistani military intelligence service, it was astonishing to see how instantly she lost her composure. From her look of terror, one would have thought that the agents of this notorious organization (busy masterminding attacks against India in Kashmir, propping up the Taliban regime in Afghanistan, and involved in the smuggling of nuclear-weapons technology to North Korea and other unstable regimes) were lying in wait for her outside the dining room at 24 Sussex Drive. Then I remembered that her own father, Zulfikar Ali Bhutto, a previous prime minister of Pakistan, had been hanged by the victors when he had been ousted by the military in a coup in the late 1970s. Some paranoids, it seems, have good reason to be worried.

Indonesia and Malaysia

In Jakarta and Kuala Lumpur, the airports, hotels, shopping malls, and main thoroughfares looked like transplants from Miami. The governments of Indonesia and Malaysia had embraced open markets twenty years earlier and had since enjoyed high rates of non-stop economic growth, together with a watering-down of their indigenous culture in favour of homogenized American-ization. They were also used to delegations from abroad coming to sell their wares and invest. Canada already conducted more business with these two than it did with all the countries of South Asia put together, despite their giant populations. Indonesia was Canada's largest trade and investment partner in the powerful Association of Southeast Asian Nations, and Malaysia was not far behind. But the size and seniority of Team Canada impressed even the most blasé locals and everyone was happy with the deals signed and contacts established.

The leaders, however, required careful handling. President Suharto, the son of poor farmers who got his start as an army officer participating in the massacre of more than half a million people, most of them Chinese, following an abortive coup attempt in the early 1960s, had been the undisputed ruler of Indonesia since 1968. He and his grown children and cronies had become very, very rich from corruption. In a bizarre and ostentatious display of wealth, the president had even built a museum to store the various extremely expensive presents that Indonesians, espe-cially members of the rich Chinese minority, seeking to curry favour, had offered him. Canada's gift, delivered a year later and unveiled as part of a trade promotion exercise, was a totem pole.

The prime minister tackled Suharto on human rights abuses in East Timor. The president, who seemed to have been waiting for the subject to be raised, launched into a lengthy explanation of the history of Indonesian rule in the former Portuguese colony. Words spilled from his mouth in a low rapid patter of Bahasa Indonesian – the national language. His interpreter, who had obviously done this before, translated simultaneously from memory. The president did not deny army excesses and promised to do better. No one could have foreseen that his country would be in financial ruin and the Indonesian leader himself driven from office in disgrace within three years.

In Malaysia Prime Minister Mahathir, despite his reputation for lecturing visitors on "Asian values" and taking offence at imaginary slights, was for once a gracious host.

Team Canada to South Korea, the Philippines, and Thailand
Canada's "Year of Asia-Pacific," the international theme adopted by the government for 1997, began in hope and confidence with the departure of another giant mission eastwards to storm its way into the markets of the future. It ended in November in Vancouver at the APEC summit amidst the Asian financial crisis and anti-globalization protests. South Korea, our first stop, was a new port of call for me, but Korea had played an early role in my life. As a newspaper carrier boy in my small Muskoka village during the Korean War, I would rush home from school to open up my bundle of papers and avidly read the latest news from the front. I later followed Korea's emergence in 1965 as an Asian Tiger and its subsequent quarter century of double-digit growth. That it was one of Canada's most important partners and that our two-way trade exceeded that with France, I also knew. I was unprepared, however, for the violence of contemporary Korean society. When we arrived, the public service was on strike and thousands of masked workers were in the tear-gas-filled streets fighting with fist and baton against the riot police. But it was the visit to the demilitarized zone that shocked me – it was a return to 1950 and to Colonel Potter, Captain Pierce, and Margaret ("Hotlips") Houlihan from the *MASH* television series, but without the comedy.

Our hosts took us to Panmunjung, on the border with North Korea, past boutiques selling American souvenirs – and bunkers and watchtowers manned by heavily armed soldiers. Leading us by a carefully marked path to avoid placing a foot in North Korea, they showed us the conference table around which the ceasefire of 1953 was hammered out. North Korean soldiers glared at us, only metres away. The premiers, their wives, and the prime minister's entourage looked around and departed – uncertain whether they had visited a tourist attraction or whether they had just seen something that would affect Canada's national interests far more than the trade ties they were promoting.

The Philippines

The Philippines, our next destination, was unique in Asia. Colonized by the Spaniards and conquered at the turn of the twentieth century and ruled virtually as a colony for half a century by the Americans, the place had for me a Latin American feel, including strong Catholicism, facility with the English language, and enormous disparities between rich and poor. For years, it had been governed by the notoriously corrupt President Ferdinand Marcos and his wife, Imelda, backed by a compliant military. All that changed in 1986. In that year, the military, led by General Fidel Ramos, threw its support behind Corazon Aquino, a charismatic candidate running on a reform agenda, forcing Marcos and Imelda into exile. Aquino in turn was succeeded by Fidel Marcos, the president who welcomed Team Canada to his country in January 1997.

Manila was raucous, dirty, and booming. As our motorcade roared into the city, I was struck by the number of businesses with names like "Toronto Massage Parlour" and others advertising "Winnipeg Style Massages"; Canadian medical massage therapy techniques, I thought with pride, must have caught on in the Philippines. If so, they were only one indication of the flourishing ties between our two countries. The Philippines had become a progressively more significant trading partner for Canada. More importantly, it was also the homeland to hundreds of thousands of industrious, highly trained Filipinos who had migrated to Canada over the years to create dynamic communities in all major Canadian cities. The prime minister and President Fidel Ramos hit it off so well that Prime Minister Chrétien mused aloud during a speech to the Canada-Philippines chamber of commerce that it was a shame that the constitution of the Philippines would not permit his friend to serve a further term in office. Corazon Aquino, whom we enlisted to dampen down the ensuing firestorm of criticism from the press, emerged from a meeting with the prime minister to tell everyone to get a life. The transgression of Canada's prime minister was not all that serious, she said, and he should not, in any case, be expected to be familiar with the nuances of local politics.

Thailand

Bangkok, the last Asian city I would visit with the prime minister, I knew well from my posting there in 1972 as a first secretary at the Canadian embassy. At that time, the city was huge, dirty, overpopulated, and poor, but things were happening. The Vietnam War was on, and the streets, bars and restaurants were filled with American servicemen on leave who knew their country was losing and did not seem to care. I had the time and taste for adventure and travelled to Chiang Mia in the north where the girls were reputed to be the most beautiful in the world. The Oriental Hotel on the Chao Phraya river, a former haunt of Somerset Maugham, with its mahogany furniture and nineteenth-century air of gentility, was one of my hangouts. In what now seems like a dream, I once was a guest on a riverboat chartered to take several hundred Thai International air hostesses from the Oriental Hotel on an evening cruise. Bangkok was the perfect place at the perfect time, and I never forgot it.

The city in January 1997 was bisected by a huge ugly expressway running over it. The traffic was as bad as it was in 1972, and the pollution worse. I discovered that we were staying at the

Oriental Hotel but it was not the one I knew more than two decades earlier. We were directed into a new super-luxurious skyscraper hotel that had been erected beside the original building and had appropriated the old name. My former lair was now a museum. As far as the eye could see, there were construction cranes – hotels and apartment complexes were being thrown up in a flurry of speculation. The ambassador told us that the economy was so red-hot that more pickup trucks were being sold in Thailand than in any other country. Fifty per cent of the world's population was within five hours of Bangkok by air, and the Thais intended to exploit their geographic advantage. At lunch, I asked for comments on a story in the *Far Eastern Economic Review* that warned of a coming economic crash in Thailand. Our Thai guests dismissed the report and the Canadian premiers squirmed in embarrassment at my lack of tact.

Mixed Results

Four years is a short period in the life of a nation. But the sustained high-level political attention in Ottawa brought about a sea change in Canadian attitudes to the Asia-Pacific region and raised Canada's profile there to an historic high. In the years I was with him, the prime minister made six tours of the Asia-Pacific area, welcomed seven heads of state or government on official visits to Canada, received virtually all regional foreign and trade ministers passing through Ottawa, and made regular follow-up telephone calls to his principal contacts. Results, however, were mixed. With over eighteen billion dollars in contracts, memorandums of understanding, and lines of credit, the results of the Team Canada missions were impressive, even if in the end a number of transactions, especially with Pakistan, were not finalized. Ties with China, now emerging as Asia's engine of economic growth, became closer, and relations with Japan, our only Asian G7 partner and second-largest trading partner after the United States, became temporarily cooler. A start was made in renewing long-neglected connections to India and Pakistan, but were upset when India resumed and Pakistan started nuclear testing in 1998. What looked like promising new linkages to the countries of Southeast Asia, Korea, and Thailand were frustrated by the Asian financial crisis of 1997 and 1998. A tentative opening to Vietnam was hindered by the hesitation of its leadership in adopting market reforms. And misunderstandings, such as those uncovered by the meeting with Prime Minister Murayama in Naples and the visit of Premier Li to Ottawa and Montreal were many as Canada became more intimate with new partners with different traditions.

10

To Russia with Love

Yeltsin's table was laden with every type of Russian delicacy imaginable — three or four different sorts of caviar, salads, pickled eels, pâtés, and olives.

In December 1991, seventy-three years after the Communist Revolution, Russia and fourteen other sovereign states emerged from the ruins of the former Soviet Union, turned their backs on Marxism, and declared their intention to embrace capitalism and liberal democracy. The new countries, in need of technical expertise, capital, and goods, invited the world in to do business. Canadians were among the first to arrive, attracted by the possibilities of selling goods and investing in projects in the energy, transportation, and mining sectors where they had expertise relevant to the needs of the new countries. They sought the support of their government to open doors and support their efforts. Prime Minister Chrétien was well-suited to help them, having travelled in the region numerous times in his previous ministerial appointments. He would visit it three times between 1995 and 1997.

My First Visit
As for me, I had long been fascinated by Russia and its people. In my formative years haunting the local library in the small Ontario village where I had been raised, and later in university, Russian authors had been my introduction to the wider world — Leo Tolstoy, Fyodor Dostoevsky, and Boris Pasternak — rich in aesthetic

genius, social commentary, religious and philosophical insight, and the art of storytelling. And who could not feel admiration for the heroism of the Russian soldiers in the Second World War? One of my family's closest aboriginal friends came back from the war to tell us of meeting and drinking with cheerful but poorly clothed Russian soldiers when units of the Canadian army linked up with advance formations of the Red Army in 1945. The Russian people had more than their fair share of oppressors, including Napoleon, Hitler, and Stalin. Their tribulations did not come to an end with the collapse of communism.

It was thus with great curiosity and anticipation that I visited Moscow for the first time in February 1994 when I was still ambassador to NATO, ostensibly to make the acquaintance of a future colleague – President Yeltsin's diplomatic advisor – before I reported for duty with Prime Minister Chrétien. We held our talks. As expected, he expressed concern about any enlargement of NATO and I departed – never to see him again. This did not matter since the real purpose of my journey had been to catch a glimpse of a nation whose military and ideological challenge to the West had dominated global politics since the end of the war. For I was a product of my times – raised in the atmosphere of life and death struggle between East and West. With two postings to NATO, assignments in the Security and Intelligence world, and two years in communist Cuba, I had lived through many confrontations with the former Soviet Union, and was present as ambassador and permanent representative of Canada in the North Atlantic Council when it collapsed in December 1991.

Moscow, I discovered, was a city of surprises. The Cold War may have been over but suspicious, cheerless grey apparatchiks dressed in Soviet-era uniforms still manned the immigration and customs counters at Moscow's airport and behaved as if the war was still on. Meanwhile, a savage type of dog-eat-dog capitalism, not seen in Western Europe since the nineteenth century, had taken over the city. On the road in from the airport, billboards advertising luxury products and casinos lined the boulevards. At the luxurious Metropole hotel, where the embassy had booked me a room, CNN, BBC, other international channels, plus the latest movies and porn channels were available at the click of a switch, just as they were in similar hotels around the world. Within seconds of my arrival, a hotel employee knocked on the door of my room to deliver pink Crimean champagne and the best of Caspian Sea caviar, compliments of the management. Yet outside on the square in front of the Bolshoi theatre, old babushkas stood in the cold trying to sell their miserable possessions to buy food. Dirty snow was piled high on Red Square and on the grounds of the Kremlin.

My first order of business was to visit Canada's embassy on Starokonyushenny Street in the old Arbat or Turkish trading area of the city to call on the ambassador. As a former director general of Security and Intelligence in Foreign Affairs just a decade earlier and as someone who had been targeted in the past by both the KGB and its ally the Cuban Intelligence Service, I looked over the building with professional interest. The KGB had been dissolved in the fall of 1991 after its chief, Colonel-General Vladimir Kryuchkov, participated in the failed coup attempt in August of the same year against then president Mikhail Gorbachev. But its successor organization, the Foreign Intelligence Service (FBS), was suspected of being just as active as its predecessor. Perhaps it was just a touch of paranoia, but I imagined that the FBS was at work listening to every conversation through microphones implanted in the walls. During the Cold War, our security officers had regularly discovered hidden microphones and had even uncovered evidence that the Soviets had drilled from a neighbouring building to implant listening devices in the basement of the mission. Soviet agents would enter the apartments of our staff members when the occupants were out, rifle through personal papers and books, and deliberately leave everything in disorder. Occasionally, staff attempting to use their telephones would hear the contents of previous conversations played back to them. The KGB wanted to ensure that Canada's diplomats were aware that big brother was watching.

The KGB had also used more traditional means of blackmail to intimidate staff and obtain information. The Russian local employees at the embassy, it was assumed, reported to the sinister Soviet security and intelligence organization. The cleaning ladies at the embassy were sometimes prepared to offer "special services" to lonely Canadians. From time to time, supposedly unilingual Russian-speaking employees, especially the drivers, displayed an unsuspected fluency in English. On occasion, gullible Canadians would be caught in KGB entrapments, surreptitiously photographed selling goods illegally on the black market or having sex with prostitutes. Usually the transgressors would rush to confess their sins to the mission security officer and be immediately recalled to Ottawa to remove them from the clutches of the KGB. Their files ended up on my desk in the years I was in charge and I, following the practice of my predecessors, always recommended that such employees be treated leniently. After all, it was in Canada's security interest to have employees admit their indiscretions to allow us to limit the damage. Their spouses, I assumed, would be less understanding, but there was nothing anyone could do about that.

Canadians probably behaved no worse and no better than our allies in Moscow in these years. In one high-profile case, a British ambassador confessed that he had crawled into bed with a particularly attractive Russian maid, but swore on a bible that he had betrayed no secrets. I think he was likewise forgiven by his authorities. Of course, no one has any idea how many Canadians were recruited by the KGB to labour for the Soviets, undetected by Western intelligence services. And no one will ever know for sure how much secret information was obtained by the Soviets by these methods. Although we did not publicize the matter, the allied security and intelligence services, including the Canadian, targeted with equal zeal Soviet and other Warsaw Pact diplomats and military staff in our capitals. And we did win the Cold War.

On this cold winter day I walked up the stairs to the official residence, located in an apartment above the chancery offices, to greet Ambassador Jeremy Kinsman, Canada's man in the new capitalist Russia. Jeremy was one of Canada's top diplomats, destined to serve in later years as ambassador to Rome, High Commissioner to London, and ambassador to the European Union in Brussels, where he would replace me in 2002 when I was called back to be Ontario's Lieutenant-Governor. I looked around the elegant nineteenth-century drawing rooms and the plasterwork on the ceilings painted gold, green, and blue. The dining room was large enough to host twenty-four guests at a sitting and had an unimpeded view of the distant Russian foreign ministry constructed years before in the grim concrete-block Soviet realist style. Many of Canada's most distinguished diplomats had sat around this table, including Arnold Smith, John Watkins, Robert Ford, Vern Turner, Geoffrey Pearson, and Peter Roberts. Each had left his mark on Canada's relations with the former Soviet Union. Watkins, sadly, was a victim of the Cold War, dying while being interrogated by the former RCMP security service in an isolated Montreal motel, his reputation sullied by accusations of treachery.

The evening before I returned to Brussels, Jeremy invited me to join him and two or three of his English-speaking Muscovite friends for a quiet meal in a local restaurant. The Russians were bitter – at least initially. While paying lip service to the new capitalist age, they lamented the decline of their country from its superpower status to one that was poor, corrupt, criminal-ridden, and violent. As the evening progressed, the conversation turned to literature and the mood changed. One was an author. The others, well versed in the arts, wanted to discuss a book that he was just completing. He at first modestly resisted, but then opened the floodgates, describing setting, plot, and character development with great enthusiasm. He did not care, he said, whether any copies of his book would be sold, but desperately wanted it to be respected by his peers and to influence the ongoing debate on the future of his country. The others eagerly jumped in, offering opinions on his creation, especially on the extent to which it reflected Russia's distinctive Slavonic soul. The discussion could have been taken from a nineteenth-century novel of an old Russian master in which passionate members of the intelligentsia debated Russia's mission in the world. I returned to Brussels the next day, happy that in the wasteland of post–Cold War Russia, at least the spirit of artistic expression and creativity had survived the many decades of communism.

Moscow 1995

Back in Moscow in May 1995 with the prime minister for the fiftieth anniversary commemorations of the end of the war, I saw just as many old people as the year before selling their belongings on the streets. There were also thousands of bemedalled Second World War veterans swigging from open vodka bottles as they marched through the streets, celebrating past triumphs when the Soviet Union had crushed Nazi Germany. Perhaps sensing that there was more glory in Russia's past than in its present and future, Jeremy took Jean Pelletier, Eddie Goldenberg, and me to visit Moscow's dead. At the Kremlin wall, we admired the graves of Joseph Stalin, Yuri Andropov, Leonid Brezhnev, the cosmonaut Yuri Gagarin as well as that of John Reed, the legendary American journalist, the hero of the movie *Reds*, who wrote *Ten Days that Shook the World* on the 1917 revolution. After a ghoulish look at the embalmed body of Lenin in his mausoleum on Red Square, we were treated to a visit to the Novodevichy cemetery, the last resting place of icons of the Soviet past such as Nikita Khrushchev (whose tomb, according to Jeremy, a connoisseur in these matters, was the most popular pilgrimage site in the complex), the famous composer Dimitri Shostakovich, long-time foreign minister Andrei Gromyko, and a variety of other figures who were constantly in the news when I was a child and young man. Our last stop was at a church where Jeremy showed us the face of modern Russia – a Russian mafia boss laid out on public view with powdered face and expensive suit, with tapers lit at the head of his open bier and gangsters serving as guards of honour. When we left Moscow, the old babushkas were still crouched on the street corners under grotesque signs advertising Western luxury products that only the new class of rapacious millionaires could afford.

Moscow Nuclear Summit – and Bucharest 1996

Moscow in April 1996 was a different world. The billboards flogging goods too expensive for most people, even in the West, and poorly clad old people selling their wares to make ends meet were still omnipresent. But the local authorities had cleaned up the city in honour of a summit of the Political Eight or P8 (the leaders of the G7 plus Russia) who were meeting to discuss a matter of the greatest importance. It was almost ten years since the explosion at Chernobyl and there were well-founded fears for the safety of the dozens of other Soviet-era nuclear reactors with the same design faults. The Russians had admitted pouring low-level nuclear liquid wastes into the Sea of Japan. The Norwegians had reported – and the Russians had not denied – that Russia continued to dump used nuclear reactor cores from old submarines into the Arctic Ocean. There was also the small matter of the sixty-eight tons of Soviet weapons-grade fissile material from old nuclear warheads that no one knew what to do with, still.

Prime Minister Chrétien, who had immersed himself in nuclear issues since his days as trade minister, took a leading role in the talks. A long-time supporter of using nuclear power to generate electricity, he had been responsible more than anyone else for convincing the Chinese government in 1994 to purchase CANDU reactors. And en route to Moscow in April 1996, he stopped off in Bucharest, Romania, to open the first unit of a

CANDU nuclear power complex in the nearby city of Cernavodă. I had never been to Romania but had the opportunity to take the measure of President Ion Iliescu when he came for lunch at NATO headquarters some years previously. I had asked myself whether someone who had worked with members of the army and security service – the Securitate – to profit from a bloody popular uprising against former dictator Ceauşescu by seizing control of the country in 1989, could be as much a democrat as he claimed. It seemed that he could. For in the interim, this former secretary-general of the Romanian Communist Party introduced reforms to set Romania on the road to a new democratic future. Leopards, it seemed, could change their spots.

The welcome President Iliescu gave to his Canadian guests could not have been warmer. He even laid on a presidential train to take the Canadian delegation from Bucharest to Cernavodă for the official ceremonies. At the site itself, there was ribbon cutting, a cluster of speeches, pride, and relief that the first phase of the project was finally finished. President Iliescu then appealed to the prime minister for Canadian support to complete another reactor unit. The prime minister responded positively and was anxious to find ways to help Romania raise the capital to fund its share of the costs. He then advanced his own suggestion. Why not create an integrated electricity grid with neighbouring Ukraine and Russia and sell them safe, surplus Cernavodă energy?

At the Moscow summit itself, after a day of talks, the leaders issued a communiqué in which the Russians said they would do better, and the rich visitors pledged more funds. Canada's main contribution was a proposal to consider using treated fuel, derived from highly enriched uranium taken from nuclear weapons, for our heavy water nuclear reactors. In a private meeting with President Kuchma of Ukraine and again during a courtesy call on President Yeltsin, the prime minister repeated the case he had made to Iliescu for an integrated electricity grid. Both expressed interest but Kuchma was too focused on the problems of obtaining funding to decommission Chernobyl to give the proposal the attention it deserved. And Yeltsin, who served us beer rather than coffee at eight in the morning, had a hangover.

Russia 1997

My final trip to Russia with the prime minister was in October 1997, this time to St. Petersburg as well as to Moscow. Jean Chrétien and Boris Yeltsin had, in the interim, developed a firm friendship, making a point of meeting bilaterally at the annual P8 summits and staying in touch by telephone. Like Chrétien, Yeltsin came from a humble background and was a populist. Yeltsin had been a stonemason and plasterer in his hometown of Sverdlovsk in the Urals. Canada's prime minister had worked in a paper mill in the summers during his university years. Boris Yeltsin, like Jean Chrétien, entered politics at an early age, assuming a senior position in his region's Communist Party in 1968, before being plucked from obscurity by Mikhail Gorbachev and brought to Moscow to head the local Communist Party structure and begin his march to the top. He, like Prime Minister Chrétien, had been written off as a spent political force, yet had bounced back to become leader of his country. Yeltsin's moment of glory was in August 1991 when he led the resistance to Moscow reactionaries who sought to return Russia to its old totalitarian communist ways, rallying the crowds from the top of a tank in the manner of Lenin during the 1917 revolution. His moment of shame occurred in October 1993 when he ordered the Russian tanks and artillery to open fire on the Russian White House, at that time home to the Russian Duma or parliament, to quell dissent from Russian legislators. And despite a bad heart, bouts of major depression, and binge drinking habits, he won election after election in the 1990s.

The previous twelve months had been bad ones for the president. In November 1996, he had undergone a difficult bypass operation. The following January, he dropped out of sight for a

prolonged period, ostensibly suffering from the flu. After Yeltsin
retired, he boasted that he had suffered from and covered up five
heart attacks in his years in office. No one, however, had been
fooled. The consensus of my counterparts in foreign capitals in
those years was that Yeltsin would die before he completed his
term of office.[43] My staff quietly prepared plans (that I kept
hidden in my office safe) for the prime minister to attend a state
funeral in Moscow at short notice. Yeltsin, however, proved
everyone wrong, deciding to stop drinking, to take care of his
health, and to pull himself together. It was therefore a very much
alive if pale and subdued Russian president, accompanied by his
watchful wife, Naina, who hosted the prime minister and his wife
on their official visit to Russia in October 1997.

The first event was an informal Sunday lunch at the presidential dacha. Zavidovo, Joseph Stalin's former hunting lodge,
stood in the middle of an immense forest, thirty minutes by helicopter from Moscow. We had arrived late the previous night
from Ottawa and our tired bodies were still on Canadian time.
One did not, however, turn down a personal invitation to lunch
from the president of Russia. Yeltsin originally wanted Chrétien
to start the day with a bear and boar hunt but the prime minister had begged off, saying that hunting was not his sport. That was
true, but he probably also remembered the photos of Brian
Mulroney posing with dead animals in the Zavidovo forest when
he had accepted a similar offer to go hunting with the Russian
president some years earlier. The howls of outrage from animal
lovers in Canada were probably heard in Moscow.

En route from Moscow, we flew over one impoverished
village after another, joined together by two-lane pothole-filled
roads. Scattered among them, like modern-day reincarnations of
the estates of the aristocracy dispossessed of their holdings in
the October Revolution, were huge western-style mansions,
many still under construction, the country homes of Russia's
new capitalist class. It could have been a late fall day at the prime

minister's country home at Harrington Lake in the Gatineau Hills at that time of the year. The trees, however, were birch and poplar rather than maple, oak, pine, and spruce. The leaves had fallen, just as they had in the Gatineau Hills, and the wet ground was golden on that grey October morning. Arriving at the dacha, we walked past chefs in military uniform standing stoically in a light rain, manning an array of spluttering barbecues. Inside it was warm Russian hospitality of a nature I do not imagine Joseph Stalin ever offered to his guests, who never knew whether they would be departing for the Gulag after dessert. The Yeltsins were accompanied by an interpreter, a protocol officer, and my opposite number – the president's diplomatic advisor (who had replaced the one I had met in 1994). They greeted Mr. and Mrs. Chrétien, the prime minister's escort officer, a Canadian interpreter, and me at the door, and took us to one end of the combined living room–dining room for drinks beside a roaring fire. The president reached for sparkling water saying that Mrs. Yeltsin had laid down the law – no more alcohol.

Then it was time for lunch. Yeltsin's table was laden with every type of Russian delicacy imaginable – three or four different sorts of caviar, salads, pickled eels, pâtés, and olives. The first course was a delicious borscht soup. There was then a succession of dishes – barbecued food was borne in from outside all afternoon – pike, carp, eel, wild boar, pheasant, venison, and duck, as well as beef and pork. The four wine glasses in front of each guest were kept full with the best that the Crimean vineyards had to offer. Too bad it was the middle of the night according to my internal clock – all I wanted to do was to climb back on the helicopter, return to the hotel, and go to bed.

Twenty courses and six hours later, we took our leave and returned to Moscow. It had been a social afternoon and the discussion was on family and other personal matters. Nevertheless, the two leaders agreed to stage a meeting at the North Pole to highlight our common northern frontiers and to announce

Russia's decision to send a delegation to Ottawa in December to sign the treaty banning anti-personnel mines.[44] Neither would happen. The prime minister would discover that Canada did not have aircraft capable of transporting and landing him safely at the North Pole; the Russian president would learn that he did not have the backing of his government to sign the treaty.

The next day, in a departure from past practice, the president offered us a choice of coffee or tea at the official talks – beer was no longer on the menu for these morning meetings. When the prime minister visited Moscow in May 1995 for the fiftieth anniversary commemorations of the end of the war, and again in April 1996 for the special summit on nuclear safety, Yeltsin had been mildly drunk. In fact, I had rarely seen him when he was completely sober. At the July 1994 Naples P8 summit, he had walked up to me at a reception to seize my hand in a rough friendly grasp, not knowing and not caring who I was. He was heavily overweight and his face was blotched, florid, and swollen, giving the impression that he had just spent the night sleeping face down on the concrete in an alley with a group of drunks. The following year at the Halifax summit, he disgraced himself by drinking too much, and collapsed in a drunken stupor in an elevator in the presence of his mortified wife and his Canadian liaison officer.

The two leaders promised to do something to increase trade from its almost derisory levels (Canada was Russia's twenty-third-largest trading partner) and to develop closer ties on arctic matters. Yeltsin, however, was dismissive of the prime minister's concerns about Russian mafia extortions against Canadian investors in Russia. He also reneged on his commitment, made less than twenty-four hours earlier, to sign the anti-personnel mines treaty. When the prime minister raised the issue, the Russian ministers of foreign affairs and finance interjected to flatly tell their leader that Russia should not and could not afford to sign on. The Russian armed forces, they said, relied on anti-personnel mines to protect hundreds of nuclear weapons storage sites – there were neither troops nor resources available to provide an equal level of alternative security. Yeltsin turned to the prime minister and said that if he could convince their mutual friend Bill Clinton to sign the treaty, then he, Boris Yeltsin, would override his ministers and ensure that Russia followed suit. He then shrugged his shoulders and smiled as if to say: "You see, I would sign now if I could but these people won't let me." The drunken Yeltsin, I thought, would never have allowed himself to be spoken to in this manner before foreign visitors, and would have fired his ministers on the spot. And before the end of the decade, it would become clear that Canadian hopes for a breakthrough in economic ties with Russia would not be realized, frustrated by mafia shakedowns, a Wild West business atmosphere, and red tape.

After Moscow, we boarded the Airbus to fly to St. Petersburg (founded in 1703 by Peter the Great as Russia's window on the west and bastion against invasion) for the final part of the official visit. Riding at top speed in a motorcade with sirens wailing is not the best way to take the measure of a city. My field of vision was made worse by a cold fall rain and by the condensation that collected on the windows of our passenger van. I caught glimpses of magnificent cream and yellow eighteenth-century buildings, more Central European in architectural style than Russian, as we rolled down Nevsky Prospect, the splendid boulevard in the heart of the city. Off in the fog, the driver told us, was the Peter and Paul fortress, used in Tsarist times as a political prison for such notable inmates as Dostoevsky, Trotsky, and Gorky. In another direction was the Hermitage, one of the greatest museums of the world, incorporating within its wings the former Winter Palace of the Tsars. Later when taken on a tour, I saw priceless treasures, but could not help wondering how much sweat the peasants of old Russia had to expend to allow their feudal overlords to purchase them.

The next day, en route to the airport, we stopped at the Piskariovskoye Memorial Cemetery for the war dead to pay our respects. Some decades earlier, I had read Harrison Salisbury's great non-fiction classic description of the siege of the city, then known as Leningrad. In *The Nine Hundred Days* he describes in poignant detail the incredible fortitude of the people who endured starvation rations, German shelling, disease, and secret-police brutality from August 28, 1941, to January 27, 1944. Almost a million people, he reported, had perished in the siege and I had found it difficult to come to terms with death on such a scale. Once at the cemetery, I began to understand. I followed behind as Mr. and Mrs. Chrétien walked down a pathway through mounds of heaped earth, each holding the remains of hundreds of thousands of civilians. The snow was lightly falling. From off in the distance, I could hear Tchaikovsky's funeral march. Young soldiers in ceremonial dress, their fur hats and uniforms slowly turning white, goosestepped in a Russian army ceremonial march down the walk ahead of the official party and stood at attention while the prime minister laid a wreath at the monument to the dead. I will remember the visit to Piskariovskoye long after dirty snow in Red Square, official talks in Moscow and St. Petersburg, lunch in Zavidovo, elegant Kremlin drawing rooms, splendour in the Hermitage, Lenin in his mausoleum, KGB dirty tricks, and even rough-hewn Yeltsin have faded from my memory.

I I

Latin America and the Caribbean

The prime minister was also at home in Latin American affairs.
The neighbourhood was huge and messy. It was, however, a Latin
world, and the prime minister was at heart a Latin.

The Miami Summit

Prime Minister Chrétien eagerly embraced Latin America, just as
he did the Asia-Pacific region and Russia, as a promising new
frontier for Canadian trade, investment, and political involvement. The Miami Summit of the Americas, hosted by President
Bill Clinton from December 9 to 11, 1994, was of key importance
in influencing his evolving views. True, the summit, the first since
Western Hemisphere leaders got together in Punta del Este,
Uruguay, in 1967, was an administrative jumble of gigantic pro-
portions. Meetings started late. The ferry transporting leaders to
their nearby island retreat became stuck in the mud. Official
chauffeurs provided by the host nation to transport dignitaries
became lost. But no one cared – all thirty-four democratically
elected heads of state or government of the Americas were there.
President Fidel Castro was the notable exception, barred from
participating because Cuba was not a democracy. President
Clinton was warm and effusive and often to be seen bonding with
one of his guests in the Latin American style, his arm around his
interlocutor's shoulder as he earnestly engaged in conversation.
The weather was warm and the mood of the leaders was upbeat.
More important, the summit was a substantive success. The
leaders quickly reached a consensus to put in place a hemispheric

free trade arrangement by 2005, as well as measures to strengthen regional democracy.

The prime minister had arrived in Miami after two discouraging days in grey, rainy Budapest at the annual summit of the Organization for Security Co-operation in Europe. The mood in the Canadian delegation in the Hungarian capital was even more morose than the general gloom in the conference centre, for word had come that Lucien Bouchard, leader at that time of the Opposition Bloc Québécois in Parliament, was dying of the dreaded flesh-eating disease, necrotizing fasciitis. He may have been a separatist but he was well-known and liked on a personal basis by almost everyone on our team from his days as ambassador to Paris and as a veteran Ottawa politician. We were all relieved when he defied the odds and pulled through, even if a leg had to be amputated. At the summit itself, some fifty European leaders, including the newly independent states of the Balkans and the Caucasus, had spent their time looking backwards, talking of war, and venting their spleen over past injustices. We had all been relieved to leave the old world of Europe, still struggling with the ghosts of its past, for the new world of the Americas.

For in Miami, the leaders looked to the future. In Miami, Canada counted in a way it had not in Budapest. And in Miami, the prime minister was a star. It did not hurt that Prime Minister Chrétien knew Florida well, was comfortable in this winter capital of Canadian snowbirds, and at home in Latin American affairs. The neighbourhood was huge and messy. It was, however, a Latin world, and the prime minister was at heart a Latin. As well, the main issue on the agenda – trade liberalization – was one that he strongly supported and on which he was more of an expert than most other leaders around the table. His new Latin American peers, for their part, liked him and invited him into their club where everyone knew each other intimately. They were anxious for Canada to put some meat on its long-proclaimed intention of fulfilling its destiny as a true country of the Americas and be more than a North American extension of Europe. Countries big and small wanted Canada's help to balance the overwhelming weight of the United States in the hemisphere – and not just in the often sterile debates at the Washington headquarters of the OAS.

South of the Rio Grande

The prime minister wasted no time in following up the contacts he made in Miami. He first of all set aside the countries of Andean South America – Venezuela, Colombia, Ecuador, Bolivia, and Peru[45] – which were plagued by corruption, high levels of criminality, thriving drug underworlds, huge class and income differences, and in some cases, endemic guerilla warfare. His priorities were Mexico and the three Southern Cone countries of Brazil, Argentina, and Chile, the largest, most dynamic countries of Latin America. He calculated that his personal involvement in getting to know their leaders was most likely to make a difference in expanding trade and investment and in pushing ahead the conversion of NAFTA into an Americas-wide free trade zone. His timing could not have been better. Mexico had just become a member of NAFTA and wanted to use Canada as a political and economic counterweight to the United States. Brazil, Argentina, and Chile had abandoned their harsh authoritarian rulers with the taste for torturing and "disappearing" suspected dissidents that had made their countries the shame of the international community in the 1970s and 1980s. Their new governments espoused liberal democracy and embraced the tenets of market economics under the globalization doctrines of the 1990s: deregulation, efficient tax collection, privatization of state enterprises, slimming down of the government sector, and the dismantling of trade and investment barriers with the outside world.

In the four years I was with him, the prime minister initiated two visits to Mexico (but was only able to go once) and led a similar number of missions to the countries of the Southern

Cone. He returned to Chile for a third visit to attend the follow-up Summit of the Americas in Santiago in April 1998. The visits he made in January 1995 and January 1998 to Argentina and Chile would be the first ever by a Canadian prime minister. The leaders of the chosen countries were received with all the honours during their return travels to Canada. The numbers racked up on the two outgoing missions ($2.76 billion and $1.78 billion respectively) would not be as spectacular as those achieved in the three Team Canada safaris to Asia, but a larger number of small and medium-sized companies participated and the number of deals concluded was impressive: 306 contracts, lines of credit, memorandums of understanding, and investment agreements. The real benefit, as it was for the Asia-Pacific region, was in creating a greater awareness in Mexico and the Southern Cone of Canada, and inside Canada of Latin America.

Mexico – and the Ice Storm
In March 1994, the prime minister arrived in Mexico just before the murder of the presidential candidate of the ruling party; the official visit never recovered. His next visit to Mexico was scheduled for January 1998 on the first leg of a Team Canada mission to Latin America. But then came the ice storm of the century. At the critical point, I was home late in the evening when Stella, my faithful mutt, put her head on my knee, pressed down hard, and fixed me with pleading eyes. It was time, she was telling me, to tear myself away from my preparations for the mission and take her for an evening walk. Outside, we both slipped and skidded down the street in a mist-like rain that had been falling for days, coating everything with layers of ice. Hydro and telephone wires were sagging and tree branches were bent but it was a scene of great beauty. It was a privilege, I felt, to live in a country where one could enjoy the rigours of four real seasons. One hour later, back inside, I was not so certain. A thunderous crack roused me from my sleepy review of Canada–Latin America trade statistics and

brought a trembling Stella back seeking comfort. The hundred-year-old tree in our front yard, unable to bear the weight of the ice, had split asunder. The lights flickered, went out – and would not come back on for ten days as power lines collapsed throughout the region. Stella and I made our way up the darkened stairs to join the other members of the family in spending a night under siege. The staccato sound of splitting limbs rent the air, ice-covered branches crashed onto the roof, and trees throughout the neighbourhood came smashing down, adding to the general destruction. I felt like Snoopy in the *Peanuts* comic strip, huddling in a First World War bunker as enemy artillery rained down.

The zone of devastation, I learned when I turned on my battery-powered radio the next morning, stretched from Kingston, Ontario, to Quebec City. Before the crisis was over, millions of trees would be destroyed, 120,000 kilometres of power lines would come down, a million Canadians would be deprived of electricity, 100,000 people would be driven into shelters, 14,000 troops would be called out, and twenty-five people would die. Meanwhile, nine premiers, two territorial leaders, and 531 business people, representing 482 companies in all were making their way to Ottawa to set out on a giant trade mission to Latin America. A worried prime minister holed up at 24 Sussex Drive with his political advisors to consider his options. They told him that it was unthinkable for him to leave the country when it was faced with a domestic crisis on such a scale.

By this time, I had abandoned our now cold and damp home, bundled wife, son, and dog into a taxi, and sought refuge in a hotel with an independent electricity supply. Calling the prime minister from my room, I told him that we could not cancel a Team Canada mission on such short notice without tremendous international economic and political costs, and it should proceed with or without him. Should he not lead the mission, however, the presidents of Mexico, Brazil, Argentina, and Chile would be deeply disappointed. Moreover, the premiers would be unhappy if the prime minister were not leading the mission. On the other hand, if he were to leave with Team Canada, there would cries in Canada that he was abandoning the nation when it needed him most; the resulting bad publicity would undermine the credibility of the mission. Why not, I suggested, ask Governor-General Roméo Leblanc to take charge of the mission in its initial stages? The status-conscious Latin American presidents and premiers would be happy with a vice-regal representative in charge. The prime minister could catch up with the rest of us in Latin America when the crisis was under control.

The prime minister heard me out in a stony silence, before muttering that he had doubts about the constitutionality of the governor-general carrying out an executive role normally reserved for a member of the government, and then hanging up. I knew what was really troubling him. Team Canada missions were dear to his heart in a way few people could understand. He revelled in the opportunity to celebrate the accomplishments of his beloved Canada abroad, accompanied by the best and brightest of Canada's entrepreneurial, academic, and provincial political class. His intellectual batteries were recharged by his contacts with foreign political, economic, cultural, communications, and academic elites. He thrived on the fast pace and heavy schedule of the programming. He rejoiced in the heavy publicity both in Canada and abroad. The thought of not participating in the Latin American program, even for a few days, must have been hard to swallow. He had no choice, however, and it was a deeply disappointed prime minister who waved goodbye as the governor-general led Team Canada as it departed for Mexico.

In Mexico it was déjà vu for me. The Mexican police, just as they had in 1994, snaked our long convoy from the airport to the city at breakneck pace through the afternoon traffic. We checked into the same massive hotel where we had stayed four years previously. We returned to the presidential residence of Los Pinos where the Canadian delegation had been received for an official reception but had been disinvited to dinner after the news of the assassination of presidential candidate, Luis Donaldo Colosio Murrieta. In my imagination, the meal set for the prime minister in 1994 had been kept warm for four years and was now being served to the premiers. And once again, the Mexican government was faced with a crisis involving the ruling Institutional Revolutionary Party. This time, local members of the party had murdered forty-five Indians in the troubled state of Chiapas where an uprising by poor indigenous people under the leadership of a charismatic leader, Sub-Commandante Marcos of the Zapatista Army of National Liberation, had been in progress since January 1994.

The media accompanying Team Canada were, of course, more interested in this bad news story than they were in the business deals. They also focused on the culture of corruption linked to massive and growing drug trafficking by a proliferation of major Mexican crime cartels specializing in the importation of cocaine from South America and its exportation to the United States that was rotting the institutions of Canada's new NAFTA partner from within. The president addressed these problems squarely in his talks with the premiers, admitting that Mexico still had a long way to go before it eliminated the roots of rural and indigenous unrest and endemic criminality. The premiers, more interested in promoting trade than discussing human rights and political issues, listened politely but did not ask questions.

Mrs. Chrétien came into her own during this trip, filling in for the prime minister during official hospitality and ceremonial occasions until he could join the others. As a long-standing lover of Latin American culture who was able to speak Spanish fluently, she was well-suited for the role. By this time, she had started attending the annual conferences of spouses of heads of state and government of the Americas[46] and knew personally most of her Latin American counterparts. As someone who did not seek the spotlight and who did not have an office and budget for a role separate from that of her husband, she had been initially reluctant to be involved. She was prepared to do her bit, however, as part of the strategy to put Canada on the map as a leading player in the Americas. Louise Léger, Canada's ambassador to Panama (and later to Costa Rica), who was the senior official at the conferences, told me Mrs. Chrétien did her country proud both in her ideas on the situation of women and children in poverty and in the friends she made for Canada. For example, she spent as much time with the Caribbean participants as with the Latin Americans, and helped bridge the cultural gap between Spanish, French, and English-speakers.

Brazil

Never having served in my foreign service career in Brazil, this South American giant was to me just a jumble of overly facile stereotypes. Pelé, the greatest football player of all time, the cult movie *Black Orpheus*, samba music, the Rio carnival, beautiful women, Copacabana beach, and Sugar Loaf Mountain clashed in my mind with *favela* slums, corrupt police, the destruction of the rain forest, and enormous social and economic disparities. I was little wiser after my trips there in 1995 and 1998 – there was just too much to absorb in too short a time. Each time, Brasilia, the soulless, artificial capital of two million people (laid out in the shape of a bent bow and arrow, and constructed on a plateau on a tropical savannah some 1,200 kilometres from Rio de Janeiro by President Juscelino Kubitschek in the 1950s), was an obligatory stop. Each time, after a long flight from the north, we descended through low-hanging clouds to arrive tired and irritable in the oppressive humidity of a southern hemisphere summer. Each time, equally fatigued and bad-tempered members of the accompanying Canadian press contingent sat grumpily through the briefings of the local ambassador and complained at being fed a diet of business-related good news stories. Each time, we travelled in minivans down wide boulevards that seemed to lead nowhere to official meetings with members of the government.

Each time, we were invited to the standard official lunch, given to all visiting delegations, with a cross-section of the curious local establishment. Each time, we attended boring official receptions at the residence of the Canadian ambassador of the type I had hosted more times in my own diplomatic life than I care to remember. And each time, we followed up our visit to the national capital with a visit to a major state city: in 1995, to Rio de Janeiro, eleven million in population and cultural capital of the nation and, in 1998, to São Paulo City, the twenty-million strong capital of the state of the same name.

My visits to these two busy port cities brought back memories of one of my first jobs in Foreign Affairs spent working as an analyst in the Foreign Intelligence division in the early 1970s. Writing reports for the then Canadian Joint Intelligence Committee on the vicious urban warfare being waged in Rio de Janeiro and São Paulo City between young left-wing revolutionaries and the brutal secret services of the dictators of the period, formed part of my duties. The issues were far removed from the reality of my everyday existence in Ottawa until the day I stumbled across information that indicated that three ambassadors in Rio de Janeiro, Canada's included, were on a kidnap list. Analysis, however, not action, was the mandate of our unit, and I had to convince my director that it was time to become operational. He gave in and allowed me to send a cryptic message to our ambassador telling him to cancel all social engagements, fortify his residence, and avoid travel unless accompanied by a small army of bodyguards. Canada's ambassador was thus spared (while the others were taken prisoner) – although he complained loud and often about the inconvenience my instructions had caused him.

From what I could see from the windows of my minivan in the high-speed motorcades that took us to the receptions and dinners offered by the state governors, the social-economic conditions that bred political violence in the 1970s had not changed in thirty years. One big difference in the 1990s, however, was that the army was in the barracks and the country was ruled by democratically elected leaders. Another was that Fernando Henrique Cardoso was president of Brazil. Next to Fidel Castro, he was the most charismatic leader in Latin America. Born into a privileged family, he made a name for himself internationally as a brilliant Marxist academic sociologist whose books heavily influenced development theory, and as a vocal opponent of the military dictatorships that ruled Brazil for so many years. After being arrested and imprisoned, he went into exile in the 1970s, returning in the 1980s to enter politics as a senator. Successively foreign and finance minister, he made his mark and became enormously popular by the measures he introduced to stabilize Brazil's currency, effectively ending the runaway inflation that had blighted Brazil's economy for so many years. He was elected president in 1994.

President and prime minister had hit it off during Chrétien's first visit in 1995 and Cardoso was disappointed that the prime minister could not make it to Brasilia in 1998. The Brazilian leader thus hurried to São Paulo City to greet his Canadian counterpart on learning that the prime minister had extricated himself from the ice-storm crisis and was flying from Ottawa to join the others for the business portion of Team Canada's mission. Their official talks in the state capital were animated and friendly, but personal chemistry was not enough to overcome fundamental differences between the two countries. Canada's Bombardier and Brazil's Embraer were fighting for the same global short- and medium-range passenger aircraft market. Thousands of high paying jobs were at stake, as was the national prestige of each country. An element of sibling rivalry was also present which meant that while relations between Canada and Brazil intensified, they did not improve. Canada was a G7 country and not bashful about mentioning this fact to those not similarly blessed. Brazil was the giant dominating country of South America and seemed to resent Canada's arrival on the Latin American scene with its energy and initiatives. Brazil's focus was on consolidating the local customs union, MERCOSUR, to which it belonged with Argentina, Uruguay, and Paraguay. Moreover, in contrast to Canada, Brazil was in no hurry to conclude a hemispheric free-trade deal. The two leaders agreed to make a last-ditch effort to resolve the Bombardier-Embraer problems by naming personal representatives to try to come up with a solution. The initiative would fail, however, and the two governments would dump the matter in the hands of the WTO for resolution.

Argentina

In my first visit to Argentina with the prime minister in January 1995, I could not get its past out of my mind. As an aboriginal Canadian, I was sensitive to its inhumane record in dealing with its native people, first slaughtering tens of thousands in the bitter frontier wars of the nineteenth century and now pretending that today's remnants did not exist. In the 1930s and 1940s, Argentina barely hid its sympathy for the Axis powers, and after the war it became a country of choice for Nazi war criminals, including Adolph Eichmann, himself fleeing war-crimes trials in Europe. And who could forget the dirty wars and the anti-Semitic violence of the 1970s and 1980s, so thoroughly documented by the survivors, when the Argentinian military tortured and killed some thirty thousand of their young people? As Canadian ambassador to NATO in the 1990s, I listened puzzled when a visiting Argentinian foreign minister claimed that his country was at heart European and for that reason sought membership in the North Atlantic Alliance. He implied an unspoken Argentinian lament for the bad luck that located his country in South America close to smelly neighbours with dark skins rather than in Europe, alongside their cultural and racial peers.

I was also aware that Argentina was the distorted mirror image of Canada – what our country might have been if our leaders had made different economic and political choices earlier in our history. On the eve of the twentieth century, Canada and Argentina were twins at opposite ends of the Americas. Our populations were roughly equal in size, as were our economies; our climates were somewhat similar and our peoples at that time were drawn in large measure from European immigrants. But the Argentinians made strategic mistakes that Canada did not make. Canada opted at an early stage for an open economic model that rewarded free trade while the Argentinians adopted the corporate state, threw up tariff barriers to the outside world, and endured a century of coups and counter coups. Argentina also indulged in a fierce machismo rivalry with Brazil that impeded trade throughout most of its history, only agreeing to membership in a free-trade association with Brazil as the century ended. Canada, unlike Argentina, never sought to go head-to-head with its giant neighbour and prospered in the security and economic shadow of the democratic, prosperous, and relatively benign United States.

However, I returned enthusiastically with Team Canada in 1998. For I discovered in 1995 that Argentina was more than its past. Buenos Aires in January was also Toronto in August – hot humid weather, wide empty boulevards with the population on the Rio del Plata rather than in Muskoka, old-world courtesy, cappuccinos Italian-style, and intimate restaurants. It was old couples dancing the tango in the park to the music from portable CD players, statues on every corner to long-forgotten heroes, barbecues, and Eva Perón a tourist attraction in her family mausoleum in the fashionable Recoleta Cemetery. It was warm hospitality from President Menem and his colleagues who twice in three years came back to their capital in the middle of their summer holidays to host dinners for the prime minister and his team at the presidential residence, meals featuring superb Argentinian beef and gaucho music.

Menem was a character straight out of a Hollywood B-movie, complete with facelift, platform shoes, slicked-back hair, and playboy image. Born Muslim in a Syrian immigrant family, he had been a fighter for human rights in his youth. He later converted to Christianity and embraced free-market economic reforms when he was elected president in 1989, selling off state enterprises and pegging the peso, the national currency, to the American dollar. At the time of the prime minister's visits, the president was riding high in the polls and the economy was doing well. Menem was, however, as shallow intellectually as Cardoso was profound. He was also, it appeared, corrupt. In 2001, two years after his term as president expired, he would spend five months in jail on arms-smuggling charges. And the Argentinian economy, bankrupted by corruption and the failure of Menem's economic policies, would almost collapse. In 2003, he would flee the country just ahead of the law along with a new wife, a model who had been Miss Universe in 1987.

Chile

Santiago was only a short hop over the Andes from Buenos Aires. At the Miami summit in December 1994, President Clinton, President Zedillo, Prime Minister Chrétien, and Chilean president Eduardo Frei announced at a hurriedly called press conference that a decision had been made to allow Chile to join NAFTA as the "fourth amigo." The deal was, however, contingent on President Clinton obtaining "fast track" approval from Congress. For under the United States Constitution, Congress has jurisdiction over commerce and its members have the authority to influence trade bills by affixing new clauses when trade agreements, negotiated by the administration, come up for approval. Under what was called the "fast track" procedure,[47] American administrations usually sought authority to present final trade packages to Congress for approval on a take it or leave it basis without amendments. President Clinton, however, never succeeded in obtaining "fast track" authority from Congress during the life of his presidency. Canada and Chile, not wanting to wait indefinitely for the administration to sort out its problems with Congress, then negotiated their own bilateral free-trade deal, signed in late 1996 and coming into effect in 1997. Chile became Canada's closest friend in South America. The Canadian mining and energy industries were delighted. They had already invested some two billion dollars in Chilean mines, refineries, gas wells, and pipelines; the total investment would double and then double again in the next three years.

During the 1995 visit, Canadian ambassador Marc Lortie and his wife, Pat – friends and colleagues of mine for many years – invited me and the members of the prime minister's team to their residence for a late evening meal after we had briefed the press and prepared ourselves for the next day. Their residence was a magnificent villa high in the hills exposed to the stars above a city hidden below in a cloud of smog. Marc told me that his next-door neighbour was Augusto Pinochet Ugarte, no longer dictator but still casting an ominous shadow over the state. Despite his crimes, he had arranged to have himself appointed senator for life, a position that provided immunity from prosecution for the crimes he had committed as dictator. I shivered involuntarily. For who of my generation will ever forget the fate of Salvador Allende, leader of a coalition of left and centrist parties who had been sworn in as president in democratic elections in 1970?

Early in the morning of September 11, 1973, the Chilean navy, under the direction of Pinochet, seized the port of Valparaiso. Allende barricaded himself in La Moneda – the historic presidency building – and was joined by civilian snipers who congregated on neighbouring buildings as the army brought up tanks, and the air force sent in bombers. After an uneven battle, Allende committed suicide. Some 2,500 people were killed in the fighting; an equal number of so-called sympathizers including priests, students, trade unionists, and advisors to Allende were rounded up, confined in a stadium, tortured, and killed. Then followed seventeen years of the same, despite the efforts of Amnesty

International, the Catholic Church, and Costa-Gavras, the famous film director. Costa-Gavras produced the internationally acclaimed film *Missing*, about a journalist, Charles Horman, who was tortured and killed by Chilean security agents at the time of the coup.

When we returned in 1998, more and more Chileans were calling for Pinochet to be stripped of his parliamentary immunity and to be made to stand trial. Nothing happened at the time, but the ground was shifting under the feet of the aging torturers, providing hope that justice would some day be done.

Forgotten in the Americas

The leaders of the small countries of the Commonwealth Caribbean and Central America actively courted Prime Minister Chrétien in these years. The prime minister of Trinidad and Tobago said only half in jest that he would be honoured if Canada's prime minister could consider himself to be the "godfather of the Caribbean." It was the same with the Central Americans, who felt abandoned by the United States and wanted Canada to be their new international protector. Although separated by language, history, and political tradition, the small states of the Commonwealth Caribbean and of Central America faced similar challenges. They desperately needed access to the protected markets of the developed world, large inflows of aid, and a country willing to champion their interests internationally. Lacking technical expertise, they wanted help in the deliberations at the World Trade Organization in Geneva and political support during the negotiations for the Free Trade Agreement of the Americas.

The prime minister would have liked, I am sure, to have been able to do more for them. He knew the English-speaking island states intimately from his days as minister of Trade and Commerce and from his frequent holidays there in the past. He met their leaders at formal summits twice in the years I was with him, and even invited them to travel with him on the Airbus from Nassau to the April 1998 Summit of the Americas in Santiago. Their premiers and presidents came for lunches and dinners at 24 Sussex Drive during their frequent private visits to Canada. He liked them and they liked him, especially his informality and sense of humour. President Cheddi Jagan of Guyana, when he lay dying at the Walter Reed hospital in Washington, stunned his family by emerging briefly from a coma to gesture for a pen and pencil. The message he scrawled before fading back into unconsciousness and death was an appeal to see Prime Minister Chrétien once again.

With twelve votes in the United Nations and other international organizations, the countries of the Commonwealth Caribbean possessed an international influence disproportionate to their size. They unhesitatingly threw their support behind major Canadian initiatives, joining us in opposing the application of American laws outside that country's borders, and backing our campaign to ban anti-personnel mines. And although Canada did not have the same historical and linguistic ties with the countries of Central America, Prime Minister Chrétien hit it off with their leaders at the December 1994 Miami summit. Responding to their invitation, he dropped in to meet them in summits in San José, Costa Rica, at the tail end of his January 1995 trade mission to Latin America. They, in turn, flew to Ottawa for a follow-up summit in May 1996.

The summits with Commonwealth Caribbean and Central American leaders alike were elaborately prepared affairs with detailed agendas and much bonhomie. They achieved little. For despite Canada's brave words in the WTO about helping developing countries gain better access for their products in the markets of the north, our record was far from perfect. We still excluded footware and textiles, disproportionally important industries in developing countries, from our shores. The leaders of the Commonwealth Caribbean also had grievances with Canada. We continued, they pointed out, to expel hardened criminals back to their countries of origin in the Caribbean – more than five hundred annually – even though many of them had emigrated to Canada as children. Their criminal justice systems simply could not cope. Most also had constituents, relatives, and friends in Canada who were angry at the huge increases in visa fees imposed by Canada for immigrant applicants. And most importantly, Canada may have been an influential middle power, but its market was too small to replace those of the United States and the European Union, the world's economic superpowers.

The troubled late twentieth-century history of Grenada illustrates the plight of these forgotten states. In March 1996, Canada and the countries of the CARICOM, the regional organization dominated by Commonwealth Caribbean states, held their biennial summit in Grenada. Arriving with the prime minister at the Grenada International airport at Point Salines, I could not help thinking of the situation of Grenada and the countries of the Caribbean Basin a little more than a decade and a half earlier, when they were in the forefront of the Cold War struggle between east and west. At that time, the prime minister of Grenada was Maurice Bishop, a young charismatic lawyer who picked up "New Left" ideas as a student in London, seized power in 1979, and tried to install a gentler version of Castro's Cuba in his country. I had met him later that same year when I was director of the tiny Commonwealth Caribbean division in Foreign Affairs and he came to Ottawa as a guest of the Cuban embassy. His request to the Canadian government was for funding to build an airport to attract more tourists to Grenada. The project was sound but there was insufficient money in CIDA's budget to cover it. Bishop turned to Castro, who sent in construction crews and equipment to help the new revolutionary government, enraging the United States, which suspected the Cubans and Russians were building a military airfield in their backyard.

Bishop was then devoured by his own revolution in the fall of 1983. At that time I was ambassador to Cuba. A fellow ambassador was Leon Cornwall, a deceptively gentle Grenadian who came from time to time to our residence in Havana for family meals accompanied by his wife, a volunteer teacher of English in Cuban schools. Leaving town for Grenada without saying goodbye, he became head of the armed forces and joined more radical members of his government in seeking to move the revolution ahead more rapidly than Bishop wanted. When Bishop resisted, the gentle Cornwall and his men killed their charismatic leader and established an even more radical left-wing government. That was the signal President Reagan was waiting for. He sent in the Marines, who expelled the Cuban construction workers and imprisoned Cornwall and the other leaders of the putsch. After establishing a new pro-American government, the Americans finished the airport for the Grenadians and showered development assistance on the newly democratic country.

And what is the moral of this story? It is that the small countries of the Caribbean Basin were often better off during the Cold War when they could play off the United States, Britain, and Canada, the three so-called metropolitan powers, against Cuba (which was bankrolled at that time by the Soviet Union) for aid and commercial concessions. I myself attended secret high-level meetings in the early 1980s between Canadian, British, and American representatives in which we mapped out strategies to deal with regional instability and coordinated increased flows of aid to shore up the fragile small island countries. The countries of Central America likewise benefited from generous but long discontinued aid packages from the Americans as part of their efforts to beat back Cuban- and Nicaraguan-supported insurgencies. Now no one cared. I sensed that the leaders pleading for Prime Minister Chrétien to take them under his wing knew that there was little Canada could do for them. They seemed, however, grateful for the time he was willing to spend listening to their problems and took him at his word when he said Canada would be sympathetic to their special needs when detailed hemispheric free-trade negotiations were eventually launched.

Unfinished Business

The prime minister had one major piece of unfinished business to conclude in his Latin American agenda. At the Miami summit, he had proposed inviting Fidel Castro to the next summit. President Carlos Saúl Menem Akil of Argentina threw a road-block in the way saying that the Cuban president had to reform his totalitarian system before he could join the club. Undeterred, Prime Minister Chrétien followed up his words with action launching a major initiative involving secret diplomacy in Ottawa, Havana, and the Vatican, culminating in a groundbreaking visit to Cuba in April 1998 to see if Castro could be induced to do precisely that.

12

Bringing Fidel in from the Cold

*I had no idea why Castro was so mad at me. . . . Whatever the
reason, the rage in his eyes made me glad that I was a Canadian
able to depart with the prime minister rather than a Cuban who
would have felt the full wrath of an unhappy leader in a police
state!*

My Secret Mission

In August 1996, thirteen years after my posting to Cuba as ambassador, I returned to Havana as a secret emissary of Prime Minister
Jean Chrétien. My mission was to persuade President Fidel Castro
to introduce market and human rights reforms into Cuba. The
idea was not as ridiculous as it sounds. A fundamental debate was
taking place at this time in Castro's Council of Ministers on the
direction Cuba should take. Vice President Carlos Lage, Castro's
unofficial prime minister, a pleasant, balding, middle-aged medical
doctor who had earned his revolutionary spurs through service
in Angola, favoured taking greater steps toward a market economy.
Raul Castro, who had served in the Sierra Maestra mountains as
a *commandante* with the original group of revolutionaries, a die-
hard communist, the president's brother, minister of defence, and
Fidel's designated successor, opposed Lage. Castro, seriously ill
with an unknown ailment, leaned toward the position of Raul but
had not made up his mind in 1996 on how far he had to go to
introduce the hated market reforms.

For Cuba was in desperate shape. Over the previous decade
all the countries in Cuba's neighbourhood in Latin America

and the Caribbean had adopted liberal democratic governments. Farther afield, Cuba's erstwhile communist partners, with the exception of China, Laos, and Vietnam (who themselves were introducing market reforms) and the hermit country of North Korea, had turned to western-style forms of government. There was every reason to assume that the crumbling of communism in Central and Eastern Europe would soon be followed by its collapse in Cuba. The only question seemed to be whether change, when it came, would be peaceful as in Poland, Hungary, and the former Czechoslovakia, or whether it would be brutally rapid and violent as in Romania where Nicolae Ceauşescu and his wife were lined up against a wall and summarily shot after a drumhead trial on Christmas Eve 1989.

The Cubans had been abandoned by their former partners. Soviet aid, equivalent to more than three billion dollars per year throughout the 1980s, was cut back beginning in 1989, ending completely in 1992. Trade with the U.S.S.R. and its satellite states, totalling 87 per cent of all Cuban imports and exports in 1988, collapsed with the disappearance of the Soviet bloc in 1991. Castro had desperately hung on, permitting farmers to sell a limited amount of their output in private markets, loosening controls on small entrepreneurs, permitting foreign investment under tight controls, and legalizing the use of dollars in special shops where Cubans could spend remittances from family members abroad. Canada's ambassador to Cuba, Mark Entwistle, told me that conditions reached their nadir in the summer of 1993, by which time the Cuban economy had contracted by 60 per cent. When he arrived in Havana in July of that year, not a car was to be seen in the streets, people walked or rode bicycles to work, there were long lineups of people desperate to obtain food outside ration shops, and there were frequent cuts in electricity. True, conditions had slowly improved in 1994 and 1995, but life for the average Cuban was harsh. Castro had become more apocalyptical than usual in his public pronouncements, talking about "socialism or death," and rushing from trouble spot to trouble spot to calm the people. The full panoply of totalitarian measures, including intimidation by neighbours and the secret police, was deployed to keep order among a population increasingly more demoralized than disaffected.

And internationally in the post–Cold War world, Cuba no longer counted. Castro withdrew the last of his troops from Africa by the end of the 1980s. With the defeat of the Sandinistas in democratic elections in Nicaragua in 1990, he had no ideological soulmates in the Americas where Cuba's form of government seemed more and more irrelevant in an age when globalization, the market economy, and liberal democracy had become the norm. Spain and France, which had maintained reasonably warm relations with Cuba in the 1980s, reduced contacts to a minimum when Castro continued his long out-of-date policy of repression against political dissidents. Even the United States, Cuba's mortal enemy, largely ignored Castro, no longer worried that the Cuban model could provoke instability in Latin America or that Cuban territory might provide bases for Soviet attack on the American homeland.

Logic thus dictated that Castro might take advantage of a Canadian initiative to save at least part of his revolution before the deluge. After all, he had already introduced some market reforms, in particular allowing foreign investment by Canadian, Spanish, Italian, and Mexican companies. However, as Prime Minister Chrétien appreciated, Castro was a dedicated revolutionary and it would go contrary to everything he had fought for to make the sort of changes I had been authorized to propose. The Cuban leader had been in power for more than thirty-seven years and regarded himself, in an opinion shared by millions around the world, as the last surviving revolutionary icon of the twentieth century, a faithful ideological child of Karl Marx and a leader cast from the same mould as Lenin, Trotsky, Stalin, Mao, and Ho, with a Latin touch from his heroes, Simón Bolívar and

Team Canada at the Taj Mahal, January 1996. A somewhat
different experience from James Bartleman's earlier awe-inspiring
visit in 1973, when he saw it alone, at dawn.

Two very different examples of Canadian young people in
Islamabad, Pakistan, 1996. Craig Kielburger, above, explains to Jean
Chrétien and James Bartleman how he came to found "Kids
Can Free the Children," the international movement that inspired
his book, *Free the Children*, and has helped thousands of kids.

Also in Islamabad, the children of the Khadr family are introduced by their mother, who pleads for Canada's help in freeing her husband, imprisoned for terrorism. Later, he and some of the Khadr children shown here were revealed as active supporters of Osama bin Laden.

Moscow, May 1995. The prime minister meets the press, with
Ambassador Jeremy Kinsman at the far left, and his diplomatic
advisor white-haired in the centre.

October 1997. A more informal visit to Russia, this time to Boris Yeltsin's
Zavidovo dacha in the birch woods outside Moscow. Beside the window sit
Aline Chrétien, President Yeltsin (sober), his Russian advisor, and an interpreter.
Facing them across the table are Caroline Chrétien, James Bartleman,
Jean Chrétien, and Naina Yeltsin.

Jean Pelletier (right), Chaviva Hosek, and James Bartleman are in the receiving line to meet President Suharto, the prime minister of Indonesia in Jakarta, November 1994. Suharto had a very poor human rights record and at the APEC summit in Vancouver in November 1997, Canadians demonstrating against him were subjected to pepper spray by the RCMP.

A prouder moment from the author's years working with the prime minister. Here Jean Chrétien addresses the Ottawa Landmines Conference, December 1997. President Cornelio Sommaruga of the International Committee of the Red Cross, Lloyd Axworthy, U.N. Secretary-General Kofi Annan, and Nobel Peace Prize winner Jody Williams look on.

February 1998 in Havana. An angry Fidel Castro did not want to discuss human rights with James Bartleman, Canada's representative, shown here with an interpreter between them.

April 1998, a still angry Fidel Castro bids James Bartleman farewell at Havana airport. Even with a different interpreter, he still did not want to discuss human rights. The author was glad to leave.

Farewell in Rome, May 1998. A farewell photograph with colleagues:
from the left, Peter Donolo, David McInnis, Chaviva Hosek, Patrick Parisot,
Jean Pelletier, Dominique LeBlanc, and James Bartleman. They did not
involve him in partisan politics, leaving him free to resume his diplomatic career.

Jean Chrétien and his diplomatic advisor.

José Martí. His speeches, broadcast live by Radio Havana Libre around the world, were as implacably anti-American as ever, and reflected a determination to protect the revolution in Cuba to the end. And despite a growing dissent movement of a size and nature that would have been unthinkable during my years in Havana, Castro himself seemed to have retained a certain level of popularity among a population proud of the accomplishments of their revolution in health and medical research, in education, and in sports.

As for me, my memories of Cuba were bittersweet. From 1981 to 1983, I was Canada's man in Havana. It was a tempestuous, difficult, and yet professionally rewarding two-year posting, my first as an ambassador. Castro accorded me exceptional access and favour, while at the same time his sinister Ministry of the Interior was given free rein to play the dirtiest of dirty tricks imaginable on me and family. It poisoned my dog and that of my first secretary, arrested my driver on trumped-up charges, and harassed Canadian embassy staff.[48] At the same time, the Cuban president, for reasons best known to himself – but most likely because he wanted to send a signal of friendship to the then prime minister Pierre Trudeau – came frequently to Canada's official residence for dinners and discussions that lasted late into the night, reminiscing about his days as a revolutionary fighter and providing insights about revolution in the Third World. As a young ambassador, anxious to make a name for myself, I was flattered by the president's attention, and headquarters found my reporting useful. Marie-Jeanne and I were nevertheless relieved when I was called back early to headquarters in 1983 to take up another assignment.

Why Cuba?

Given the limited prospects for success, why would the prime minister make change in Cuba a foreign-policy priority? Our interests were not heavily engaged. Two-way trade amounted to less than $700 million per year (the bulk composed of exports of raw nickel for refining in Canada) or the equivalent to less than one-half of a day's transactions with the United States. Direct investments in hotels, the nickel industry, and other areas were less than $500 million, a relatively small sum compared to those elsewhere in Latin America which included $9 billion in Chile alone. True, more and more Canadian tourists were visiting Cuba (some 125,000 in 1995 compared to 25,000 when I was posted to Havana), but Canada had long since lost its place to Italy, Spain, and Mexico as the largest source of visitors. Political relations had not been close since the Trudeau years, the high point being the official visit of the prime minister and his wife to Cuba in 1976 during which Margaret sang to Castro and Pierre shouted "Viva Castro" to the crowd. The two leaders genuinely liked each other, perhaps because both were visionaries and romantics at heart. John Downing, a *Toronto Sun* editor who was part of the press contingent with the Trudeaus in Cuba, told me that Canada's prime minister spoke to him after returning from a snorkelling-fishing expedition with Castro. Trudeau was, he said, in awe of the "life force" of the Cuban president, who thought nothing of cleaning fish while treading water in shark-infested lagoons.

The two countries, however, remained so far apart on human rights, political freedoms, and foreign policy that the warmth of the relations between leaders was never reciprocated at the level of officials. When Cuba dispatched troops to Angola, the late foreign minister Mark MacGuigan phased out Canada's aid program and downgraded relations, despite Trudeau's objections. The Trudeau era gave way to the Mulroney one in 1984 and relations cooled. Mr. Mulroney's desire to strengthen ties with Washington, plus an incident during which my successor in Havana in 1984 fell asleep and snored gently during one of Castro's long-winded exposés at three o'clock in the morning on the evils of American capitalism, meant that the Canadian ambassador, guilty of *lèse-majesté*, was no longer in favour, and Castro no longer dropped by for all-nighters. Castro, however, seemed to have some regard for Mulroney, mentioning to me several times in the course of my talks with him in 1996 and 1998 how much he appreciated receiving a kind note from him during the Earth summit in Rio in 1992.

Policy of the Chrétien Government

The victory of the Liberals in 1993 brought to power a Canadian government prepared to be more sympathetic to Cuba. Led by Foreign Minister André Ouellet and Secretary of State Christine Stewart and supported by the prime minister, the government made Cuba eligible for Official Development Assistance once again after a sixteen-year hiatus. It then launched an intensified program of official contacts at the level of public servants and accorded greater trade and investment assistance, including help with trade delegations, to the Canadian private sector seeking to do business in Cuba. It was hoped that closer ties would prepare the ground for Canadian companies to take advantage of the trade and investment opportunities certain to follow when Cuba eventually adopted a market economy. To provide balance, the Canadian government also directed the embassy in Havana to strengthen its links with Cuban dissidents, and continued to take a high-profile role in the United Nations' criticism of Cuba's human-rights record. It was assumed that the many Canadians who knew Cuba from their holidays there over the years would welcome helping the Cuban people, although not necessarily the Cuban government, in their hour of need.

Prime Minister Chrétien took a strong personal interest in Canada's policy toward Havana, frequently raising the matter with me to seek my views, however dated. He did not have a romantic view of the revolution but wanted to help Cuba achieve a soft landing in the post–Cold War era and to increase the odds that the transition to liberal democracy, when it came, would be along the lines of the peaceful Hungarian rather than the violent Romanian model. He actively lobbied the other heads of state attending the first Summit of the Americas in Miami in December 1994 to establish "normal" diplomatic and trade relations with Cuba, pressed President Bill Clinton to eliminate Washington's trade embargo, and advocated (unsuccessfully) allowing Cuba to attend the next Summit of the Americas. At the fiftieth anniversary of the United Nations in New York in October 1995 the two leaders shook hands and had a brief conversation during which President Castro invited the prime minister to visit Cuba, and talked for some time in Spanish with Mrs. Chrétien, to whom he displayed old-world courtesy and charm.

In the remaining months of 1995 and the beginning of 1996, contacts between Canada and Cuba were stepped up, with high-level meetings between foreign ministers, parliamentary visits, and greater CIDA activity. The Cuban government, for its part, took a further series of modest measures to open its economy to foreign investment and to give greater freedom for small entrepreneurs to operate.

Meanwhile, in the United States, the strong anti-Castro Cuban community in Florida and New Jersey had been waiting since the end of the Cold War for the Castro regime to collapse. In 1996, six years after the fall of the Berlin Wall, they were growing impatient and decided to give history a shove by enlisting senators Helms and Burton to present draft legislation in the United States Senate to block foreign investment in Cuba, to stifle economic growth, and, they hoped, to increase opposition to Castro. Under the draft legislation directed mainly at Canadian, Mexican, and Spanish investors, American citizens would be authorized to sue in an American court any foreign national or company that purchased or made use of property that had been nationalized by the Cuban government after the revolution. Moreover, any individual found by the United States government to have exploited assets or property in Cuba belonging to an American would be denied entry into the United States.

The Canadian embassy in Washington strongly protested to

the State Department, saying that it was contrary to international law for one country to apply its laws extraterritorially to other countries. Foreign Affairs in Ottawa called in senior members of the American embassy and I telephoned the American national security advisor, Tony Lake, to make the same point. We were assured that the president would veto the bill. Not to worry. The Cuban air force then shot down two small American civilian aircraft piloted by anti-Castro Cuban exiles from an organization called "Brothers to the Rescue" who were on a mission dropping propaganda pamphlets on Havana on February 24, 1996. In the ensuing uproar, President Clinton signed the bill into law, saying that the Cuban behaviour left him with no choice; any presidential veto would have been subject to a Congressional override. He did, however, insert a provision giving himself the authority to grant six-month waivers for implementation if he was satisfied that members of the international community were making an effort to respect the spirit of the legislation.

Canada strongly protested to the Cubans for downing the aircraft and to the Americans for passing Helms-Burton. Ricardo Alarcón, President of the Cuban National Assembly, visited Ottawa and was received by the prime minister, who rejected Alarcón's attempts to justify Cuba's behaviour. Prime Minister Chrétien also told Alarcón, who repeated Castro's invitation to visit Cuba, that Canada looked forward to the day when there would be an end to human rights abuses and the installation of democracy in Cuba. Alarcón looked stunned, not expecting the head of government of an ostensibly friendly country to speak so candidly about such a sensitive issue. Perhaps he did not believe what he had heard.

Mission to Cuba

In early August, preparatory to chairing interdepartmental meetings to discuss the future of Canadian peacekeeping in Haiti, I visited Port-au-Prince for discussions with the Canadian force

commander, United Nations officials, and local Haitian authorities. A Canadian embassy official pulled me away from my mac-
aroni and cheese lunch at the Canadian military mess to take an
urgent call from the prime minister. He had, the prime minister
told me, been giving considerable thought to Canada's policy
towards Cuba and thought the time had come for him to visit
Havana for face-to-face discussions with Castro. Aware that
inquisitive electronic spy organizations from a half dozen countries made it their business to monitor all international telephone
calls having to do with Cuba, I suggested that we postpone our
discussion until I returned to Ottawa.

Back in Canada's capital, the prime minister told me that he
had just spent time in Florida where he had discussed Cuba with
a number of local Cuba watchers. They had told him that prior
to the destruction of the Brothers to the Rescue aircraft and the
retaliatory Helms-Burton legislation, there had been an emerging consensus, even among members of the exile community, that
Castro, for the first time since coming to power, might be interested in introducing democratic reforms and opening up his
closed society. There was a chance, according to the local experts,
that Castro might be tempted to follow the Chinese model by
introducing a market economy while keeping the lid on political reforms. Perhaps, the prime minister told me, it was time for
him to visit Cuba and talk directly with Castro. Who could tell?
If we did not try, we would never know if a Canadian initiative
would succeed.

My advice, for good or bad, was that a visit by Canada's prime
minister at that time would be premature. We were making
progress in forging closer ties with Cuba under our policy of
gradualist constructive engagement, but Castro should be made
to pay a price for the international credibility a visit by Canada's
leader would bring. Moreover, the United States was in the final
stages of a presidential campaign; it would not be in our interest
to have Canada's policy toward Cuba become a campaign issue.

Why not send me to Havana instead to see if Castro would be willing to deepen Cuba's relations with Canada and begin a dialogue on market and democratic reforms and human rights? If sufficient progress were achieved, he could follow up with a personal visit. I was no friend of the Castro regime but thought the initiative worth a try.

The prime minister agreed and told me to get Castro on the telephone. He wanted to be certain that the president took my mission seriously. And now that the prime minister had decided to act, he did not care who listened in to his telephone conversations. Ambassador Mark Entwistle relayed the request to his astonished Cuban contacts – it was unheard of for Western leaders to speak to Castro on the telephone. They acted promptly, however, contacting Castro, who was on vacation in Oriente province. The call took place within twenty-four hours. The president, speaking in guarded language through an interpreter, said that he would be pleased to meet with the emissary at the time and place of Canada's choosing. He made no comment when the prime minister told him that he of course would recall Jim Bartleman from his days as ambassador to Cuba in the early 1980s. Castro obviously did not remember me. Apparently I had not made as big an impression on the "maximum leader" as I had intimated to the prime minister.

I was nevertheless elated. At last my latent talents as a skilled diplomatic negotiator would be put to the test and recognized! Perhaps my "secret" mission would one day go down in the history books as the key to opening up Cuba to the winds of democratic change. One day, historians might compare my journey to that of Henry Kissinger when he visited China in July 1971, preparing the way for the visit of Nixon that changed the course of the Cold War. Never mind that my mission was no longer secret, the prime minister's call having assuredly been listened to by electronic intercept stations of the Americans, the British, the Russians, and probably the French and Mexicans as well. True, Castro did not seem to remember me, but perhaps that would give me a tactical advantage in the negotiations. When the best place I could obtain to fly to Cuba was in economy class in a seat marked by coffee stains, spilt wine, and cigarette burns on a dilapidated Cuban Airways aircraft, I consoled myself that true secret emissaries deliberately travelled by inconspicuous means. I even interpreted Foreign Minister Lloyd Axworthy's insistence that I be accompanied by Paul Durand, director-general for Latin America in Foreign Affairs, as an indication of my high status, not (as some might ungraciously think) as a sign that he did not trust me to act alone.

On arrival in Havana, Durand and I were met by senior officials of the Cuban government and quickly taken to meet Vice President Lage, who sought to find out exactly why I was in Cuba. Was I bearing a message from the Americans? Was the Canadian prime minister about to arrive? Was Canada about to announce a major new aid program? I resisted all attempts to ferret out the purpose of my mission. That was reserved for the ears of the president himself! The Cubans did not give up. We were taken to see Foreign Minister Roberto Robaina, a young man with black shoes, black socks, black pants, and black open-neck shirt with rolled-up sleeves, Miami-vice style, and a gold chain around his neck. The only thing he lacked was an earring and tattoo. He did not impress me, being a mere foreign minister. I dealt only with presidents, or if really necessary, with vice presidents. My lips remained sealed.

We were finally taken to see Ricardo Alarcón, who actually remembered me from the days when he was a senior official in the Foreign Ministry responsible for relations with Canada in the early 1980s. He was tough, and pressed me hard on the purpose of my mission. I resisted, telling him that I would discuss my business only with President Castro himself. Alarcón gave up and said that the president had returned from Oriente province and would meet me over dinner at the residence of the Canadian ambassador that evening. The discussion would be of a social nature only. The president would receive us in his office for official talks the next day. On returning to the official residence, Entwistle, Durand, and I quickly converted a memorandum, prepared some months earlier in Foreign Affairs on areas for future Cuba-Canada co-operation, into a *bout de papier* or working paper to leave with the Cubans at the conclusion of the talks. I wrote in a strong reference to human rights and we baptised the document the Fourteen-Point Plan.

Untimely Advice from Pierre Trudeau

Entwistle then gave me some disquieting news. He had had, he said, a good opportunity to take the measure of Castro when he had dropped by his residence less than two months earlier to see his old friend Pierre Trudeau who was in Cuba on holiday. Castro had been visibly tired. His seventieth birthday was less than two months away and he seemed worn out and dispirited. Significantly, he was in a reflective mood and ready to listen. Castro wanted Trudeau's counsel, and the two old warriors discussed at length the pressures the president was under to make fundamental changes in the way he governed Cuba. Trudeau's advice was startling. He told Castro that while he would have to modernize his country eventually, he should go slowly and not rush reform. Otherwise, he would put his accomplishments in jeopardy. After all, it had taken centuries for democratic institutions to become established in the West. Trudeau's words had made a great impression on the president, who remained silent and contemplative for some time before resuming the conversation.[49] Suddenly my task had become much more difficult.

Castro as Grandfather

President Castro, accompanied by Lage and Alarcón, arrived on schedule for dinner at the official residence of Canada's ambassador, to be greeted by Entwistle, Durand, and me. Castro looked older than his seventy years and spoke slowly in a distracted manner. He greeted me warmly at the door, putting his arm around my shoulder, and moved without prompting to his favourite chair in the living room. I had the impression before the discussion began that he knew the purpose of my visit, probably from the listening devices planted by the Cuban Ministry of the Interior in the walls of the residence, and was in no hurry to talk business. In contrast to the monologues he had engaged in during his visits to the residence in my era, the president asked me questions and seemed genuinely interested in what was going on in the wider world. He seemed to be groping in the dark to find answers that would fit his ideological view of the world. What for example had caused the collapse of communism in Eastern Europe? What had given rise to a one-superpower world and rendered his revolution irrelevant? When I sought to engage him on the subject of my visit, he gently said that we could get into that on the next day. He was more interested in knowing what I wanted for lunch than in my message and smiled when I told him that I would love to have a traditional Cuban meal of roast pork, beans and rice. The president then departed early, walking slowly to the door like a tired old grandfather who had just done his duty in receiving respectful visitors and now just wanted to go to bed. I preferred the old Castro, full of himself and raging against the injustices of the world.

The Dialogue

The next day, we met in Castro's office from ten in the morning until five in the afternoon with lunch served at our conference table. Lage, Alarcón, and the Cuban ambassador to Canada, Bienvenido Garcia Negrin, accompanied the president. Durand and Entwistle backed me up. Introducing my message indirectly, I said that the prime minister had sent me to tell the president that he appreciated his invitation to visit Cuba, which he hoped to be able eventually to accept. In the meantime, Canada's prime minister wanted to see Canada–Cuba relations strengthened. Ties had already been reinforced since his government had come to power in 1993. An unprecedented number of contacts between Canadian ministers and Cuban officials had taken place. We were helping Cuba through CIDA in modernizing its national bank and tax-collection system, and there had been parliamentary exchanges. More, however, should and could be done. Canadians realized that Cubans had gone through difficult times since aid and trade between Cuba and the former Soviet Bloc had been cut and Cuba was forced to face the challenges of globalization by itself. But all countries and not just Cuba were having to adapt their economic – and even in some cases their political structures – to face the new reality. And all countries of the Americas except Cuba were now liberal democracies. The prime minister wanted Canada to help Cuba continue with its process of adaptation already started with the reforms it had put in place, such as its recent laws opening up Cuba to foreign investment.

The prime minister was concerned, however, that the shooting down of the American civil aircraft and the putting into place of the Helms–Burton legislation could lead to a setback in Cuban efforts to modernize and to become integrated into the democratic world of the Americas. He wanted Castro invited to the follow-up sessions of the Miami Summit of the Americas, the goal of which was to bring about one vast free-trade area ranging from the Arctic to Patagonia. I then said that I would leave behind a list of possible areas for future collaboration including a suggestion that we initiate a dialogue on human rights. This latter subject was sensitive but was of great importance to the Canadian government and people. We had constructive exchanges with countries as diverse as China and Indonesia and should be able to initiate a similar dialogue with Cuba.

Castro avoided replying directly and launched into a diatribe against the United States, which, he said, was forcing Cuba to

maintain a state of siege, with controls over its population to protect itself against American aggression. He then began a lengthy
monologue lasting the rest of the morning on his achievements
of the past thirty-seven years, recounting in great and painful
detail the entire course of Cuba's involvement in Africa. With a
hint of bitterness, he said that more than two thousand Cuban
soldiers had died fighting for the independence of Angola and
Namibia. Carrying on in the same vein, he observed that today
the Namibian government would not even allow Cuban ships to
fish in its waters. He also wryly observed that the Cubans had been
forced to make compromises in the past for the greater cause.
Cuban troops in Angola, for example, found themselves protecting the oil wells of American oil companies who provided the
foreign exchange used by the Angolan government to pay Cuba
to fight its domestic enemies, who in turn were in the pay of the
CIA and the South African government.

Growing morose, he admitted that Cuba had lost the ideological war against the United States in the Third World. Castro
gave the impression of being a beaten man, uncertain as to the
direction he should take his country. He had trouble concentrating, often losing the thread of his thought. His steadfast interpreter, still as elegant as she was when I last saw her more than a
decade before, had heard the president's stories so often that she
simply filled in the blanks and carried on without hesitation.
Meanwhile, Alarcón, obviously bored, read the newspaper, and
Lage contemplated the ceiling at great length. Such liberties
would never have been tolerated in the old days.

In the afternoon session, I tried to put the conversation back
on the rails by noting that Canada was master of its foreign-policy
agenda with Cuba and would pursue it independently of the
United States. I also repeated my message that the world had
changed and that countries that did not open their borders to the
free flow of people, ideas, and trade would become marginalized.

The president made several efforts to reply to substantive points of my message but drew back each time. Finally, he said that he would review our conversation and the paper that I proposed leaving behind with "the comrades in the Council of Ministers." He would send a special envoy to Canada in due course with Cuba's response. Castro then subjected me to a four-hour grilling on what was going on in the world. He was either out of touch or was pretending ignorance. He was aware that I had accompanied the prime minister to all G7, P8, APEC, Commonwealth, and Francophonie summits in recent years during which the theme of adapting to globalization had dominated the proceedings. What were the main conclusions of the discussions? What were the positions of individual leaders? What was the nature of the North-South divide?

The Cubans Accept

Three weeks later, the Cuban ambassador called on the prime minister in Ottawa to convey a message from Castro that he considered that our discussions had been fruitful. Several weeks later, Castro's personal envoy, Vice President Lage, arrived to say that Cuba accepted our offer to deepen relations based on the proposal contained in the paper we had left behind and was prepared to begin a serious dialogue on human rights. Prime Minister Chrétien welcomed the news but was more forceful with Lage than I had been in speaking to Castro on human rights, saying that he would like to see the people of Cuba elect their leaders as was done in Canada. He added that the American policy of isolating Cuba gave President Castro a tool to stay in power. When the United States had open relations with Cuba, change would occur. Lage made no comment but might have wondered whether Canada's aim was to help Castro adapt to globalization or to ease him out of office. He was, however, left in no doubt regarding Canada's political and human rights objectives.

The Axworthy Mission

In December 1996, the prime minister returned to the charge, telling me he thought the time was ripe for him to visit Cuba. I recommended against, saying that we should wait until the Cubans had signed the plan of action and then delivered on their commitments, before we rewarded them with a visit at his level. In January 1997, therefore, it was Foreign Minister Axworthy who went to Havana to sign the joint Fourteen Point Declaration. It was, in all main aspects, identical to the paper Durand and I had left behind in August 1996 committing the two countries to work together in the following areas: the administration of justice and the judicial legal system; exchanges between the House of Commons and the Cuban National Assembly; strengthening of a Citizen's Complaint Commission in the Cuban National Assembly; broadening and deepening of co-operation on Human Rights; supporting activities of Canadian and Cuban non-governmental organizations; macroeconomic co-operation with the initial focus on taxation and central banking; negotiation of a Foreign Investment Protection and Promotion Agreement; collaboration on narcotics interdiction; international terrorism; negotiation of memorandums of understanding on health, audio-visual co-production, and sports; joint research and co-operation especially on demining; and the provision to Cuba of food aid.

Rome and Havana

One year later, in January 1998, I reviewed the results of our opening with colleagues from Foreign Affairs and with Canada's ambassador to Cuba to see whether a visit by the prime minister would now be worthwhile. Both Canada and Cuba, they told me, had worked hard in pursuing the ambitious work plan throughout 1997. The Cubans, as expected, had focused on concluding the various memorandums of understanding where they could obtain material benefit and access to Canadian food aid. They had likewise been amenable to Canadian suggestions that they sign international conventions dealing with international terrorism that cost them nothing politically and economically. Whenever human rights issues were raised, however, they had stalled. They were happy enough to attend seminars in Canada as long as Canada paid their expenses and were, when pushed, willing to accord a limited freedom of action to certain non-governmental organizations in Cuba. There was, however, no meeting of minds. The Cubans repeated the Cold War communist double-talk that the Party reflected the will of the people, and that democratic elections and liberties in the developed world were but smoke-screens for the interests of capitalists. They insisted that social and economic rights of the group took precedence over the political rights of the individual. The Cubans also resented Canada's continued high-profile role promoting human rights in the United Nations and our co-sponsorship of resolutions in Geneva and New York specifically criticizing Cuba's record.

Canadian officials found Cuba's tactical manoeuvring to be hypocritical and their arguments justifying the lack of individual freedom in Cuba to be specious. Even more galling, from the Canadian perspective, was the damage Cuba (in company with China, India, Indonesia, Sudan, and Iran) continued to inflict on the effectiveness of the U.N. rights system by their successful and self-serving efforts to deprive it of resources and limit its freedom of action. This group of countries, among the worst violators of human rights in the United Nations, clearly did not want international observers poking around in their prisons.

Pope John Paul II then paid his highly publicized visit to Havana during which he seemed to have made some progress on human rights. I accordingly made arrangements in early February through Canada's ambassador, Fernand Tanguay, to visit the Vatican to meet with Archbishop Tauran, foreign minister of the Vatican, to see if there were any lessons we Canadians could learn. Tauran said that apart from pastoral benefits, Castro had agreed to accord greater freedom to the Catholic Church and to release a large number of political prisoners. He now feared a crackdown on dissidents, however, now that the papal visit was out of the way. A visit by the Canadian prime minister, he said, would not lead to any dramatic change in the nature of the Cuban state, but would encourage reformers and hearten those Cubans hoping for eventual democratic reform.

I briefed the prime minister, saying that limited progress only had been achieved with the Fourteen Point Declaration and it was unlikely Castro would go much further in making reforms. But a visit would, at the least, help consolidate the opening made by the pope. I also told him that Castro was not well. Ambassador Keith Christie, who had replaced Mark Entwistle in 1997, had confirmed to me that the president, seriously ill, had dropped out of sight in the summer of 1997, not reappearing until the fall and looking terrible. Some Cuban watchers, basing their theories on his speech patterns at the time, believed Castro had suffered a stroke. The president had slowly recovered and been reasonably fit for the visit of the pope in January 1998.

The genial Carlos Lage then reappeared in Ottawa to renew his invitation from his president to the prime minister. At the luncheon the prime minister offered him to reciprocate the hospitality accorded to me by Castro, Lage argued that sufficient progress had been made to justify a visit. The prime minister, who knew better, was noncommittal but agreed to send me once again to Cuba for another session with the president. He wanted to see if Castro would be prepared to make further concessions.

Return to Havana

Accompanied this time by Michael Kergin, Foreign Affairs assistant deputy minister for the Americas and a former Canadian ambassador to Cuba, I returned to Havana on February 24, 1998. Just before we left, the Havana embassy sent an urgent message saying that the Cubans wanted to expel to Canada twenty-one political prisoners. Castro had promised the pope during his visit that he would free them, but did not want to release them in Cuba, presumably because they could be a disruptive influence with their freedom-loving ideas. In Havana, we were summoned to the office of Lage at seven in the evening, where the vice president peremptorily demanded that I outline what we hoped to accomplish to allow him to prepare the president. He was in no mood to hear me say that my message was for Castro's ears only and I spoke frankly. Making no mention of the request that we accept the prisoners, I told him that Prime Minister Chrétien was prepared to make a low-key visit to Cuba but had conditions. Lage frowned and said that we should stand by for dinner that night with Castro in his private quarters in the palace. We should prepare for an all-night session.

At ten, the vice president telephoned to say that the president was waiting for us. We drove though darkened streets lined with magnificent mansions falling into ruins, and past the few still functioning streetlights that illuminated dozens of young women in spandex pants and low-cut blouses pursuing the world's oldest profession – one that was supposed to have been banished forever from revolutionary Cuba. The presidential palace itself was shrouded in shadows. A tough, unsmiling, and heavily armed member of Castro's personal bodyguard corps stepped out of the gloom in front of a sentry box to demand that we state our business. Taking our passports, he disappeared into the dark, returning five minutes later to hand back our documents and to tell us to proceed. In my imagination, the scene could have been taken from the great novel *The Autumn of the Patriarch*, by Castro's close friend, Nobel Prize winner Gabriel García Márquez. In that book, an aged leader lives isolated from his people and from the reality of chaos and moral decline outside his palace in a far-off, marginalized Latin American country until he is eventually over- thrown in a bloody insurrection, paying the price for his tyranny and his neglect of the modern world.

There was no one to greet us at the elegant entrance to the palace and we waited silently until Lage, at the wheel of an old Soviet-built Lada, sped up and took charge. Leading us through unlocked doors into the lobby, he used a house telephone to call someone in the bowels of the massive building. Eventually, the doors to an elevator opened to reveal a retainer of the president whom I had not seen for fifteen years and who had grown old with his master. Like the silent valet in Edgar Allan Poe's "The Fall of the House of Usher," he wordlessly beckoned to us to join him. The elevator then moved quietly to an upper floor where the door opened and a scowling Cuban president confronted us.

This patriarch was in a foul mood. Fidel Castro had not liked my message that there were conditions attached to a prime-ministerial visit. The mellow, reflective Castro I had met in August 1996 was gone. In his place stood a weakened old lion, so thin his tightly tucked-in shirt hung loosely on his ribs. His yellow eyes protruded from their sockets, his cheeks were hollows beneath prominent cheekbones, wisps of beard stuck out at odd angles, his skin was sallow, and he exuded a medicinal odour from between false teeth that clicked when he talked. His mood was one of intense irritation. When he sat down, his right leg pulsated in an up-and-down motion and his left arm twitched. He held his left arm with his right to try to still it and leant toward me with baleful eyes.

"I'm tired of visitors who come asking the impossible. They are no better than the foolish Don Quixote. By the way, are you or are you not going to take the twenty-one prisoners. I want to rid Cuba of a few more rapists and killers!"

I looked into the president's baleful eyes, thinking of Zaka, our wonderful family pet poisoned by Cuban Ministry of the Interior thugs on Castro's orders in 1983. I was certain that Castro had long forgotten the incident, part of some obscure Cuban attempt to intimidate me at the time, but my wife, children, and I had not. I wondered how could one of the most charismatic leaders of the twentieth century, who had devoted his life to seeking justice for the downtrodden of the Third World, behave so callously? To him, animals and people were just pawns to be pushed around in the service of a by-now discredited ideal. Perhaps he simply liked to play God, handing over people as if they were just so many sides of beef, rather than men, women, and children, each with his or her inherent dignity.

Having consulted the minister of immigration before leaving for Cuba, I was ready with an answer to his question, saying that Canada preferred political prisoners to be released in their home-lands and not to be sent into exile. In this case, however, if the choice was prison or exile, we would take them, provided that they confirmed directly to one of our immigration officers that they really wanted to go to Canada. And under no circumstances would we accept rapists or killers.

Castro snorted and said that he had been joking. (He was not. Canadian immigration officers discovered criminals on the Cuban list, whom they refused to process.) The president then started a long monologue, not tolerating the slightest interruption for about four hours. His views, in contrast to those of our encounter in 1996, were clear and decided. He described at great length the visit of John Paul II, who obviously had made an enormous impression on him. He contrasted the noble and humanitarian face of John Paul II and the Vatican with the petty nature of the local church and its leadership. He was furious at the Cuban Church for seeking to exploit the pope's visit and, he said, "his good nature" to seek a greater role in Cuban society.

Castro continued to transfix me with unfriendly eyes, and moved so close that his spittle splattered my face. I had the impression, however, that he was not really talking to me. He was engaged in a stream-of-consciousness dialogue with himself that would have done James Joyce proud. My sense was that he had forgotten why I and my colleagues were there and was oblivious to the presence of his devoted vice president. He seemed to be seeking to draw conclusions from the visit of the pope and was unhappy that he had, perhaps in a fit of enthusiasm, accorded too much liberty to the local Church.

Around two o'clock in the morning, the old retainer signalled to the president that dinner was ready. I then made my move. When the president was momentarily distracted from his monologue by having to struggle to his feet and lead us to the table in an adjoining room, I told him that Prime Minister Chrétien had sent me to say that he would like to pay a working visit to Cuba in the mid-March to end-of-April period. His preference was to come in the latter part of April, after the Summit of the Americas meeting in Chile. Some progress, I said, had been accomplished in implementing the Fourteen Point Declaration, but more could have been done on human rights. Cuba's release of political prisoners following the pope's visit had constituted a forward step. Could not more be done in the context of the prime minister's visit, such as releasing other higher profile prisoners and undertaking to sign the United Nations Covenant on Economic, Social and Cultural Rights? I emphasized that human-rights issues were of great importance to the Canadian people and to the prime minister personally, and that continued progress would lead to even closer Canada-Cuban relations.

Castro's eyes flashed but he made no reply. Instead, on sitting down, he began another long, meandering account describing the role of Catholicism and African folk religions in Cuba over the past four hundred years. This was followed by several hours on Cuba's role in Africa, repeating what he had told me two years earlier. This time there was no self-pity. History would show that Cuba had played a noble and crucial role in the struggle for decolonization and he had no regrets. The old retainer, assisted by one waiter, silently passed around the food and kept our water glasses filled, obviously well-versed in providing simple businesslike meals in the middle of the night. Meanwhile, Castro took tiny bites of food and chewed each of them for ten to fifteen minutes before swallowing. From time to time, he would stop eating and push his dish away. The interpreter and Lage would then urge him to continue eating. He had to be strong, they said; the revolution needed its leader. Castro was obviously still suffering from the strain of the pope's visit and the illness that had floored him the previous summer. As the night wore on, however, he became progressively more comfortable with his Canadian visitors and we with him. He accepted questions and comments with greater grace, his face took on colour, his eyes became friendly, and he was highly animated towards dawn.

His guests, for their part, could hardly keep their eyes open. Lage coped by staring without blinking at the ceiling for lengthy periods, his eyes as wide open as possible. I could not do the same since Castro held me in his gaze as he ranted on, at times incoherently. I therefore drank cup after cup of strong black Cuban coffee and visited the washroom every hour, mainly for the exercise. Castro who drank no coffee but sipped periodically from a glass of pure rum, left the room only once during the night for the toilet, giving me a chance to glance around the room. The table, obviously moved in to accommodate his dinner party, dominated the small, intimate room. I assumed that Castro had a bedroom nearby but did not see it. The walls were lined with well-stocked bookshelves and there was a desk in one corner. We were, I sensed, in the holy of holies of the Cuban power structure. In Hanoi some months before, on my mission to free a Canadian from a Vietnamese prison, I had visited the private quarters of Ho Chi Minh, the Asian revolutionary closest in spirit to Fidel Castro. His bedroom and study had been preserved as a shrine for the ideological faithful and as a tourist attraction. Ho, I saw, had lived like a monk, sleeping on a camp cot in a bare little room open to the elements. His study was tiny, furnished only with a hard chair and a desk that looked like it had been requisitioned from a typing pool. I wondered if Castro's study would one day share a similar fate, becoming a destination for busloads of tourists and schoolchildren after the revolutionary hero's death.

Castro, however, was no monk and his study, while not ostentatious in its furnishings, could have been that of a Cuban middle-class lawyer before the revolution. The president, although he had had many mistresses throughout his life (and occasionally boasted about his sexual conquests), also lived a conventional private life, with spouse and children. He also, I remembered, had studied law. Had he stuck to his profession, there would not have been a Cuban revolution and he would probably have had a similar study in a capitalist Cuba. I started to feel sorry for the old warrior; his best days were behind him and he was now ill. For that reason, I ignored all my years of training when I found myself confronted in his bathroom with an array of his personal medicines and other medical paraphernalia neatly arranged on the shelf above the washbasin. Had I taken note of the contents, the mystery of Castro's illness would have been known. I didn't have the heart to do so. I was his guest.

Around six in the morning, with the morning light starting to penetrate the room, Castro asked me to repeat my proposal. I did so, but my fervent hope that he would provide some sort of reply to allow me to go to bed was frustrated when he changed the subject to provide his opinion on globalization. At the end of a tortuously long, often confusing and detailed analysis, he concluded that it was merely extreme economic liberalization marginalizing poor countries and worsening the lot of the disadvantaged of all societies. He had made up his mind since we last talked in 1996. Then just before eight, the president, by now relaxed and smiling, with his guests barely conscious, made his pronouncement. He wanted the Canadian prime minister to visit, but Cuba was not prepared to make concessions: "Don't ask Cuba to do anything which would damage it, and Cuba will not ask Canada to do anything that would embarrass it." We Canadians then excused ourselves and went home to bed. Castro,

I was told, then went off for his daily regime of sleep and CNN-watching; Lage, poor soul, had to go to work.

Following the submission of my report on returning to Ottawa, the prime minister decided to proceed with a working visit on April 27 and 28. In so doing, he hoped to reinforce Canada's policy of constructive engagement, in particular our desire to advance the cause of human rights. He was by now under no illusion that Castro wanted our help to ease the transition of his country to a market economy or was really interested in lessening Cuba's isolation in the hemisphere at the cost of loosening his totalitarian control. Castro had, however, freed a number of political prisoners and restored a certain degree of religious freedom in the wake of the pope's visit. A visit could well help consolidate this opening and give heart to the dissident community. The prime minister was also curious. He wanted to take the measure of Castro the man and the historical figure.

The Prime Minister in Havana

Thus began the first official visit to Cuba by a Canadian prime minister since that of Pierre Trudeau in 1976. From the start, it was a clash of two different personalities with diametrically opposing visions of the future. The jousting started at the airport arrival ceremony, broadcast on all Cuban radio and television channels. Castro, radiating new-found vigour, welcomed the Canadian prime minister by delivering a vicious anti-American diatribe during which he pledged fidelity to the principles of the revolution. On the flight down from Ottawa, I had prepared the prime minister for a tough propagandistic statement from Castro, telling him the press would be watching him closely to see if his body language conveyed sympathy for Castro's message. It would be best, I said, to look enigmatic. Castro's speech was so violent, however, there was no need for the prime minister to restrain his enthusiasm. Everyone, the prime minister, his advisor, and media on the Canadian side were surprised that Castro would exploit the arrival ceremony for such blatant propaganda purposes.

The prime minister then delivered a calm, measured speech containing the messages he would convey to Castro repeatedly over the next thirty hours: "The winds of change are blowing through our hemisphere. . . . And we must all adapt. . . . This is an expression of confidence . . . to a more dynamic, more democratic, more prosperous hemisphere . . . that is becoming a family . . . with shared goals, shared values, shared hopes and dreams. . . . And we are committed to working to achieve greater social, economic, and political justice throughout the region."

The two leaders then got into Castro's big Soviet-era limousine and led the way to the newly restored National, a beautiful pre-revolutionary hotel overlooking the sea on Havana's famous Malecon drive. The official talks began later in the morning, with the prime minister and me on one side of the table and Castro and Lage on the other. The winds of history, great ideas, and the principles of the Cuban revolution were the themes of Castro's opening remarks. He assumed that the prime minister would be overwhelmed with the brilliance of his analyses and allow him to dominate the discussion. The prime minister, however, stopped the president in full rhetorical flight. I want, the prime minister said, to discuss the Fourteen Point Declaration. Could the Civilian Complaints Commission be empowered to investigate human-rights complaints? Could foreign non-governmental organizations be granted greater freedom of action? Would Cuba sign the United Nations Covenant on Social and Economic Rights? He then passed over a list of four high-profile dissidents languishing in a Cuban jail for the past year without being charged and asked Castro to release them.

Castro's face betrayed all manner of emotion, passing from astonishment to anger and then to bitterness. He said nothing for some time, picking up and throwing down distractedly the cue card with the names of the four dissidents scrawled in my barely legible handwriting. "I have never been so humiliated," he said in a barely audible voice. He would have walked out the door, I believe, had he not been in his own office. The dialogue never recovered, although the leaders remained at the table for two hours and fifteen minutes. The president had been prepared to release three low-level prisoners as a sort of human gift but the prime minister had just raised the stakes. It was at this point that Castro probably decided that the policy of constructive engagement with Canada had reached the limits of its usefulness. The Canadians were taking human rights far too seriously.

Although other bilateral and international issues were then discussed, there was no meeting of minds. The prime minister mentioned that Canada had been happy to resume our aid program. And to commemorate his visit to Havana, CIDA intended to announce that it would provide funding to allow Cuba to provide new textbooks and scribblers for its schoolchildren for a year. Castro and Lage sat silent and tight-lipped. They were not about to say thanks to a visitor who had not listened to Castro's thoughts on the future of humanity. Eventually, after stroking his beard attentively, always a sign that he was thinking hard, Castro turned to Haiti and proposed that Canada fund a program to pay Cuban doctors to administer to the desperately poor in that country. While not rejecting Castro's suggestion, the prime minister made one of his own. Why should Canada and Cuba not collaborate in clearing anti-personnel mines in Angola and Mozambique? Cuban forces had operated there for over a decade. Canada could fund a program and Cuban soldiers could remove the mines.

Castro looked devastated. He would later tell a national Cuban television audience that he had rarely heard a more imperialist proposal. Imagine! Canada suggesting that Cubans do the dirty work in the minefields, while the Canadians sat off to one side garnering all the credit!

Castro glanced at me angrily from time to time as the ill-fated talks progressed, as if I were to blame for his game plan going wrong. Finally, the meeting dragged to a conclusion and the prime minister and I got up to leave. Prime Minister Chrétien proceeded out the door and I prepared to follow when I felt the hands of the president on my shoulders from behind, squeezing hard and shaking me.

"I hope you are satisfied, Bartleman!" He hissed out the words in Spanish, his voice cold, high pitched yet low enough not to attract the attention of Prime Minister Chrétien who was already striding rapidly ahead to meet the assembled Canadian press contingent. I had no idea why Castro was so mad at me. Perhaps he felt I had not conveyed his message to the prime minister not to ask Cuba to do anything during his visit that could damage it. Whatever the reason, the rage in his eyes made me glad that I was a Canadian able to depart with the prime minister rather than a Cuban who would have felt the full wrath of an unhappy leader in a police state! I also thought his sentiments were a touch unkind to someone who had spent a night with him so recently.

After the press conference, we all moved on to an official lunch hosted by the prime minister and Mrs. Chrétien for Cardinal Jaime Lucas Ortega y Alamino, fully covered by the press, the first time Castro had ever allowed the media to report on such an event. Michael Kergin and I then met with Cuba's leading dissidents not in jail, demonstrating to them that they were not alone in their struggle for political justice. I had enormous respect for their courage, appreciating that they risked many years of prison just for talking to us. That evening over dinner, Castro had calmed down but the contest between the two leaders continued. Discussing issues as diverse as the Euro, the reform of the Bretton Woods institutions, and the future of the European Union, Castro as usual threw out a myriad of statistics and facts. The prime minister matched him, statistic for statistic.

Castro resorted to revolutionary rhetoric, describing his vision of the future where the disinherited would triumph through all-or-nothing revolutionary action. The prime minister said that he shared the same goal but proclaimed his faith in solving problems pragmatically one at a time. Castro was pessimistic regarding the future; Chrétien believed greater wealth was being created now through capitalism than at any time in world history. On globalization, Chrétien argued that countries had to adapt or their populations would suffer. Castro, using arguments which presaged those that anti-globalization crusaders would adopt at the Seattle WTO meeting a year later, retorted that the wealth being generated through globalization was not being shared with the poor. The so-called democracy that had appeared in Latin America was just a cover, he said, for monopolizing wealth by selfish neo-liberals. Chrétien said Castro was being simplistic; there were at least three types of liberals in the world including the centralist Canadian variety. Mrs. Chrétien weighed in from time to time in Spanish, ensuring that the mood remained friendly.

An ebullient Castro bade farewell to Prime Minister and Mrs. Chrétien at the airport late the next morning. As I said goodbye, the president drew me toward him, grinning. "Your prime minister and I had a good discussion in my car on the way to airport. And do you know why?"

I said that I had no idea and smiled expectantly, hoping that he had overcome his fit of pique at me of the day before. But I had no such luck.

"*Because you weren't there, Bartleman, that's why!*"

I decided I would drop Cuba from my list of vacation destinations for the foreseeable future.

The good will between the leaders stimulated by the vigorous, candid, and friendly discussions of the previous evening did not disguise the fact that the Canadian initiative to engage Cuba in a policy of constructive engagement had gone as far as it could, at least as long as Castro was alive. Following the prime minister's visit, the four dissidents whom the prime minister had sought to have released were sentenced to long prison terms after a secret trial, in defiance of Canadian and world opinion. Relations

between the two countries then descended, as the prime minister decreed, into the deep freeze. As I write this some years later,
Fidel Castro is still in power. His predictions about democracy
in Latin America being accompanied by predatory neo-liberalism
seem, unfortunately, to have been confirmed with the passage of
time. On the other hand, the Cuban model, source of so much
hope to the disenfranchised of the region for so many decades,
remains a bankrupt alternative, with the Cuban people still the
victims of a gigantic social engineering experiment. For Castro
has taken no significant steps to change the tight state control of
the economy or to concede democratic liberties to the people of
his country.

Was then Prime Minister Chrétien's initiative in the latter part
of the 1990s a failure? Castro did nothing to open up either his
economy or his repressive political system. On the other hand the
luncheon with the archbishop helped consolidate the gains for
the Church registered by John Paul II and our meeting with the
dissidents could only have encouraged them. In addition, our
efforts, however tentative, to implement the Fourteen Point
Declaration exposed hundreds of Cubans to another way of
managing an economy and governing a state that will not be forgotten when the transition comes, as it inevitably will, some day
after the passing of Castro. The prime minister had the courage
to take a risk for a noble cause and positioned Canada on the
moral high ground for a major role in post-Castro Cuba. But I,
alas, will not be able to tell my grandchildren that I played the role
of a Kissinger in the Caribbean!

SUMMITRY AND THE ANTI-GLOBALIZATION MOVEMENT

13

The Anti-globalization Movement

A light came on in the prime minister's eyes. "Pepper? Pepper, I put it on my steak! Ha ha ha!"

The New Diplomacy

Prime Minister Mackenzie King, who was his own foreign minister for most of his time in office, travelled every two or three years at most – and by leisurely steamer – to international conferences, usually in London, the centre of Canada's universe in those days. His successor, Prime Minister Louis St. Laurent, was more active, making what was called a "world tour" in 1954. Prime Minister John Diefenbaker made a similar one in 1958 following his election victory in 1957. From Prime Minister Pearson onwards, however, prime ministers were on the road more and more often as jet-plane travel proliferated and their involvement in foreign affairs increased dramatically. G7 summits started in the mid-1970s, shifting even more responsibility for the management of the big foreign-policy issues of the day to heads of state and government and away from their foreign ministers. The role of foreign and trade ministers evolved, as a consequence, to one of support for the activities of their leaders and to the pursuit of niche areas for initiatives they could pursue largely by themselves. By the time Prime Minister Chrétien came to office in 1993, leaders had become both the chief diplomats and the chief salespersons of their countries.

Why did this happen? As early as the 1960s it was becoming apparent that the lines between domestic and foreign policy were becoming blurred. In 1970, Prime Minister Trudeau's ground-breaking "Foreign Policy for Canadians" proclaimed that foreign policy was in fact only an extension of domestic policy. By the 1990s, the lines had become completely tangled. With globalization and the revolution in information technology, leaders found it easier than at any other time in history to stay in touch with each other. Goods and services, currency transactions, information, cultural products, disease, criminals, migrants, and pollution poured across borders in a manner never before seen in history. In order to manage the internal affairs of their countries, leaders had to become players internationally. And – something too often forgotten – it was more *fun* dealing with foreign affairs than with domestic issues. The stages were larger than the ones available at home. And who could resist twenty-one-gun salutes, military honour guards, state dinners, elaborate cultural performances, and self-congratulatory gossip with peers?

They enjoyed belonging to the most exclusive club in the world. There were fewer than two hundred heads of government or heads of state with executive power for the six billion people on the planet. To be sure, there were enormous differences among them. There were democrats in all their varieties, strongmen of authoritarian and military bent, and despots of diverse religious persuasions. A few were big fish in small puddles, many were medium-sized fish in medium-sized puddles, others were small fish in small puddles, and only one, the United States, was a huge fish in a huge puddle. Each, however, was usually the most powerful individual in his or her nation and represented a sovereign country with a vote in the United Nations. And the leaders of the 1990s transacted their business at summit meetings, transformed into modern-day medieval fairs. Here leaders gathered together regularly to network, to seek support for their national initiatives, to sell products, to rub shoulders with the presidents and prime ministers of the great powers, and to be the centre of media attention.

I accompanied Prime Minister Chrétien to thirty-five such conferences from 1994 to 1998, including two that he hosted: the Halifax G7 meeting of June 1995 and the November 1997 Vancouver APEC summit. They could not have been more different. Halifax was a substantive and public relations success and Vancouver was not. At the first, the anti-globalization movement had not yet put its act together; at the second, its adherents were out in full force. Straddling the two was the Edinburgh Commonwealth summit, where I first saw the new international protest movement bare its teeth.

The Halifax G7 Summit

In June 1994, the people of Nova Scotia's capital turned out in their thousands to cheer Bill Clinton, Boris Yeltsin, Jacques Chirac, John Major, Helmut Kohl, Tomiichi Murayama, Jacques Santer, Lamberto Dini, and Jean Chrétien as they passed by in their motorcades to receptions, dinners, and official meetings. All of them, except Boris Yeltsin, met together on the first day of the two-day conference to discuss macroeconomic issues as the G7. The next day, they gathered with Yeltsin to review global political, social, and environmental issues as the P8. Chirac, freshly elected as president of France, jockeyed as expected for the limelight. Clinton was as warm and friendly and Kohl as stolid as ever. Major was thrilled by the entertainment – the Cirque du Soleil – perhaps because it recalled his own family's history in the circus. Murayama, Santer, and Dini said little, and Yeltsin got drunk but sobered up when it was time for him to speak.

A watershed in the recent history of these annual meetings, Halifax was the most intimate and businesslike gathering in years and became a model to be followed in future summits. And Prime Minister Chrétien was happy with the results. The leaders devoted attention to the reform of the International Monetary Fund and the World Bank – a goal the prime minister had been pursuing ever since coming to office. The prime minister's colleagues were initially skeptical about devoting much time at Halifax to the matter. Then the Mexican economy almost collapsed in late 1994, forced to the wall by a currency crisis fuelled once again by speculators. This caught the attention of the G7 leaders, who came on side. At the summit itself, they agreed on a work plan to strengthen the international institutions, particularly by measures to increase the transparency of their operations.

Eventually some reforms would be put into place, but the suspicion would grow that the problem could not be fixed by trying to stuff the globalization genie back into the bottle through the reimposition of some sort of controls, such as a tax on currency transactions. What if the real culprits were the tough love, neo-liberal remedies themselves, the ones so favoured by the Bretton Woods institutions in dealing with governments in trouble: slashing government expenditures and cutting subsidies, even at the cost of public misery and revolt? The matter the prime minister put on the table in Halifax would be debated by world leaders for the rest of the decade – as new financial crises arose in Latin America, Russia, and East Asia. The same issues would also become a focus of attention by the anti-globalization activists and add fuel to their burning perception that the governments and international financial institutions alike put the interests of the establishment ahead of those of the people in the new world order.

The Edinburgh Commonwealth Summit

The Commonwealth summit was in session in Edinburgh, Scotland, from October 23 to 26, 1997, and more than fifty heads of state and government were in town. A "People's" or parallel summit was held at the same time. Tens of thousands of representatives of non-governmental organizations came to the Scottish capital to debate many of the same issues being discussed by the leaders in their official talks and to take to the streets to publicize their causes. The activists, the British officials told us, would be peaceful. We took our hosts at their word, and the day after arriving in Edinburgh, the prime minister visited an exhibition put on by a leading participant in the People's summit, an anti-personnel mines organization, to lend it moral support. He told the cheering, applauding crowd that his priority at the forthcoming sessions would be to lobby other world leaders to get them to sign the anti-personnel mines treaty in Ottawa in December.

The crowd was not applauding later in the week when I travelled with the prime minister from our hotel to the summit site. Crowds of protestors forced their way through the police lines to beat their hands on the roof of our car, to shake their fists, to scream slogans, and even to spit on the windows. One demonstrator I will never forget. He was about thirty years old, his hair and beard were red, his eyes were wild, and his face was flushed and twisted with rage as he yelled: "You bastards! You bloody bastards!"

If we had met socially, I am certain that he would have displayed the politeness for which the British are renowned. He and the other protestors, however, had no idea that the prime minister of Canada, supporter of one of their favourite causes, was in the car and they probably would not have cared if they had known. They were no longer people but members of a mob imbued with collective passion. In their eyes, we likewise were not individuals but symbols of a despised new world order. Anyone attending the summit, in their view, was an apologist for globalization and deserved fierce criticism.

The Anti-globalization Movement

Gentle or violent, each of these faces of the anti-globalization movement was as legitimate as the other. The movement had, in fact, as many facets as the causes which its adherents espoused. Hundreds of thousands of concerned citizens from across the globe were seeking to stop unfair trading practices and to right wrongs, whether against Third World debt, women, aboriginal peoples, the environment, or any of a host of issues. Ironically, it was the Internet (then just coming into its own, and itself a central player in the hated globalization process) that allowed them to unite, and gave synergy to their efforts. And summit meetings where the most powerful global political figures met regularly in what the protestors assumed were unholy conclaves to plot more injustice, were the rods attracting their lightning.

There was, of course, more to the anti-globalization movement than that. The Cold War, for all its dangers and stupidities, was also a clash of ideologies with a moral dimension. Marxism spoke of a world order in which "goods would be distributed to each according to his need and from each according to his means." Liberal democracy eschewed the raw dog-eat-dog capitalism denounced by Marx in the nineteenth century and portrayed itself as the system most likely to bring the greatest good to the greatest number. The moral component, however, disappeared with the end of the ideological struggle. The Cold War ended with the fall of the Berlin Wall in 1989 and was replaced by an often heartless pursuit of wealth in the globalized world of the 1990s. Francis Fukayama proclaimed the end of the Cold War–bipolar era, and hailed the triumph of liberal democracy and the market economy in a world of growing prosperity. For their part, senior representatives of the World Bank and the International Monetary Fund quoted statistics to prove that hundreds of millions of people had been lifted out of poverty in countries that had opened their borders to freer trade over the years.

But the politically aware members of the anti-globalization movement were not fools. They were able to quote other statistics to make the case that the gap between rich and poor in developing and developed countries alike was increasing. They pointed out that the vaunted reduction in tariffs agreed in the 1986–1994 Uruguay Trade Round and the establishment of the WTO in 1995 with its dispute settlement mechanisms were of little use to many developing countries, since they lacked the expertise to navigate in the complex new trade policy environment. Moreover, they pointed out, aid flows had plummeted at the end of the Cold War when the developing world was no longer of strategic value to anyone. And the developed world apparently had no intention of opening its markets to the agricultural products of the Third World. Meanwhile, big corporations, whose goal was simply to make money, often had more influence with governments than did special-interest groups with moral purposes. To make matters worse, they saw that their leaders were standing by as communicable diseases decimated populations and as life expectancies, child mortality rates, and literacy levels collapsed in most sub-Saharan countries. And, as is spelled out in the chapter on Eastern Zaire, in many failed states of Africa, the only outside support provided to peoples in need came from the non-governmental organizations themselves, such as Doctors Without Borders, CARE International, and Oxfam.

It was this profound sense that the Cold War had been replaced by a world devoid of any sense of morality that so animated the red-haired individual spewing obscenities and spittle in my general direction on October 24, 1997.

The Vancouver APEC Summit

Thirty months after Halifax and one month after Edinburgh, Canada hosted the sixth Asia-Pacific Economic Co-operation[50] conference in Vancouver in November 1997. The welcome accorded the distinguished visitors, other than from the prime minister and the business community, was cool. The assumption that somehow Vancouverites would prove to be as enthusiastic about the presence in their city of the leaders for the Asia-Pacific as the Haligonians had been when they hosted the G7 summit just two years previously was wrong. Alas, Vancouver was used to the great and famous. Did not Bill Clinton meet Boris Yeltsin there in 1993? Was not Vancouver called the "San Francisco of the North"? Had it not become Hollywood North, with world-class film stars frequenting its fashionable bar and restaurant scene? Was Vancouver International airport not one of the busiest in the entire Pacific Northwest? Was Vancouver not the most beautiful and desirable city in which to live in all of Canada? And who needed the hassle of closed highways, constant motorcades, lost business, and parking nightmares associated with a big summit, anyway!

As it was, the mood of the visitors matched that of the Vancouverites. Eighteen grim leaders came to the resentful city. For the past six months, a financial firestorm of the type the prime minister had sought to guard against by his initiatives in Halifax, had been consuming many of the countries of Asia. On July 2, 1997, the Thai *baht* had collapsed. The International Monetary Fund arranged a seventeen-billion-dollar rescue package, but the contagion spread to Korea. The largest bailout package ever put together by the Fund kept Seoul's economy alive on life support, but the infection spread to Indonesia and its neighbours in Southeast Asia. The prime minister as host was forced into a crisis-management role. Supported by President Clinton, he made repeated statements to the press to calm the currency markets, saying that the economic fundamentals of the region remained strong, and that the markets were overreacting and the economies would eventually bounce back. He also met individually with every head of state or government, spending as much time reassuring his rattled guests as discussing the agenda of the forthcoming conference.

The Protestors
The substance of the summit already derailed, the train then ran slowly off the tracks and onto the streets. We had expected that the raw emotion we encountered in Edinburgh from the anti-globalization movement would be seen again in the capital of British Columbia. No one foresaw, however, the growing power of the anti-globalization forces. Vancouver, in effect, marked the

halfway point between the rough but relatively restrained demonstrations in Edinburgh and the full-scale rioting at the Seattle
WTO ministerial meeting in November 1999. And the strategy
adopted to cope with the street – a combination of effective polic-
ing and gestures of good will – proved to be inadequate.

We assumed, mistakenly, that the RCMP would be able to do
its job, providing security for everyone within the framework of
Canadian law that provided for peaceful protests. The police,
however, faced with dealing with the largest single international
event in their history, were overwhelmed. Foreign Minister Lloyd
Axworthy and Trade Minister Sergio Marchi did their best to
lance the boil of protest in a constructive way. Their main concern
was, understandably, not security but finding an appropriate way
of dealing with the legitimate worries of the anti-globalization
movement. Marchi obtained the approval of Canada's partners to
release a number of previously classified documents to the public,
thus enhancing the transparency of the APEC process. Axworthy
dug two hundred thousand dollars out of Canada's aid budget to
help fund a People's summit. But the radicals were not mollified.

We also underestimated the strength of one single-issue organization, the East Timor Alert Network, dedicated to freeing East
Timor from Indonesian rule. In 1975 Portugal pulled its troops
out of East Timor, a colony it had occupied since 1520. The
indigenous inhabitants declared independence, but President
Suharto sent in the Indonesian army to annex the territory in a
bloodbath in which tens of thousands of people were killed.
Supporters of independence carried on the fight through an
international campaign to force Indonesia to relinquish control.
Although there were apparently only two Canadian citizens of
East Timorese origin in Canada, their cause had been adopted by
the anti-globalization movement. And they saw the participation
of President Suharto in the APEC summit as an opportunity to
attract attention to the cause.

Finally, we misread the prime minister's attitude on the need to have the president of Indonesia attend the summit. When the Indonesians in the summer of 1997 began to threaten that their president might boycott the conference if his safety and personal dignity could not be safeguarded, Canadian ministers and officials with responsibility for the success of the conference sprang into action. After all, President Suharto was the leader of the largest country in Southeast Asia, the longest-serving member of any APEC government, a recent and strong supporter of the cause of free trade, and the head of a government with whom we wanted to establish closer trade and investment ties. Canada's ambassador to Indonesia, Gary Smith, made representations in Jakarta. Foreign Affairs officials in Ottawa called in Benjamin Parwoto, the local ambassador. Foreign Minister Axworthy, in Indonesia in July, assured the president that he had no need to fear for his security. Nothing seemed to work. The Indonesians continued to threaten that their leader would not come unless we could provide guarantees that his dignity, as well as his security, would not be violated.

What, Me Worry?

I was not unduly concerned, not yet anyway. My plate was filled to overflowing in August 1997. My team and I were busy working with Foreign Affairs organizing fall official visits for the prime minister to Russia and the United Kingdom, to the Commonwealth and Francophonie summits, and planning major state visits to Canada by the leaders of China, Japan, and the Philippines, not to mention another Team Canada mission, this time to Latin America in January 1998. We were also heavily involved on the policy side, especially in the campaign to ban anti-personnel mines and in efforts to determine how Canada should best respond to the Asian financial crisis. In September, I would accompany Mrs. Chrétien to Calcutta for the funeral of Mother Teresa. Subsequently, I would become progressively more involved in the preparations of the Canadian position our negotiators would take to Kyoto on climate change. While the Vancouver APEC summit was the most important single event on the prime minister's fall schedule, it was but one of many.

Moreover, by August 1997, I had been in my job long enough to know that there was no such thing as a problem-free official visit or summit, whether the venue was in Canada or abroad. Meticulous planning, involvement in the policy-making process, and close consultation with the prime minister minimized the scope for error. However, some things could not be planned for, simply could not be anticipated. Who, for example, could have foreseen the assassination of the leading candidate for the presidency on the first day of the prime minister's visit to Mexico in March 1994? How could we have foreseen that Premier Li of China would act like a spoilt child during his visit to Canada in October 1995? We could have anticipated that the White House would have been furious with the prime minister's open-mike joking in Madrid but the president, in any case, held no lasting grudge. Incidents like these were my daily fare on almost every visit and I enjoyed the challenge of coming up with solutions. When travelling abroad, I worked closely with the members of the accompanying PMO team to nip problems in the bud. In Canada, more often than not I worked directly with the prime minister to solve problems and he had faith in me. Sometimes too much!

On APEC, I had arranged for Len Edwards, the senior official from Foreign Affairs on Asian matters and special representative for the APEC summit, to brief the prime minister in late August. Len did so, mentioning but not expressing undue anxiety about the concerns of Suharto. Early in September, however, he and other colleagues from Foreign Affairs, under pressure from the Indonesians, started calling me with increasing frequency to say they were deeply worried the president would not come. His absence, they said, would badly damage the summit. The Australian High Commissioner[51] in Ottawa, Greg Wood, whose opinion I highly valued, then contacted me to urge that all the stops be pulled out to ensure that Suharto would attend. The Indonesians, in the opinion of his authorities, were not bluffing. Suharto would refuse to go to Vancouver if he or his handlers thought that his dignity would be "offended by events taking place in the streets."

Australia, Greg said, did not have the economic options of Canada, which was located next door to the world's richest and most accessible market. Its destiny was in Asia, and the trade liberalization implied in the APEC process was the key to obtaining access to regional markets that otherwise could turn protectionist and shut out Australian products. Indonesia was Australia's closest neighbour and was central to Australia's "Asia First" policy. For decades, relations between Canberra and Jakarta had been bad, fuelled by differences over East Timor and Irian Jaya. In recent years, however, there had been a rapprochement between the two neighbours and trade had been booming. It was essential, therefore, that Indonesia's leader come to Vancouver and remain closely involved in the APEC process.

I Worry

Len Edwards and Greg Wood had got my attention. I knew that there was nothing anyone could, or indeed should do about Suharto's concerns about having his "dignity being offended by events in the street." When Premier Li came to Canada in 1995, we had ignored his request to ban demonstrators and had found other ways to ensure the success of the visit. But I believed we should focus on reassuring the Indonesians at the highest level about the president's security. They would have to determine for themselves if our arrangements would lead to an offence against his dignity. I reckoned that if the prime minister himself were to speak to the Indonesian ambassador to reassure him on this point and then telephone the Indonesian president to do the same, Suharto would come. It was late on a Friday afternoon in

September when I came to this conclusion, however, and I hesitated to call the prime minister on a matter that was not of critical importance. I therefore included a note outlining my worries together with proposed speaking points to use with the ambassador and included it in the pack of documents sent to the prime minister's residence for his weekend reading. At my request, the prime minister's executive assistant then pencilled in an appointment for him to receive the ambassador and me first thing on the Monday morning.

I left my office early on Monday to enjoy the walk to the Centre Block of Parliament. It was the first day of fall, the weather was glorious, the air was fresh, and the leaves on the maple trees on Parliament Hill were starting to change colour. I had taken this path hundreds of times, dating back to 1967 when I was a junior-protocol officer in Foreign Affairs and it had been my job to usher heads of state and government visiting Canada during our centennial year into the Parliament buildings to meet Prime Minister Pearson. I had once helped Pierre Trudeau, then relatively unknown and clad in shorts and sandals, to persuade a skeptical security guard that he really was Canada's minister of Justice. In later years, as Canada's ambassador to Israel, I had accompanied the president of that country when he called on Prime Minister Mulroney and addressed a joint session of the House of Commons and Senate. And for the past three years, I had made this trip in all seasons, in all types of weather and at all times of the day and night to consult with the prime minister on problems big and small.

I was in a relaxed mood. Although I had recently been absent from Ottawa for a week to attend the funeral of Mother Teresa in India, my team in Ottawa had kept on top of all our issues. I had also, I thought, come up with the perfect solution to deal with Indonesia's difficult president. My track record in solving problems of this sort was excellent and I had no doubts that the prime minister would accept my proposed solution. It would not take long to deal with the matter, I assumed. Perhaps I would be able to review with him the details of his forthcoming trip to Russia. I flashed my pass to the guards, went up two flights of stairs, and, at peace with myself and the world, went in to see the prime minister at one minute to nine.

An angry prime minister greeted me. "Is this the ambassador who has been harassing members of the East Timorese community in Canada?" I avowed that he was.

"Then I don't want to see him." The prime minister added a choice selection of highly unparliamentary language to be sure I understood. "And you can tell him that if Suharto doesn't want to see demonstrators, then he should stay at home."

Ignoring what the prime minister had just said, I went to fetch the ambassador, who had been cooling his heels outside in the hall. To this day I don't know what possessed me to engage in this gross act of *lèse-majesté*. True, I was preoccupied with the need to have Suharto attend the summit and was certain that a word from the prime minister would guarantee his participation. If I had been thinking properly, however, I would not have disobeyed him as I did. Perhaps I was still jet-lagged from my trip to India. The prime minister, faced with his unwanted visitor, cast an uncomprehending glance at me and did the courteous thing. He offered his fawning visitor a seat and read out to him the speaking points that I had prepared, intoning the following words regarding Indonesia's leader: "His personal security is assured and steps will be taken to preserve his comfort. . . . Please convey to the president my intention to telephone him personally in the coming days to discuss his participation in the Vancouver APEC meeting."

As the enormity of my behaviour sunk in, I nervously left the room with the ambassador, and never mentioned the security or comfort of the president of Indonesia to the prime minister again. I certainly did not ask the PMO switchboard to book a telephone call from the prime minister to Suharto. But for what it was worth, my scheme worked. Nothing further was heard from the

Indonesians on the president's safety and embarrassment. Suharto came to Vancouver, participated in the sessions, and departed. The sixth meeting of the Asia-Pacific Economic Co-operation conference was relatively uneventful for Indonesia's president. The same could not be said, however, for his Canadian host.

Pepper Spray

My last cameo appearance in what would be known as the APEC scandal occurred on the last day at the summit itself. On November 25, I did not accompany the prime minister to the summit site, but remained in my hotel room watching the developments in the streets on television. Toward the end of the afternoon, I saw demonstrators clash with police and heard the commentator mention the use of pepper spray. Not knowing the substance, I assumed that it must be some mild crowd-control agent. The police, I naively thought, were going easy on the demonstrators. Excellent. Then it was time for me to join Peter Donolo at the front door to greet the prime minister when he returned to the Convention Centre to debrief us on the just-completed official talks, and to confer with us prior to meeting the press. Neither Peter nor I mentioned pepper spray. And, of course, the first question asked by a journalist was: "What about the pepper spray, Prime Minister?"

Deaf in one ear, the prime minister cupped his hand behind his good one and asked the journalist to repeat his question.

"The pepper spray! The pepper spray!"

A light came on in the prime minister's eyes. "Pepper? Pepper, I put it on my steak! Ha ha ha!"

The prime minister had displayed a terrible lack of sensitivity toward the demonstrators, said editorial writers and protestors alike. Even so, in normal circumstances, the story would have petered out after a few days. But it turned out that the police handling of the summit had been ham-handed. And pepper spray, it transpired, was *oleoresin capsicum*, made from the hottest peppers in the world and was actually one of the harshest crowd-control agents in the police inventory, leaving people temporarily blinded and struggling for breath. Fifty-two submissions from individuals alleging that they had been unjustly arrested, unfairly strip-searched, and illegally doused with pepper spray were filed with a commission responsible for investigating complaints against the RCMP. A three-member panel was established to investigate the allegations and was itself soon mired in controversy as a counsel, a commission chairman, and even a federal solicitor-general were forced to resign for making inappropriate public comments.

The hearings became a tamer version of the celebrated O. J. Simpson trial or an afternoon soap opera, with the public and political opposition anxiously awaiting new revelations each day of RCMP wrongdoing on the television evening news. On university campuses across the country, students, whether supporters of the various anti-globalization causes or not, were revolted by what they perceived as the excessive use of police force to protect a motley band of corrupt leaders from Asia with blood on their hands. From the beginning, complainants also alleged that the prime minister had instructed his director of operations, Jean Carle, to order the RCMP to use all means, including excessive force, to curb the demonstrators. A secondary line of attack opened up with the publication in the press of my records of his meeting with Ambassador Parwoto in the late summer of 1997. These documents in turn were taken as evidence that the prime minister had been involved in a conspiracy to restrict the rights of demonstrators. I was among the 153 witnesses called before the commission, and accepted my share of responsibility for the fiasco. Unsurprisingly, the complainants castigated me for not indicting the prime minister and a Toronto newspaper published a cartoon on its editorial page depicting me as a puppet being manipulated by a malevolent Jean Chrétien.

In all, there were 170 days of hearings, 710 exhibits entered, and 40,000 pages of testimony produced, all at great cost to the taxpayer. In the end, the commission chair, Justice Ted Hughes, in his report of July 31, 2001, was not gentle with Jean Carle and described a "police performance that did not meet an acceptable and expected standard of competence, professionalism, and proficiency." He also described "individual instances of police conduct that were inappropriate to the circumstances and, in some cases, inconsistent with respect for the fundamental freedoms guaranteed by the Charter of Rights." However, he also found that: "The efforts by Prime Minister Chrétien, Mr. Axworthy, Mr. Bartleman . . . to allay President Suharto's security concerns were proper, acceptable, and to be expected of the host of a significant international event such as the APEC conference."[52]

And finally, at the risk of ending my memoir with a touch of the maudlin, there is the story of the bag. Someone gave me a cloth bag at the APEC conference press centre. It was a black, cheap, mass-produced product with a shoulder strap and emblazoned with a Vancouver APEC logo, of the type handed out by the thousands as souvenirs at summit meetings around the world. The bag, however, was an omen of bad luck. After emptying out the glossy brochures provided as filler by the British Columbia tourist bureau extolling the warm welcome Vancouverites always accorded visitors, I gave it to my son. Laurent, a university student, was almost ostracized by his classmates when he used it to carry his books to class. He swiftly gave it back, and I took to using it to carry personal possessions such as my passport, wallet, and reading materials. I had it with me when I was viciously beaten during a hotel-room robbery in Cape Town some years later, when I was High Commissioner to South Africa.[53] Blood poured from my broken nose as I fumbled through the bag's pockets searching for anything that would satisfy my assailant, who continued to hit me as he demanded "The money! The money! Give me the money!" I have kept the bag, its APEC logo now stained a dark brown, as a macabre reminder of Vancouver 1997 and of what can happen when one is travelling on a rollercoaster.

Epilogue

It was a farewell in the field as I finished my last trip abroad with the prime minister – to Slovenia, Bosnia, Italy, and the Vatican.

As I put these words to paper, less than a year has passed since Jean Chrétien stepped down as prime minister. At this early stage, some critics consider the 1990s to be a black hole in terms of Canadian foreign-policy achievement and hold Canada's leader responsible for this alleged sorry state of affairs. This school blames him (fairly) for depriving Canada's military and diplomats of the resources they needed to do their jobs, and (unfairly) for presiding over a decline in Canada's place among the nations that had actually been ongoing for decades. Critics, perhaps nostalgic for the Trudeau era, allege that Chrétien lacked charisma, claim that his decision-making was whimsical, avow that he was intuitive rather than intellectual, and assert that his leadership on the great issues of the day was handicapped by an inability to articulate great ideas in his public speeches. One commentator, Andrew Cohen, author of the best-seller *While Canada Slept: How We Lost Our Place in the World*, has even said that Mr. Chrétien was the most parochial prime minister since Mackenzie King.[54]

On the other side are those who point to the strengths he brought to the conduct of foreign policy – his sense of humour, his avoidance of cant and pretence in public utterances, his ability to take tough decisions and live with the consequences, and his exceptional and sustained personal popularity that made him the envy of leaders around the world. Noel Sokolsky, Dean of Arts at the Royal Military College, has said that the Chrétien era was one of the most active in recent decades.[55] I am on the side of Sokolsky but am not by definition an objective observer since I was there. I was also Mr. Chrétien's advisor for less than half of his time in office and cannot comment as an insider on the big foreign-policy challenges that came up in his remaining years in office, in particular the Kosovo and Afghanistan military campaigns, his management of relations with George W. Bush, his response to the September 11, 2001, tragedy, his opening to Africa, and his refusal to commit troops to Iraq. In my opinion, however, his early foreign-policy initiatives were key in setting the course for what would come later. And Chrétien's record for these years speaks for itself.

There were, of course, failures and miscues, described throughout my account. The most serious of these was in not doing more for Rwanda during the three horrible months of genocide in the spring of 1994. The positive side of the ledger, however, overwhelmingly outweighs the negative. In a famous analogy, the British philosopher Isaiah Berlin, quoting the Greek poet, Archilochus, said that great men could be foxes "who knew many things" or hedgehogs "who knew one big thing."[56] In my opinion, contemporaries of Jean Chrétien such as Tony Blair, Bill Clinton, and François Mitterrand were foxes – as much at home among foreign ministers and the foreign-policy elite as among the rank and file in their countries, but with their energies dissipated by trying to juggle too many policy balls at the same time. Canada's leader, however, like Helmut Kohl, Jacques Chirac, and Boris Yeltsin were hedgehogs – political animals who derived their strength from being close to the pulse of their peoples and who communicated emotionally as well as intellectually with the crowd. Chrétien was a natural member of the latter group, a man of deep convictions, seizing on one or two big ideas and doggedly pursuing them to a conclusion. And in terms of ideas, the greatest for Chrétien was his love for Canada. When he took office, he

had, to paraphrase de Gaulle, "une certaine idée du Canada." For
Chrétien, Canada would not be Canada without being a successful multicultural exception among the racially divided nation
states of the 1990s, and a leader among the middle powers. And
Jean Chrétien was as passionate about Canada as Charles de Gaulle
was about France. He could not stand the thought that his beloved
country, crushed by debt and unemployment as it was when he
came to power, might tumble down into the ranks of the Third
World. He thus pursued integrated foreign- and domestic-policy
goals from the outset to lead Canada out of the recession of the
early 1990s by export-led growth. This contributed to the decade
of prosperity, social peace, relative political harmony at home, and
credibility abroad that will, I suspect, be seen by future historians
as his greatest contribution to his country.

Other ideas that he pursued tenaciously were his efforts to
embrace globalization, rather than trying to hide from it. He was
one of the first to recognize that Canada's growing population
of Chinese, Indian, Filipino, and Latin American citizens gave us
a natural advantage in establishing links of privilege with their
countries of origin, and that these links in turn made these new
Canadians more comfortable in their adopted homeland. The
highly popular campaign against anti-personnel mines would
not have come to a successful conclusion were it not for the priority he attached to the initiative over a three-year period. His
role in encouraging NATO enlargement to take in the countries
of Central and Eastern Europe, and correct a historical wrong,
will eventually be recognized as one of his leading successes. And
no leader could have done more to encourage Canadians to
embrace their Pacific and Latin American destinies, in particular with China, even if only time will tell whether the seeds he
planted will take root.

Looking back, I feel immensely lucky. I arrived in Ottawa to
be part of the action in early 1994 just after one political generation had run out of steam and had given way to another, still

filled with optimism and excitement. I was in on the ground floor when Team Canada was created and participated in its missions when it was blasting Canada's way into new markets, and was gone before it ran out of worlds to conquer. I was present during the honeymoon period of federal relations with all provinces except Quebec, and was privileged to come to know Canada's premiers as a result of travelling each year with them on lengthy trips to Asia and Latin America. I was at Chrétien's side when shrewd investments of prime-ministerial time brought disproportionate returns in new links with the Asia-Pacific and Latin American regions. There were occasions when I helped steer him away from the edge of precipitous foreign-policy cliffs, but that was part of my job. I did not turn out to be a Henry Kissinger, but Jean Chrétien functioned quite well without a foreign-policy giant alongside him.

I will never forget taking my leave in Rome in May 1998 after more than four years as the prime minister's diplomatic advisor. There would be formal goodbyes later in Ottawa before I rejoined the foreign service. But that hot night in the Italian capital, after the final official meeting I would attend as his diplomatic advisor, was special. I had been battling a debilitating depression for years and had finally plucked up the courage to tell the prime minister that I wanted off the rollercoaster to return to my first love – traditional diplomacy in a Canadian embassy or High Commission. He agreed and it was a farewell in the field marked by an immense sense of relief after I finished my last trip abroad – to Slovenia, Bosnia, Italy, and the Vatican. The prime minister joined the members of the PMO team in a small Italian restaurant for a late-night dinner to say *au revoir*. I had developed good working ties with Mr. Chrétien, but our relationship was as advisor to leader, and in no way personal. Moreover, the PMO had never sought to involve me in partisan politics, and the way was clear for me to depart on a posting as High Commissioner to South Africa.

And I left with my memories – the dying Mitterrand, the hopeful Rabin, the happy Princess Diana, the resolute John Paul II, the conciliatory Clinton, the vindictive Sandy Berger, the raging Castro, the tipsy Yeltsin, the evil Li Peng, the smooth Berlusconi, the furious Brian Tobin, the traumatically injured General Dallaire. And the places: Paris, Rome, New York, and London in all seasons, shell-shattered Sarajevo, polluted Beijing, overcrowded Mumbai, traffic-clogged New Delhi, ultra-modern Tokyo, artificial Brasilia, baking Sharm el-Sheikh. Not to mention the bedlam in Mexico City following the assassination of Luis Donaldo Colosio Murrieta, Mother Teresa's funeral, the anti-personnel mines crusade, Her Majesty receiving guests on board the *Britannia*, Fidel Castro strangling me, snarling "I hope you are satisfied, Bartleman!," boring state dinners, adrenalin rushes, motorcades, and friendships to last for what remains of my lifetime.

Appendix One

Visitors to Canada: November 1993 – May 1998

1993

November 16-19 – Prime Minister Yitzhak Rabin of Israel

November 29-December 1 – Secretary-General Chief Emeka Anyaoku of the Commonwealth

1994

January 23-28 – President Jean-Bertrand Aristide of Haiti

March 10 – Chairman Eduard Shevardnadze of Georgia

March 21-22 – Director General Peter Sutherland of the General Agreement on Tariffs

April 10-13 – Prime Minister Francisque Ravony of Madagascar

April 19 – Vice President Ejup Ganic of Bosnia-Herzegovina

April 21 – President-elect José Maria Figueres Olsen of Costa Rica

May 8-9 – Ambassador Madeleine Albright, American ambassador to the U.N.

June 20-23 – President Carlos Menem of Argentina

July 13-15 – Prime Minister Percival Patterson of Jamaica

July 19 – Vice President Albert Gore of the United States

August 16-19 – Secretary-General Boutros Boutros-Ghali of the U.N.

August 27-September 1 – Prime Minister Edward Fenech-Adami of Malta

September 10-13 – President Lech Walesa of Poland

September 14-18 – Prime Minister Jean-Luc Dehaene of Belgium

September 28 – October 1 – President Ali Hassan Mwinyi of Tanzania

September 28-October 5 – Prime Minister Chuan Leekpai of Thailand

October 4-7 – Prime Minister Faustin Twagiramungu of Rwanda

October 16-21 – President Nicéphore Soglo of Benin
October 23-27 – President Leonid Kuchma of Ukraine
October 23-27 – President Mitsuo Sato of the Asian Development Bank
October 27-29 – President Enrique Iglesias of the Inter-American Development Bank
November 22 – President Ernesto Zedillo of Mexico
November 23 – Prime Minister Yitzhak Rabin of Israel

1995

February 11-14 – Chancellor Franz Vranitzky of Austria
February 19-21 – Secretary-General César Gaviria Trujillo of the Organization of American States
February 23-24 – President William Clinton of the United States
March 1-2 – Secretary-General Willy Claes of NATO
March 20-24 – United Nations High Commissioner for Human Rights José Ayala-Lasso
March 27-30 – Prime Minister Akezhan Kazhegeldin of Kazakhstan
April 2-4 – Director-General Peter Sutherland of the World Trade Organization
April 6-8 – King Hussein of Jordan
April 26 – Prime Minister Lamberto Dini of Italy
June 14-17 – Halifax G7 Summit
June 17-18 – Chancellor Helmut Kohl of Germany
July 4-8 – Foreign Minister László Kovács of Hungary
July 4-9 – President Blaise Compaoré of Burkina Faso
September 11-14 – Prime Minister Goh Chok Tong of Singapore
September 22-24 – Prime Minister John Bruton of Ireland
September 27-30 – Secretary-General Chief Emeka Anyaoku of the Commonwealth
October 4-7 – Prime Minister Viktor Chernomyrdin of Russia
October 12-13 – Premier Li Peng of China
October 16-21 – President Kim Young Sam of Korea
November 21-23 – Secretary-General Boutros Boutros-Ghali of the U.N.

1996

March 22-24 – President René Préval of Haiti

April 30-May 3 – Governor Christopher Patten of Hong Kong

May 1-4 – President Abdou Diouf of Senegal

May 8-9 – Prime Minister Janez Drnovsek of Slovenia

May 15-17 – Heads of State of Central America

May 25 – Secretary-General Boutros Boutros-Ghali of the U.N.

May 27-June 2 – Director-General Renato Ruggiero of the World Trade Organization

June 9-11 – Prime Minister Alain Juppé of France

June 10-14 – President Ernesto Zedillo of Mexico

June 13-25 – President Cheddi Jagan of Guyana

October 6-10 – Prime Minister Daniel Duncan of Ivory Coast

October 9 – Prime Minister Basdeo Panday of Trinidad and Tobago

November 17-18 – President Eduardo Frei of Chile

December 17-18 – Prime Minister John Bruton of Ireland

1997

February 20-23 – Prime Minister Václav Klaus of the Czech Republic

April 11 – Secretary-General Javier Solana of NATO

April 10-14 – Prime Minister Rafik Al-Hariri of Lebanon

April 21-24 – President Fernando Cardoso of Brazil

June 12-16 – Prime Minister Pavlo Lazarenko of the Ukraine

June 23-28 – President Luigi Scalfaro of Italy

September 3-5 – Secretary-General Chief Emeka Anyaoku of the Commonwealth

November 24-25 – Vancouver APEC summit

November 26-27 – Prime Minister Ryutaro Hashimoto of Japan

November 26-29 – President Jiang Zemin of China

November 27-30 – President Fidel Ramos of the Philippines

December 1-4 – Secretary-General Kofi Annan of the U.N.

December 4 – Prime Minister Jean-Claude Juncker of Luxembourg and Jacques Santer, President of the European Commission

1998

February 11-15 – Vice President Carlos Lage of Cuba

February 15-17 – President Enrique Iglesias of the Inter-American Development Bank

March 9-10 – Secretary of State Madeleine Albright of the United States

May 3-5 – Bernard Kouchner, Minister of Employment of France

May 24-30 – President Emil Constantinescu of Romania

May 26-28 – Secretary-General Donald Johnston of the OECD

Appendix Two

Prime-Ministerial Travel: November 1993 – May 1998

1993
November 18-20 – Seattle APEC summit

1994
January 5-6 – London
January 6-9 – Paris
January 9-12 – NATO summit, Brussels
March 23-25 – Mexico City
June 2-5 – United Kingdom
June 5-8 – France D-Day Fiftieth Anniversary
June 9-10 – Bosnia-Herzegovina
July 5-6 – Bonn
July 7 – Vatican
July 8-10 – Naples G7 summit
September 8-9 – Reykjavik
November 5-10 – Team Canada China
November 10-13 – Hong Kong
November 13-16 – APEC summit, Bogor, Indonesia
November 16-17 – Hanoi
November 30-December 4 – HIV/AIDS summit, Paris
December 5-7 – OSCE summit, Budapest
December 9-11 – Miami summit

1995
January 19-30 – Trade Mission Latin America: Port of Spain,
Montevideo, Buenos Aires, Santiago, Brasilia, Rio de Janeiro, San José

March 23 – IMF and World Bank consultations, Washington
April 5-6 – Dallas speech to editors
May 4-May 11 – Europe VE Day: Netherlands, London, Paris, Moscow,
    Caen, Trouville
June 15-17 – Halifax G7 summit
June 18-21 – Chancellor Helmut Kohl visit to Iqaluit
October 20-23 – U.N. Fiftieth Anniversary, New York
November 6 – Funeral of Yitzhak Rabin in Israel
November 9-14 – Auckland and Queenstown Commonwealth summit
November 14 – Wellington official visit
November 14-16 – Canberra official visit
November 16-19 – APEC summit, Osaka
December 1-4 – Francophonie summit, Cotonou

1996
January 9-19 – Team Canada: India, Pakistan, Indonesia, Malaysia
March 4-5 – Canada-CARICOM summit, St. George's, Grenada
March 12-13 – Summit of the Peacemakers, Sharm el Sheikh, Egypt
April 16-18 – Bucharest official visit
April 19-20 – Moscow nuclear summit
June 25-27 – Vatican and Canada–EU summit
June 27-29 – G7 summit, Lyon
July 18-19 – Atlanta Olympics
November 22-26 – APEC summit, Manila
November 26 – Shanghai
November 26-30 – Japan official visit
November 30-December 2 – OSCE summit, Lisbon

1997
January 9-20 – Team Canada: Seoul, Manila, Bangkok
January 21-24 – France official visit
February 1 – Toronto summit on hostage situation in Peru
April 7-9 – U.S.A. official visit
June 19 – G7 summit, Denver
June 23-25 – Summit of the environment, New York
July 6-9 – NATO summit, Madrid
October 18-22 – Moscow and St. Petersburg official visit

October 22-23 – London official visit
October 23-27 – Edinburgh Commonwealth summit
November 12-16 – Francophonie summit, Hanoi
November 21-25 – APEC summit, Vancouver

1998
January 15-23 – Team Canada: Mexico City, Brasilia, São Paulo, Buenos
   Aires, Santiago
March 2-3 – New York Disability awards
April 16 – Canada-CARICOM summit, Nassau, Bahamas
April 17-18 – Summit of the Americas, Santiago, Chile
April 26-28 – Official visit Havana, Cuba
May 12-14 – London
May 15-17 – Birmingham G8 summit
May 17-18 – Slovenia official visit
May 18 – Bosnia-Herzegovina visit to troops
May 18-23 – Italy official visit
May 19 – Vatican official visit

Appendix Three

Summits: November 1994–May 1998

NATO. Brussels, Belgium. January 6-9, 1994.

Canada-Europe. Bonn, Germany. July 5-6, 1994.

G7. Naples, Italy. July 8-10, 1994.

APEC. Bogor, Indonesia. November 13-19, 1994.

HIV/AIDS. Paris, France. November 30-December 4, 1994.

OSCE. Budapest, Hungary. December 5-7, 1994.

Americas. Miami, USA. December 9-11, 1994.

Central American leaders. San Jose, Costa Rica. January 29-30, 1995.

G7. Halifax, Canada. June 15-17, 1995.

United Nations Fiftieth Anniversary. New York, USA. October 20-23, 1995.

Commonwealth. Auckland, New Zealand, November 9-14, 1995.

APEC. Osaka, Japan. November 16-19, 1995.

Francophonie. Cotonou, Benin. December 1-4, 1995.

Canada-CARICOM. St. Georges, Grenada. March 4-5, 1996.

Peacemakers. Sharm el Sheikh, Egypt. March 12-13, 1996.

Central America leaders. Ottawa, Canada. May 15-17, 1996.

Nuclear summit. Moscow, Russia. April 19-20, 1996.

Canada-Europe. Rome, Italy. June 25-27, 1996.

G7. Lyon, France. June 27-28, 1996.

APEC. Manila, Philippines. November 22-26, 1996.

OSCE. Lisbon, Portugal. November 30-December 2, 1996.

Canada-Europe. Ottawa, Canada. December 17-18, 1996.

Peru hostage-taking summit with P.M. Hashimoto and President Fujimori. Toronto, Canada. February 1, 1997.

G8. Denver, USA. June 19, 1997.

Canada-Europe. Denver, USA, June 21, 1997. United States.

Environment. New York, USA. June 23-25, 1997.

NATO. Madrid, Spain. July 6-9, 1997.

Commonwealth. Edinburgh, Scotland. October 23-27, 1997.

Francophone. Hanoi, Vietnam. November 12-16, 1997.

APEC. Vancouver, Canada. November 21-25, 1997.

Canada-Europe. Ottawa, Canada. December 4, 1997.

Canada-CARICOM. Nassau, Bahamas. April 16, 1998.

Americas. Santiago, Chile. April 17-18, 1998.

G8. Birmingham, United Kingdom. May 15-17, 1998.

Canada-Europe. Birmingham, United Kingdom. May 17, 1998.

Note: Prior to my arrival as his advisor, the prime minister attended the APEC summit in Seattle from November 18-20, 1993.

Endnotes

1. The United Nations, with its bloated bureaucracy and ineffective decision-making procedures, and presided over by Secretary-General Boutros Boutros-Ghali, the snobbish, prickly Egyptian diplomat who took over in 1992, bears part of the blame for the failure of the international community to deal effectively with the crises of the 1990s, most notoriously the genocide in Rwanda in 1994.

2. In March 1991, Mohammed al-Mashat, a former Iraqi ambassador to the United States, was admitted to Canada. Given al-Mashat's background as an apologist for Saddam Hussein, there was an uproar in Canada. Who, press and opposition parliamentarians demanded, was responsible for the decision? Until this time, it had been Canadian practice for ministers to assume responsibility for the actions of public servants who worked for them. In this case, the finger was pointed at Raymond Chrétien, the senior Foreign Affairs official, even though he had advised the chief of staff to his minister, Joe Clark, of the decision to admit al-Mashat ahead of time. The case is now a standard part of university courses on Canadian public policy.

3. In 1944, the Canadian government established a universal family allowance program of modest cash payments to help mothers provide for their children's basic needs.

4. Jacques Roy, Bill Jenkins, Alan Sullivan, Robert Fowler, Reid Morden, Ernest Hébert, Anne-Marie Doyle, and Paul Heinbecker.

5. I would not, I soon discovered, be expected to provide such independent advice on budgetary and defence procurement matters, given their domestic political sensitivity. Such advice was given to the prime minister by members of the PMO.

6. Battalions and regiments are units commanded by lieutenant

colonels and are comprised of sub-units: batteries of artillery, companies of infantry, and squadrons of armour, communications, and engineers commanded by majors.

7. See World Bank report *Assessing Aid* (New York: Oxford University Press, 1998).

8. Foreign Affairs, Defence, and CIDA, accordingly, were not spared when the government slashed the budgets of its departments to meet budgetary targets in the mid-1990s.

9. The University of Toronto G8 Information Centre provides an excellent factual summary of the origins of the G8 as follows: "Starting with the 1994 Naples Summit, the G7 met with Russia at each summit (referred to as the P8 or Political 8). The Denver summit of the Eight was a milestone, marking full Russian participation in all but financial and certain economic discussions; and the 1998 Birmingham summit saw full Russian participation, giving birth to the G8 (although the G7 continued to function alongside the formal summit. At the Kananaskis summit in Canada in 2002, it was announced that Russia would host the G8 summit in 2006, thus completing its process of becoming a full member."

10. See Chapter Six.

11. In his introduction to *Human Security and the New Diplomacy* (Montreal: McGill-Queen's University Press, 2001), Lloyd Axworthy says that "The human security agenda is a basis for a new way forward. It attempts to deal with new and newly transformed threats to the lives and safety of individuals, both at home and abroad. . . . Some have taken soft power to mean weakness, or lacking hard power. That is a wrong, and perhaps politically motivated, rebranding of an essentially positive phrase. Soft power relies on diplomatic resources, persuasion, information capacity, and creative use of selective military tools rather than coercive force to promote a country's interests or project its influence on the world stage. It means maximizing our talent for coalition building, developing ideas, and making use of the multilateral system. Exercising soft power is not a retreat from any great hard power tradition and it does not reduce Canada's influence abroad."

12. See the first volume of my memoirs, *Out of Muskoka* (Manotick, Ontario: Penumbra Press, 2002).

13. See the second volume of my memoirs, *On Six Continents* (Toronto: Douglas Gibson Books, McClelland & Stewart, 2004).

14. Lester Pearson fought to turn NATO into a North Atlantic Community, with close economic and political as well as military ties among its signatories, when the original treaty was being drafted in 1948. He persuaded the others to include a provision providing for a non-military dimension, but the Americans and the Europeans were reluctant to use NATO for anything other than security purposes. Canada's dream died with the 1957 Treaty of Rome when Germany, France, Italy, and the Benelux countries launched the European Economic Community, opting for an economic future that did not include Canada.

In the 1970s, Canada made another effort by negotiating a "contractual link" with the European Economic Community. The resulting "Framework Agreement" signed in July 1976 was impressive in its ambition but modest in its accomplishments. In addition to providing for regular meetings between foreign ministers, a Joint Co-operation Committee and a myriad of subcommittees and working groups were set up to remove obstacles to trade and to find ways to deepen economic ties. The business communities on both sides of the Atlantic ignored the initiative, and trade between Canada and Europe continued its downward slide. No one was surprised when the Europeans took no notice when Prime Minister Chrétien floated the idea once again of a free-trade deal between Canada and the new Europe in a speech to the French senate in November 1994. Canada's search for an economic and political counterweight to the United States would continue, but this time in Asia and Latin America.

15. I am grateful to John Noble, minister of the Canadian embassy in Paris during these years, for these details.

16. So close did their ties become, the president would even host a farewell gala in Paris for Prime Minister Chrétien when he left office in December 2003.

17. Mitchell Sharp started his career in the public service, rising to become deputy minister of Finance before moving on to his illustrious political career.

18. Michael Adams, *Fire and Ice: The United States, Canada and the Myth of Converging Values* (Toronto: Penguin Canada, 2003).

19. From 1995 to 1998, for example, the prime minister, fully occupied with Asia and Latin America, accepted only six official invitations to European countries while attending seven obligatory summit meetings on European soil. The record for incoming visitors was somewhat better: fifteen European leaders were received by the prime minister in Ottawa. Few, however, were of the stature of the leaders received from Latin America and the Asia-Pacific region.

20. In subsequent rants in the coming months on his personal Web site, he attacked me as the ineffective yet malign instrument of wrongheaded Canadian government policy.

21. The Europeans may not have been entirely wrong. Bill Rowat, deputy minister of Fisheries, later told me that Brian Tobin considered proposing that Canada declare Canadian sovereignty over the Nose and Tail.

22. Brian Tobin, *All in Good Time* (Toronto: Penguin Canada, 2002).

23. In *All in Good Time*, Tobin repeated his "gutless" slur, but dropped his reference to me as a hated central Canadian, perhaps because he had moved to Toronto by that time. He also described me as a dove, probably the worst epithet he could think of, but I accepted it as a compliment.

24. See Chapter Eleven of the second volume of my memoirs, *On Six Continents* (Toronto: Douglas Gibson Books, McClelland & Stewart, 2004).

25. The German airforce destroyed the Spanish city of Guernica on April 26, 1937, in savage bombing attacks that shocked the world.

26. I am convinced that Canada could have become a member, had we pushed hard to be included. We did not, I believe, out of a concern that we could find ourselves even more deeply embroiled in the Balkans.

27. On March 31, 1995, the United Nations peacekeeping operation in the former Yugoslavia was reorganized and renamed. Overall command was called the United Nations Peace Force (UNPF); the forces in Bosnia inherited the designation United Nations Protection Force (UNPROFOR); and the force in Croatia was renamed the United Nations Confidence Restoration Operation (UNCRO).

28. Clinton named his vice president American representative on a U.S.A.–Russia Economic and Technical Co-operation Commission,

to work with Prime Minister Viktor Chernomyrdin to strengthen bilateral relations. He also asked him to co-chair a similar type of commission with Thabo Mbeki, at that time deputy to President Nelson Mandela. In his autobiography, *My Life* (New York: Alfred A. Knopf, 2004), Clinton provided his reasons for delegating this type of responsibility to Gore. "In the post–Cold War world, with America the world's only military, economic, and political superpower, every nation wanted our attention, and it was usually in our interest to give it. But I couldn't go everywhere. As a result, Al Gore and Hillary made an unusually large number of important foreign trips."

29. Prime Minister Chrétien jokingly used to say that when the American president called asking for a favour, his predecessor answered the telephone by immediately saying "Yes, hello." He, Jean Chrétien, however, answered such calls with a "Hello, yes." Canada's prime ministers throughout the years have had to live with the reality that the friendly giant to the south expected Canada to support it internationally on all the big issues and there would be costs if the answer was "no."

30. In his autobiography, *My Life*, Clinton would say that "We spent a lot of time with Prime Minister Jean Chrétien and his wife, Aline. Mr. Chrétien would become one of my best friends among world leaders, a strong ally, confidant, and frequent golfing partner."

31. A pastry made with flour, yeast, milk, and salt, shaped vaguely like the tail of a real beaver, boiled in oil, and served with a dusting of sugar and a touch of cinnamon. Jam is optional.

32. Queen Elizabeth II is Canada's head of state, and her personal representative in Canada is the governor-general.

33. An American colleague later told me that some fifty civilian and military officers engaged in preparing the positions for the American negotiators in Oslo listened in to the conversations between Prime Minister Chrétien and President Clinton, seeking ideas to break the internal American deadlock.

34. Dean Acheson as quoted on page 364 of John English's *The Worldly Years: The Life of Lester Pearson 1949-1972* (Toronto: Alfred A. Knopf Canada, 1992).

35. This was a favourite theme of Fidel Castro when I was on a posting in Havana in the early 1980s. Castro was fond of telling visitors from Canada that should revolutionaries seize power in Haiti, they would

expect Havana to support them economically, but their needs would be too great for Cuba to do so.

36. In 1999, the prime minister committed Canada's air force to support NATO's intervention in Kosovo – without a United Nations Security Council authorization. In 2001, he sent in Canadian troops as part of a Security Council–mandated intervention to clear the Taliban from Afghanistan. In 2003, he refused to send forces to support an American invasion of Iraq that was not blessed by the Security Council. In one of the major initiatives of his last years in office, he embraced the cause of humanitarian intervention, and announced on September 2000 the creation of a blue-ribbon panel to prepare a report for the United Nations. The resulting document, *Responsibility to Protect, Report of the International Commission on Intervention and State*, was issued in December 2001.

37. President Clinton did not, of course, act solely on his own initiative. The issue was considered a domestic one and the prime minister's senior domestic political advisor, Eddie Goldenberg, worked closely with American ambassador, James Blanchard, to choreograph his interventions. See Ambassador James Blanchard's book on his years in Canada, *Behind the Embassy Door: Canada, Clinton and Quebec* (Toronto: McClelland & Stewart, 1997).

38. Roméo Dallaire, *Shake Hands with the Devil* (Toronto: Random House of Canada, 2003).

39. See World Bank report *Assessing Aid* (New York: Oxford University Press, 1998).

40. Nik Gowing, "Dispatches from Disaster Zones," conference paper prepared for the European Community's Humanitarian Office, May 27, 1998. Gowing, an internationally recognized expert on the role of the media in conflict management, describes how inexperienced officials from humanitarian organizations provided inaccurate reports to the media and to United Nations headquarters, making a bad situation appear even worse.

41. Drawing on lessons learned from the deployment of the hospital in 1995, Defence had created a novel organization, the Disaster Assistance Relief Team or DART, with prepackaged components ready for deployment in emergencies.

42. Ernesto Che Guevara, *The African Dream, The Diaries of the Revolutionary War in the Congo* (London: The Harvil Press, 2000).

43. Strobe Talbot, deputy secretary of state under Clinton for seven years, responsible for relations with Russia, described Yeltsin's medical prognosis at this time as follows: "The medical and political prospects could hardly have been bleaker. Yeltsin seemed to have recovered from the heart attacks that felled him . . . but the likelihood of another one within a year was rated at 25 per cent, and the chance that it would be a fatal attack was estimated at twenty-five times the average for a man of his age." Strobe Talbot, *The Russia House* (New York: Random House, 2002).

44. Yeltsin, who blew off two fingers from his left hand years earlier in a grenade accident, seemed to have been particularly impressed by the prime minister's description of the horrendous damage mines inflicted on farmers and children in the Third World.

45. The prime minister's only involvement in Andean South America, in the years I was with him, was involuntary. On December 17, 1996, leftist guerillas of the Tupac Amaru Revolutionary Movement (MRTA) attacked the residence of the Japanese ambassador in Lima, capturing several hundred guests, including Canadian ambassador Anthony (Tony) Vincent, and his wife, Lucie. Canada was then dragged into the often sordid world of power struggle typical to the region between revolutionary ideologues prepared to go to any means to achieve their goals and governmental forces of repression prepared to do the same.

I knew the region well, having served as a junior officer in the late 1960s in Bogotá, Colombia, travelling extensively in Ecuador and Peru. I returned to Peru in 1981 to take temporary charge of a Canadian embassy (see *On Six Continents*) overwhelmed with the problems of protecting itself against an urban terrorist threat and in managing more than a hundred Canadians being held prisoner in the notorious local jail for drug trafficking. At that time government forces and adherents of the Shining Path guerilla organization were locked in fierce combat. Tens of thousands of innocent civilians would be killed in the crossfire. In time, using scorched earth tactics, the Peruvian government managed to beat back the Shining Path. In the interim, a sister revolutionary organization, the one that seized the Japanese embassy, had risen to take its place. It now demanded the release of all its members held in prison before it would release its prisoners in the embassy.

It was 11:15 p.m. on December 17 when I was informed of the crisis. Gar Pardy, director-general of consular affairs, telephoned to give me the bad news. He would, he said, brief the foreign minister in the morning. I told him that the prime minister would want to be informed immediately. And he was, despite being awakened from a sound sleep. He approved a press release condemning the terrorist action and expressing sympathy for the Vincent family. "Call me any time of the day or night," he told me.

Lucie was then released. Then Tony himself, together with diplomats from France, Germany, and Greece, was set free – on condition they pass messages to the Peruvian government and return to resume their captivity. That is when Tony showed everyone what he was made of. The other diplomats scampered for safety and did not return. Tony resolutely decided to fulfill his part of the bargain and return to the Japanese residence after speaking to the Peruvian authorities.

I managed to get Tony on the telephone before he returned to captivity. "Before you act, I want you to speak to the prime minister."

The prime minister was full of admiration, telling him: "You are a brave man, Tony, but you need not go back to a possible death."

"But I gave my word, Mr. Prime Minister," said Tony. "Besides, perhaps by returning I might help save lives. The guerillas may decide to use me as a negotiator."

This part of the story has a moderately happy ending. The terrorists released him again. The prime minister of Japan called to express his gratitude. But on April 22, 1997, Peruvian security forces stormed the Japanese embassy, freeing the remaining hostages and killing all the terrorists. The Peruvian government probably never had intended to strike a deal with the hostage-takers. But from December to April, they gave every appearance of trying to find a negotiated settlement and Tony Vincent played a central and honourable role in that effort. At the request of the guerillas, Tony was brought in at an early stage as one of three guarantors (the other two were the Roman Catholic Church and the International Committee of the Red Cross on a guarantor commission) sitting in on the talks with the government. As such, he came to Toronto in February to brief Prime Minister Chrétien, who hosted the leaders of Japan and Peru planning strategy for the crisis. The prime minister repeated to Tony that he was a "gutsy guy," someone that he and all Canadians were very proud of.

Tony returned to Lima, where he continued to visit his former captors in a mediator's role. He had, in fact, just left the compound before the assault was launched. Prime Minister Hashimoto of Japan, who had hoped for a non-violent end to the occupation, called the prime minister to express Japan's appreciation for Tony's efforts, and Foreign Affairs had another hero.

Sadly, Tony died at an early age in 1999 while serving as Canada's ambassador to Spain.

46. According to the Summit of the Americas Information Network: "The Conference originated in 1980 when the First Ladies of Central America decided to meet to exchange experiences and integrate goals, projects, and mechanisms for action and co-operation among their nations. It became an annual event in 1991 and a hemispheric event in 1994, with the first-time participation of Canada and the United States. . . . Eight . . . conferences were held in Chile (1998), Panama (1997), Bolivia (1996), Paraguay (1996), Saint Lucia (1994), Costa Rica (1993), Colombia (1992), and Venezuela (1991). The Conference of Spouses traditionally focuses on social welfare themes, such as health, education, violence, and the increased participation in society of women and children." The 1999 conference was held in Canada with Mrs. Chrétien as the co-host, together with CIDA president Huguette Labelle.

47. The name "fast track" was changed to "trade promotion authority" in 2002.

48. The gory details are outlined in my memoir *On Six Continents* (Toronto: Douglas Gibson Books, McClelland & Stewart, 2004).

49. I thank Ambassador Mark Entwistle for giving me permission to include the details of Castro's discussion with Trudeau in this book. Note that Castro travelled to Montreal to attend the funeral of his old friend on October 3, 2000.

50. Members are referred to as "economies" rather than "countries" because of the participation of the three Chinese economies – the People's Republic of China, Chinese Taiwan, and Hong Kong – not all of which are recognized as countries by the international community.

51. Commonwealth countries exchange High Commissioners rather than ambassadors. The practice dates from the time when all Commonwealth members had the same head of state. When India and Pakistan became independent in the immediate post-war period and did not recognize King George VI as head of state, but as head of the Commonwealth, the practice was continued among all members of the growing Commonwealth.

52. In Article 32 of his Interim Report, Justice Ted Hughes outlined the efforts of the Canadian government to ensure the Indonesian president's attendance as follows: "In July 1997, Foreign Minister Lloyd Axworthy went to Jakarta and met separately with President Suharto, with Indonesia's Foreign Minister Alatas, and with the Human Rights Commission. Ambassador Smith was present at each meeting. He testified that Mr. Axworthy told President Suharto his security would be assured at the APEC conference and that Mr. Axworthy conveyed the same message to the Indonesian Foreign Minister.

On September 3, 1997, Mr. Axworthy wrote a letter to Foreign Minister Alatas which contained the following passage:

> With respect to security arrangements for the APEC Economic Leaders Meeting (AELM) in Vancouver in November, I would like to extend to you my assurance that the security concerns of the Indonesian government will be given the utmost consideration. In addition, as promised during our discussions in Jakarta, I have conveyed the security concerns of President Suharto to Prime Minister Chrétien.
>
> A senior Royal Canadian Mounted Police officer will be assigned as personal security officer to your President and, together with dedicated bodyguards, will accompany the President during the entire time he is in Vancouver . . . and will also be at his disposal. With a police escort that will be provided throughout and additional route security measures, I am confident that we will provide for free and unobstructed movement of the President.

On September 12, Ambassador Smith personally delivered the letter to senior officials in the Indonesian Foreign Ministry and orally assured them that President Suharto's safety would not be compromised. In September 1997, Mr. Bartleman had become concerned about President Suharto's possible boycott of the APEC conference. He recommended a meeting between Prime Minister Chrétien and the Indonesian Ambassador to Canada, Mr. Parwoto [sic]. The meeting took place on September 22, 1997, at the Prime Minister's offices. Mr. Bartleman testified that the Prime Minister went right to the point, concentrating on security issues, and that the Prime Minister told Mr. Parwoto [sic] that the safety and dignity of all leaders attending the APEC conference, including President Suharto, would be assured during their visit to Vancouver.

On October 3, Prime Minister Chrétien wrote to the heads of the APEC economies, formally inviting them to the November 1997 meetings. On the advice of his officials, and because of the continuing uncertainty regarding President Suharto's attendance, the following paragraph was inserted into President Suharto's invitation alone:

> I understand you have had discussions with my Minister of Foreign Affairs on the arrangements for the Vancouver meetings. I have directed my officials to spare no effort to ensure that appropriate security and other arrangements are made for your stay in Canada as our guest. I recall warmly my participation in the 1994 meeting you hosted and the leadership you provided in developing the Bogor Declaration, which has been so crucial in advancing APEC's agenda. I hope that I may count on your support, advice, and encouragement to ensure that the Vancouver meeting is also a success.

On October 7, 1997, Ambassador Edwards personally delivered Prime Minister Chrétien's letter to President Suharto in Jakarta. Ambassador Smith was also present. (Although they discussed the APEC conference, President Suharto did not raise the security issue on this occasion.) As the ambassadors were leaving, a senior Indonesian government minister indicated to Ambassador Edwards that he would see him in Vancouver. The Canadians took this as a sign that the Indonesian delegation would attend the APEC conference as, of course, they did.

Later the same day, Ambassadors Edwards and Smith attended on Foreign Minister Alatas and others. The Indonesians indicated their continuing concerns about what would occur in Vancouver. As recorded in a report on the meeting prepared and approved by Ambassador Smith:

> (Mr. Edwards) noted that the Canadian host would take all the precautions necessary to protect the dignity of its guest. Canadian law does not permit, however, the banning of peaceful demonstration or expression of views.

Propriety of Canada's Effort

I have two comments to make on the sequence of events I have just described.

Firstly, the efforts of Prime Minister Chrétien, Mr. Axworthy, Mr. Bartleman, and the two ambassadors to allay President Suharto's security concerns were proper, acceptable, and to be expected of the host of a significant international event such as the APEC conference. As explained by Ambassador Edwards, it was particularly important to Canada that President Suharto attend the APEC conference. It is unrealistic to expect that as host of the APEC conference the Prime Minister's Office would take no interest whatsoever in the security concerns of a foreign leader, particularly where failing to provide appropriate assurances might result in a boycott, to the detriment of the conference in general and Canada's economic aspirations in particular. . . .

Secondly, the message communicated by Ambassador Edwards to Foreign Minister Alatas . . . is consistent with the message that I accept was conveyed consistently by Canadian officials to Indonesian officials over the months leading up to the APEC conference: although President Suharto's security and dignity would be protected, there was no guarantee that he would not encounter peaceful protests advancing political views inconsistent with his own. I agree with the following two paragraphs of the written submission of counsel for the Attorney General of Canada, the first of which is based on the evidence of Ambassador Edwards and Mr. Bartleman. . . .

> Indonesian officials were given no assurances beyond the protection of Suharto's security and dignity. Indonesian officials were informed that the Canadian Government could not guarantee that they would not see demonstrators, although protestors would not be permitted in close proximity."

53. See the first volume of my memoirs, *Out of Muskoka* (Manotick, Ontario: Penumbra Press, 2002).
54. Andrew Cohen, *While Canada Slept: How We Lost Our Place in the World* (Toronto: McClelland & Stewart, 2003).
55. Noel Sokolsky, *Realism Canadian Style: National Security Policy and the Chrétien Legacy. Policy Matters* 5, no. 2 (Montreal: Institute for Research on Public Policy, 2004).
56. Sir Isaiah Berlin, *The Hedgehog and the Fox* (New York: Simon and Schuster, 1953). According to Berlin, "Taken figuratively, the words can be made to yield a sense in which they mark one of the deepest differences which divide writers and thinkers, and, it may be, human beings in general. For there exists a great chasm between those, on one side, who relate everything to a single central vision, one system less or more coherent or articulate, in terms of which they understand, think and feel . . . and on the other side, those who pursue many ends, often unrelated and even contradictory, connected, if at all, only in some de facto way, for some psychological or physiological cause. . . ."

Acknowledgements

Besides Jean Chrétien I thank Gordon Smith, deputy minister of Foreign Affairs and later Executive Director of the Centre for Global Studies at the University of Victoria; Michael Kergin, assistant deputy minister for the Americas in Foreign Affairs and my successor in the summer of 1998 as diplomatic advisor to the prime minister; Raymond Chrétien, ambassador to Washington and later ambassador to Paris; Dr. Tommie Sue Montgomery of Trent University; John Noble, minister at the Canadian embassy in Paris and later Director of Research and Communications, Centre for Trade Policy and Law, Carleton University; Jean Pelletier, Chief of Staff to the prime minister; Chaviva Hosek, Director of Policy and Research in the Prime Minister's Office; Michael Shenstone, former assistant deputy minister for International Security Affairs; John Graham, Chair of the Canadian Federation of the Americas; and David Malone, Director-General Global Relations Foreign Affairs and later President of the International Peace Academy New York for reading and in some cases providing detailed comments on the entire manuscript.

I also thank Lieutenant-General (retired) Roméo Dallaire, United Nations Force Commander during the genocide in Rwanda in 1994, for reviewing the chapter on Rwanda and Eastern Zaire; Jill Sinclair, Foreign Affairs director of arms control, for checking the sections on anti-personnel mines; and Vice-Admiral (Retired) Larry Murray, acting Chief of Defence Staff in 1996, for his comments on the Rwanda and the fish war chapters. I am also grateful to Dr. Janice Gross Stein, Nanda Casucci-Byrne, Vania Cecchin, Sandra Black, Major (Retired) David Hyman, Alan Bowker, and Arthur Menzies for their encouragement. And finally, I express appreciation to Jean-Marc Carisse for allowing me to use his photographs and to Guy Tessier, photo archivist of Library and Archives Canada, for helping me to assemble a portrait essay. Everyone cited in these acknowledgements should be absolved of responsibility for any lack of objectivity, for which I take full credit, and for any errors, for which I accept the blame.

Index

DISTANCE *by* Jack Hodgins
"Without equivocation, *Distance* is the best novel of the year, an intimate tale of fathers and sons with epic scope and mythic resonances. . . . A masterwork from one of Canada's too-little-appreciated literary giants."
Vancouver Sun

Fiction, 5⅜ × 8⅜, 392 pages, trade paperback

RAVEN'S END: A novel of the Canadian Rockies *by* Ben Gadd
This astonishing book, snapped up by publishers around the world, is like a *Watership Down* set among a flock of ravens managing to survive in the Rockies. "A real classic." Andy Russell

Fiction, 6 × 9, map, 5 drawings, 336 pages, trade paperback

BROKEN GROUND: A novel *by* Jack Hodgins
It's 1922 and the shadow of the First World War hangs over a struggling Soldier's Settlement on Vancouver Island. This powerful novel with its flashbacks to the trenches is "a richly, deeply human book – a joy to read." W.J. Keith

Fiction, 5⅜ × 8⅜, 368 pages, trade paperback

THE MACKEN CHARM: A novel *by* Jack Hodgins
When the rowdy Mackens gather for a family funeral on Vancouver Island in the 1950s, the result is "fine, funny, sad and readable, a great yarn, the kind only an expert storyteller can produce." *Ottawa Citizen*

Fiction, 5⅜ × 8⅜, 320 pages, trade paperback

THE SELECTED STORIES OF MAVIS GALLANT *by* Mavis Gallant
"A volume to hold and to treasure" said the *Globe and Mail* of the 52 marvellous stories selected from Mavis Gallant's life's work. "It should be in every reader's library."

Fiction, 6⅛ × 9¼ , 900 pages, trade paperback

TEN LOST YEARS: Memories of Canadians Who Survived the Depression *by* Barry Broadfoot
Filled with unforgettable true stories, this uplifting classic of oral history, first published in 1973, is "a moving chronicle of human tragedy and moral triumph during the hardest of times." *Time*

Non-fiction, 5⅞ × 9, 442 pages, 24 pages of photographs, trade paperback

HOW I SPENT MY SUMMER HOLIDAYS *by* W.O.Mitchell
A novel that rivals *Who Has Seen the Wind.* "Astonishing . . . Mitchell turns the pastoral myth of prairie boyhood inside out." *Toronto Star*

Fiction, 5½ × 8½, 276 pages, trade paperback